ALDERSGATE RECONSIDERED

KINGSWOOD BOOKS

ALDERSGATE RECONSIDERED

Edited by
Randy L. Maddox

KINGSWOOD BOOKS
An Imprint of Abingdon Press
Nashville, Tennessee

ALDERSGATE RECONSIDERED

Library of Congress Cataloging-in-Publication Data

Aldersgate Reconsidered / edited by Randy L. Maddox
p. cm.
"Most of these essays . . . were presented originally at the January 1988 Minister's Week at Candler School of Theology, Emory University, in Atlanta, Georgia."—Pref.
Includes bibliographical references.
ISBN 0-687-00984-7 (alk. paper)
1. Wesley, John, 1703–1791—Congresses. 2. Conversion—Case studies—Congresses. 3. Methodist Church—Doctrines—Congresses.
I. Maddox, Randy L.
BX8495.W5A72 1990 287'.092—dc20 90-44090

Printed in the United States of America
on acid-free paper

To the Memory of
Albert Cook Outler,
Exemplary Wesley Scholar

Contents

Preface

The occasion of its 250th anniversary (May 24, 1988) sparked a scholarly debate about the nature of Aldersgate and its importance, both for Wesley and for his contemporary descendants. The present work was motivated by the conviction that the issues involved in this discussion have significance beyond the confines of Wesley scholarship. At the center of the debate are questions such as: "What really accounted for the dynamic spirituality of Wesley and his early followers?" and, "How can such vital Christian commitment be renewed today?" These questions should interest all of Wesley's contemporary descendants, as well as the larger Christian community.

The purpose of this volume, accordingly, is to make the discussion of Aldersgate spawned by its 250th anniversary more widely available. We have undertaken three specific tasks towards this end.

First, in the Introduction we provide a typological overview of the major contributions to the recent discussion of Aldersgate.

Second, we have collected several contributions to this debate that have not yet been published. Most of these essays—by Roberta Bondi, Richard Heitzenrater, Theodore Runyon, Jean Miller Schmidt, and David Watson—were presented originally at the January 1988 Minister's Week at the Candler School of Theology, Emory University, in Atlanta, Georgia. Our appreciation is extended to Candler for making the essays available for this project. The essay by Stephen Gunter was prepared specially for this volume.

Third, we have prepared a Select Bibliography and a Tradition-History of the discussion of Aldersgate, both covering the full temporal range of Wesley Studies, in order to place the recent discussion in its historical context and to enable readers to continue their own investigation.

A word of explanation on the style of references is in order. When reference is made to materials in the Select Bibliography, we will use the APA style (Author, Date, pp. #). All other materials will be referenced in the MLA form of endnotes.

Finally, a comment on the dedication. If 1988 will be remembered in the history of Wesley studies as the 250th anniversary of Aldersgate, 1989 will be recalled as the year we lost one of the most respected Wesley scholars—Albert Cook Outler. It is no exaggeration to say that this volume would not have been possible without the groundbreaking work of Outler, pioneering the discipline of Wesley scholarship and providing many of its most basic tools. In recognition of that debt, all profit from this volume will be donated in Dr. Outler's name to the Oxford Institute of Methodist Theological Studies—one of the many scholarly enterprises he helped nurture.

Randy L. Maddox
Sioux Falls, SD

Introduction

ALDERSGATE—SIGNS OF A PARADIGM SHIFT?

Randy L. Maddox

The year 1988 marked the 250th anniversary of the May 24th evening when John Wesley felt his heart "strangely warmed" at a religious society meeting on Aldersgate street in London. This event was commemorated worldwide by the various ecclesial traditions that are descended from Wesley's subsequent ministry.[1]

This anniversary also provoked a flurry of scholarly reflection upon the nature and significance of Aldersgate, both as a component in Wesley's personal spiritual development and as a normative pattern for his descendants. Among other places, Aldersgate was a focus of discussion at the annual meetings of the Wesley Fellowship (March 1987), the Wesley Studies Section of the American Academy of Religion (November 1987), the Wesleyan Theological Society (November 1988), and the Methodist Sacramental Fellowship (1988). The material from these meetings was later published.[2] In addition, there were several books released commemorating the anniversary of Aldersgate. Some of these focused specifically on the topic of Aldersgate while others dealt more generally with Wesley and his influence.[3]

If there is any generalization that can be drawn from these various studies (and the ones included in this volume), it is that there is far from a consensus among Wesley's contemporary heirs about the significance of Aldersgate, either for his life or as a standard for current "Wesleyans." Indeed, the present discussion might best be characterized as an "interpretive revolution" concerning Aldersgate. That is, there is a widespread dissatisfaction with the current dominant interpretation of Aldersgate and a search for a new interpretation that is more adequate both for understanding Wesley and for guiding contemporary spirituality.

A Typology of the Current Discussion

Thomas Kuhn's analysis of scientific revolutions suggests an organizing typology for the current interpretive revolution concerning Aldersgate.[4] Kuhn argues that changes in major interpretive models (paradigms) in the sciences—e.g., the change to a Copernican model of the universe—take place neither instantaneously nor easily. Rather, after a period of time in which a particular paradigm has possessed such dominance that it becomes the norm for all "regular science," there arises a growing chorus of "nonconformist" voices pointing out the lacunae, distortions, and other inadequacies of the reigning paradigm. The typical response of regular science to such charges is either: (1) to ignore them, (2) to defend the standard paradigm vigorously as it stands, or (3) to propose minor *ad hoc* adjustments to the reigning paradigm, in an attempt to preserve its major claims. If any of these strategies convince the nonconformists, the debate subsides and an interpretive revolution is avoided. But what happens if regular science cannot answer the critique of the nonconformists? Perhaps the most significant insight of Kuhn is that it takes more than an awareness of the problems of the current paradigm to effect a scientific revolution. There must also be an alternative candidate paradigm that is able to incorporate the central elements of the old paradigm while also successfully explaining those phenomena which the old paradigm could not. Hence, a science may remain in turmoil for some time until such an alternative paradigm emerges. Therefore, the envisioning and testing of such alternatives becomes the major task for furthering the science.

Kuhn's analysis suggests, by analogy, that the various contributions to the current debate concerning Aldersgate can be organized into three basic categories: (a) those suggesting problems with the reigning interpretation of Aldersgate, (b) those defending the standard interpretation against such charges, and (c) those proposing an alternative interpretation of Aldersgate.

Critiques of the "Standard" Interpretation of Aldersgate

Since some of the contributions to the current discussion of Aldersgate take the form of critiques of the "standard" interpretation, it is necessary first to remind ourselves what that interpretation is. Briefly put, this standard interpretation assumes that Aldersgate was the time of Wesley's *conversion experience*.[5] That is, it was a specific subjective *experience* by which Wesley was *converted* from a pre-Christian moralist into a true Christian believer. Perhaps the classic example of this interpretation is Thomas Jeffery's biographical study of Wesley's "quest" for a "satisfying religious experience" and the "true gospel of salvation by faith" (Jeffery 1960, pp. 11, 358, 387–9).

The critiques of this currently dominant interpretation of Aldersgate have focused on two levels, corresponding to the two-fold significance of the event: (1) questions about its adequacy for explaining Wesley's own example and understanding of spiritual life, and (2) criticisms of its appropriateness as a contemporary Methodist paradigm for spiritual life.

Critiques of the Interpretation of Aldersgate as Wesley's "Conversion Experience." In the opening salvo of the current debate, Theodore Jennings issued a stringent critique of the "conversionist" reading of Aldersgate (Jennings 1988). Briefly, Jennings argued that the conversionist reading took over uncritically Wesley's own immediate post-Aldersgate interpretation of the event, and ignored the fact that Wesley later qualified or rejected this interpretation (p. 10; cf. Jennings 1988b, p. 104).[6] He then gathered together the various aspects of Wesley's biography that appear to conflict with the conversionist reading. Essentially, he claimed that Aldersgate did not make that significant or immediate a change in Wesley's life. Both before and after Aldersgate Wesley pursued holiness; and, both before and after Aldersgate Wesley struggled with doubt (p. 16). If one must locate a decisive turning point in Wesley's life, it would be in 1725, not 1738 (p. 20). Jennings' real concern is not such a biographical one, however. It is a theological concern. He is persuaded that the conversionist reading of Aldersgate fundamentally distorts Wesley's mature theology of Christian discipleship. It replaces the mature Wesley's emphasis on the "gradual process of God in the soul" with an emphasis on an isolated "moment" of conversion (p. 20); and, it subjectivizes and individualizes piety, at odds with the mature Wesley's "social Christianity" (p. 21).

Michel Weyer reinforced many of these same points in an essay which, if less strident, is more detailed than that of Jennings (Weyer 1988a). Weyer again emphasizes the "retractions" that the later Wesley made to the most conversionist language in the original account of Aldersgate (p. 36). He highlights the evidences for Wesley's spiritual development *prior* to Aldersgate (pp. 10ff), and the evidences of Wesley's continuing spiritual struggles *after* Aldersgate (pp. 28ff).

As a result, he places Aldersgate *within* the process of Wesley's quest for *holiness* (p. 33), rather than as the *culmination* of his quest for an *experience of forgiveness* (as per Jeffery).

An even milder critic of the biographical adequacy of the standard reading of Aldersgate is John Lawson (1987). Like Jennings and Weyer, Lawson points out the continuities between the pre- and post-Aldersgate Wesley, as a way of rejecting any strong conversionist reading of the event (pp. 20ff). His primary concern, however, is to question the legitimacy of an emphasis on the importance of *experience* at Aldersgate, stressing instead the rational basis of Wesley's faith (p. 3). Lawson details Wesley's intellectual activity leading up to and following Aldersgate as a corrective to the standard concentration on Wesley's subjective feelings. For Lawson, Wesley was a rational moralist on both sides of Aldersgate (p. 30).

J. Brian Selleck (1988) provided a unique addition to the criticisms of the reigning conversionist paradigm. This standard understanding of Wesley's spiritual life typically contrasted internal "felt" religion with external religion. As a result, one assumed implication of Aldersgate was Wesley's rejection of his previous liturgical and sacramental spirituality. Selleck provides convincing detail of the role of liturgy and sacrament in the Aldersgate event itself and in Wesley's later spiritual life, as a way of rejecting any reading of the event which is anti-liturgical, anti-church, or anti-sacramental (p. 40).

One further participant who raised significant questions about the adequacy of understanding Aldersgate as Wesley's conversion was John Vickers (1988). Vickers agrees with the others that any satisfactory account of Aldersgate must do justice not only to the change it may have occasioned, but also to the significant continuity in Wesley's life surrounding it. His unique contribution is the reminder that the abstract of Wesley's *Journal* that contained the Aldersgate account was meant to counteract Moravian "stillness." Hence, the major point of the narrative for Wesley must have been its stress on the vital importance of actively searching for faith through all the divinely appointed means, not the character of the "experience" *per se* (p. 10).

Critiques of the Conversionist Reading of Aldersgate as a Paradigm for Contemporary Methodist Spirituality. The first two essays in this volume provide a different focus for evaluating (and rejecting) the standard understanding of Aldersgate. They inquire into the effects of adopting this understanding as the paradigm of contemporary spirituality.

Roberta Bondi argues that the paradigm of spirituality imposed upon contemporary Methodism by the standard interpretation of Aldersgate is inadequate, and even destructive. It does not take seriously enough the complexity of human life or the need for spiritual disciplines in developing an authentic Christian life. Significantly, she then looks to the mature theology of Wesley and the practice of the early Methodists for an alternative spirituality that is truly life-giving. In essence, the destructive effects of the standard paradigm become evidence for the fact that it could not have been Wesley's own mature understanding.

David Lowes Watson's essay corroborates that of Bondi. He argues that the standard reading of Aldersgate assigns a single religious experience a disproportionate importance, while undervaluing the role of the General Rules, class meetings, and other spiritual disciplines in nurturing and forming Christian life. While Wesley viewed the gift of the inner witness of the Spirit (which he received at Aldersgate) as the *power* of Christian discipleship, he consistently stressed the *form* of disciplined Christian life as the source and nurturer of this power. You cannot have the power without the form. Thus, if contemporary Wesleyans have lost the *power*, it is not because we need to seek more "experiences," but because we have discarded Wesley's spiritual guidelines and disciplines.

A similar critique of the conversionist reading of Aldersgate appears to be implicit in John Newton's and Donald Soper's commemorative lectures given to the Methodist Sacramental Fellowship.[7] In their analysis of what contemporary Methodists owe the Wesleys there is little stress on the need for a "conversion experience." Rather, they note such characteristics as their sacramental spirituality, their "sung" theology, etc.

Defenses of the "Standard" Interpretation of Aldersgate

Examples of Kuhn's three suggested reactions of the "reigning position" to the "nonconformist" critique are evident in the current discussion of Aldersgate as well.

Ignoring the Criticisms of the Standard Interpretation. Even though questions about the conversionist interpretation of Aldersgate began emerging already during the 225th anniversary celebration in 1963,[8] some of the 1988 contributions present a conversionist reading of the event with little or no notice of these questions.[9] Indeed, two of the contributions were simply representations of material given on the 225th anniversary.[10]

Vigorous Defense of the Standard Interpretation. Kenneth Collins emerged as the most vigorous defender of the conversionist interpretation of Aldersgate in the recent discussions. He fired an answering volley to Jennings' opening salvo, decrying the "dangerous new wave in Wesley studies" that questions whether Aldersgate was Wesley's conversion (Collins 1988, p. 98). He then turned his attention to Albert Outler, whom he views as the source of this "new wave" (Collins 1989a). Finally, he developed an extended defense of the standard interpretation, arguing that it is true to Wesley's own understanding and has been the position of Wesley scholars ever since, until this "new wave" (Collins 1989b). Collins marshals all the standard arguments for the conversionist reading. Unfortunately, he does not respond directly to some of the critics' most important questions about this reading. In particular, he continues to focus on Wesley material that is immediately post-Aldersgate (or, at most, "mid-life") Wesley, scarcely mentioning the later Wesley and the qualifying footnotes in the last edition of the *Journal*.[11]

Minor Adjustments to the Standard Interpretation. Still other participants in the current discussion have wanted to retain the central claim that Aldersgate was Wesley's conversion while trying to make some modifications in the standard interpretation so that it would not be as vulnerable to charges of emotionalism, subjectivism, or individualism.

A good example is the essay by James Nelson (1988). Nelson assumes throughout his essay that Aldersgate was the time when Wesley was justified and regenerated (i.e., converted). However, he goes to great lengths to "de-subjectivize" the event. In the first place, he argues that when Wesley said he felt his heart "strangely warmed," he meant "warmed by an external or foreign influence." That is, the emphasis was not on the quality of the warming but the identity of the one who warms—God (pp. 13–14). Likewise, he argues that the crucial factor which Wesley appropriated from the Moravians, leading to Aldersgate, was their spirituality which emphasized God's radical intrusion into the human situation. This spirituality helped Wesley modify an overly subjective model of conversion inherited from the Puritans.

A similar line of attack can be found in Frances Young (1988), who assumes that Aldersgate was the time of Wesley's "adoption," but spends most of his time arguing that "the emotional element was far less central than the 'myth' has suggested" (p. 39).

Proposals of an Alternative Paradigm

As we noted earlier, a successful interpretive revolution requires more than an awareness of inadequacies in the current standard interpretation. It also requires an alternative interpretation that can be argued to be more adequate than the current standard. Given the twofold significance of Aldersgate, this adequacy would have to be demonstrated both in terms of its ability to enlighten the spiritual/theological development of the "whole Wesley," and in terms of the implications of the paradigm for contemporary belief and spirituality. One of the remarkable aspects of the recent discussion of Aldersgate is the degree to which there is agreement among those proposing such a new paradigm.

The Place of Aldersgate in Wesley's Religious and Theological Development. The key to the proposed alternative paradigm of Aldersgate is that the perspective of the *late* or mature Wesley is taken as determinative. There is no better articulation of this reading than the essay by Richard Heitzenrater in this volume (an extensive development of Heitzenrater 1988). For Heitzenrater, as for the mature Wesley, Aldersgate was not the beginning of Wesley's Christian life but one significant development in his spiritual pilgrimage. In particular, it was the time wherein he received a profound assurance of God's freely-given love. From this event Wesley would develop a stronger commitment to the gracious nature of salvation and to the witness of the Holy Spirit. And yet, the irony of Aldersgate was that much of Wesley's immediate interpretation of the event proved to be inadequate. The reality of his subsequent Christian life did not live up to his initial "great expectations." A crucial reason for this was that he was trying to understand (and experience) a Lutheran theology in the context of his own Anglican and Arminian assumptions. Hence, Wesley's understanding of Aldersgate underwent significant modification over the course of his life. To recognize this fact does not make the event less significant. It simply suggests that we should learn from the "wisdom" of the whole of Wesley's experience concerning the event. It also helps explain why Wesley did not hearken back to Aldersgate as a model experience to be universalized (cf. 1988, p. 6).

Very similar accounts of the role of Aldersgate in Wesley's life and theology were presented by Karl Heinz Voigt (1988) and Michel Weyer (1988b). As Voigt put it, Aldersgate was not Wesley's conversion, but his *"Erfahrung der evangelischen Glaubensgewissheit"* (p. 21).[12]

The Implications of Aldersgate for Contemporary Belief and Spirituality. Several of the discussions of the implications of Aldersgate for contemporary belief and spirituality also consciously adopt the perspective of the mature Wesley rather than that of the immediately post-Aldersgate Wesley. An excellent example is the essay by

Theodore Runyon in this volume. Runyon is sensitive to the criticisms of Aldersgate as Wesley's conversion, but argues that the event was nonetheless theologically significant for Wesley: it crystallized his deeper concern for "experience" in Christian life and theology. Having made this point, however, Runyon quickly adds that Wesley's early post-Aldersgate assumptions about that experience were too heavily influenced by his Moravian contacts. Indeed, the burden of Runyon's essay is to show how the mature Wesley developed a more complex, less subjective, understanding of experience than that first expressed at Aldersgate under the influence of the Moravians! He then proceeds to recommend this refined understanding of the proper role of experience (*orthopathy*) as one of the important contributions Wesley can make to contemporary theology and spirituality.

A parallel type of argument can be found in the several essays on Aldersgate contributed by Methodist scholars in Germany. Manfred Marquardt sets the tone by claiming that the significance of Aldersgate for Wesley and for today is the experience of the certainty of salvation (1988, p. 49). However, he immediately adds that the mature Wesley saw that such certainty was not guaranteed and did not rule out a legitimate place for temptation and doubts (*Anfechtung*) in Christian life.[13] Likewise, Dieter Sackmann assumes that Aldersgate was the time Wesley received the certainty of salvation (*Heilsgewissheit*), but spends the bulk of his time arguing that the mature Wesley had to learn the lesson of Luther that *Anfechtung* always accompanies *Heilsgewissheit* (1988, pp. 58–62). Similar points can be found in Klaiber 1988 and Weyer 1988.

Summary. What the various proposals for a new understanding of Aldersgate agree upon, in other words, is that it should not be viewed as *the* decisive experience that marked the beginning of Wesley's authentic Christian life. Rather, it was *an* important further step in his spiritual development when his intellectual convictions about God's gracious acceptance were appropriated more deeply at an affectional level. However, it was also an event that Wesley initially read too much into. As such, it is Wesley's *mature reflections* on Aldersgate that should be most significant for those who seek a contemporary expression of "Wesleyan" theology and spirituality.

Gaining Historical Perspective on the Standard Interpretation

The theme of changes in understandings of Aldersgate is central to much of the current discussion. On one level, this theme focuses on changes in Wesley's own understanding of the event, arguing that the mature Wesley reconsidered many of his early post-Aldersgate claims. On a second level, there is a call for a contemporary change from the current standard interpretation to the new proposed understanding. There is yet a third level at which changes in understandings of Aldersgate need to be considered.

In her contribution to this volume, Jean Miller Schmidt raises the historical question of the origin and longevity of the current standard interpretation of Aldersgate. Her research points out that the current tendency to focus on Aldersgate as the crucial event in Wesley's life is a relatively recent phenomenon, not evident before the twentieth century![14] Likewise, she argues that a strong conversionist reading of Aldersgate is first found in Luke Tyerman (1870). Thereby, she demonstrates that the current standard interpretation is hardly a self-evident or perennial one. Rather, it is characteristic of a specific historical situation.

The contextuality of readings of Aldersgate is illustrated even more dramatically by Stephen Gunter's essay, which surveys how Aldersgate has been interpreted by one particular branch of the Wesleyan tradition—the holiness denominations. In their attempts to warrant their distinctive emphasis on entire sanctification as a definite second experience of grace, many have claimed Aldersgate to be such an experience! The difference between this interpretation and the standard conversionist interpretation is striking. Even more striking is the related realization that Aldersgate has become a focus for partisan debates within the Wesleyan traditions.

This realization sets the agenda for the Tradition-History of Aldersgate provided by Randy Maddox. The thesis of Maddox's survey is that the variety of opinions concerning the significance of Aldersgate that populate the history of Wesley studies cannot be accounted for simply by the ambiguities in Wesley's references to the event. They are also a function of the shifting theological concerns within the history of the later Wesleyan traditions. The goal of his survey is to provide a greater awareness of the influence of contemporary concerns on interpretations of Aldersgate and, thereby, to nurture a greater hermeneutic sensitivity in the continuing discussion.

Chapter 1

Aldersgate and Patterns of Methodist Spirituality

Roberta C. Bondi

Aldersgate is a sacred event for United Methodists on two levels. According to our legend, it was the occasion when our founder, John Wesley, had an experience that both changed his life and provided his heirs with a paradigm for their own spiritual lives. As the legend runs: before Aldersgate, Wesley was a man full of doubts and anxieties, unsure of his faith and of the love of God. At Aldersgate, when his heart was "strangely warmed," his doubts were resolved, his anxieties over. From this point on he was a new man, a simple lover of God who was now prepared to become the great preacher and director of the Methodist Revival. Therefore, Wesley's heirs have taken what happened to him at Aldersgate as the controlling image for understanding our *own* patterns of Christian spirituality. Having once become Christian (i.e., having had our hearts warmed), we believe that we ought also to be the kind of people who love God and our neighbor in a simple and spontaneous way.

This standard Methodist interpretation of Aldersgate is open to critical investigation on both levels of its significance. Indeed, recent studies have raised serious questions about the historical accuracy of isolating and emphasizing Aldersgate as Wesley's "conversion experience." Other significant religious events preceded Aldersgate in Wesley's own spiritual life and his struggle with doubt, for example, did not immediately disappear following Aldersgate.[1]

Admitting the cogency of many of these questions about the adequacy of the standard interpretation for explaining Wesley's own experience, I want to raise some related questions about the adequacy of this interpretation on its second level, where it presents a paradigm for contemporary Methodist spirituality. What does an "Aldersgate spirituality" do to us? What happens when we expect that, from the day we become Christian, we ought to be full of simple love for God and neighbor?

In the following pages, I will argue that the effects of "Aldersgate spirituality" are, in fact, very destructive. This is not, however, a rejection of the importance of John Wesley for contemporary Methodist spirituality. Quite the contrary! I believe that there is a much more authentic spirituality in the theology of John Wesley and the practice of early Methodists than that offered by the standard Aldersgate legend. It is this alternative spirituality which is most properly called "Wesleyan spirituality," and which has such life-giving promise for Wesley's heirs.

Because models of the spiritual life are ways of organizing every level of our private and corporate lives, it is impossible to provide an exhaustive examination of Aldersgate spirituality in this essay. Thus, I will limit the discussion to two of the most fundamental characteristics associated with this paradigm. The first is the expectation that we should be straightforward, simple, and loving people who relate to ourselves, other people, and God in an uncomplex and unambiguous way from the day we become Christian. The second is a logical consequence of the first: the conviction that our prayer should always be appropriate to the kind of simple people we ought to be—a spontaneous expression of our heart, arising out of our deep feelings of love and gratitude toward the God who has saved us.

"Aldersgate Spirituality" and Human Complexity

Let us begin by admitting that United Methodists have a problem with human complexity. We are fascinated by the notion of a "simple childlike faith." We canonize the "simple" shepherds at Christmas, or the "innocent" Mary, the mother of Jesus. We recall with nostalgia our own religious experiences of youth camp. We remember the older saint whom we may have known in our past who embodied a perfect trust in God and an unquestioning acceptance of anything life could dish out. We fantasize about people who pray with so much trust that God will grant their requests for healing or for help.

The flip side of our fascination with simple faith is our fear of complexity. We believe that, simply because we are Christian, we ought to have lives and hearts free of ambiguities. We ought not to have family conflicts, trouble with the children, divorces, difficulties with parents, job troubles, money troubles, even illnesses. We suggest to those who attend our churches that we are only comfortable with straightforward, unconflicted images of happiness, innocence, success, and health. Even though we know better at some level, we tend to associate these unconflicted images with being Christian. Problems indicating real ambiguities in our lives embarrass us in front of each other and shame us, so much so that many people stay away from our churches during their periods of hardship.

I encounter this uncomfortableness with complexity constantly in my dealings with students. It is not at all uncommon for a good student to express discouragement about the state of her Christian faith with some such words as:

> I am so confused. I am full of mixed emotions about myself (or my mother, or my spouse, or school, or my calling, or my job, or whatever), and I am torn by doubts. I'm learning things at Candler that throw everything I believe about God up in the air. Why did God put me in this situation anyway? I am angry and restless, and I can't concentrate on my prayers. I am constantly distracted by the chores I need to do, what we'll have for supper, or the sermon I have to write for Sunday. All I do is end up feeling guilty. Maybe I'm not even a Christian any more. Maybe I've lost my faith.

To this student the very existence of complexity in her life, particularly in her thoughts and feelings, suggests that she is a failure as a Christian, and perhaps even as a human being. Her worries may be ours, and they are certainly the worries of many people in the local church. They are important and very painful; and they deserve to be considered seriously.

We need to acknowledge that we are complex people, all of us. There are very few of us who are simple. I imagine that even the shepherds had more than their share of mixed emotions and ambiguities in the situation in which they found themselves—serenaded by angels and summoned to a cold, dark stable. Certainly, however innocent Mary was, while she *said*, "behold, the handmaid of the Lord," the fear and confusion that accompanied those early months of pregnancy must have continued throughout the ministry of her son, his crucifixion and resurrection. How else could it have been for the mother of our particular Messiah? It is the nature of human life to be complex, and an Aldersgate spirituality that expects us to be something other than what we are can only hurt us. What we need is a way of understanding the Christian life that takes our ongoing complexities seriously, allowing us to understand them and to claim them as central both to who we are and to who we want to be.

Properly understood, simplicity and complexity ought not to be opposed to each other. In the process of the integration of our lives, the movement is from complexity to simplicity. On investigation, the expectation of this movement can be shown to be fundamental to Wesley's own theology. The ideal of simple, (that is, integrated) love is there in Wesley, but he believes that we arrive at it only at the end of a long journey. The process is not simple, and neither are we as we make the journey toward it. This point can be demonstrated best by a focused consideration of that distinctive Wesleyan belief: the doctrine of Christian perfection.[2]

On first consideration, the decision to critique Aldersgate spirituality from the perspective of "Christian perfection" might appear to be a leap from the frying pan into the fire. The expectation of an Aldersgate spirituality that we be simple lovers of God and each other, free from complexity and ambiguity, is hard enough. The paradigm of "perfection" in a Wesleyan spirituality would surely be impossible. And certainly it would be, unless we understand "perfection" in the way Wesley did.

For Wesley, the call to perfection did not mean what it suggests to us; namely, a call to perfectionism: the need to control every detail in our lives, a demand that we never sin, never be tempted, always do everything right, never have a demoralized thought, always put others first in all circumstances, and never think of ourselves. I repeat: this is what perfection did *not* mean for John Wesley or those who influenced him.

At the beginning of his "Thoughts on Christian Perfection," Wesley defines what he *does* mean by perfection:

> [Christian perfection means] loving God with all our heart, mind, soul, and strength. This implies that no wrong temper, none contrary to love, remains in the soul and that all the thoughts, words and actions are governed by pure love.[3]

In itself, historically speaking, Christian perfection is not an unusual doctrine. Wesley found this doctrine in his reading of the Bible ("be perfect as my Father in heaven is perfect"), in the Anglican and Catholic traditions, and, above all, in the writers of the early church. For these early writers, as for Wesley, to talk about perfection was another way of saying that love is the *goal* of the Christian life. It was a paraphrase of Jesus' great command, "You shall love the Lord your God with all your heart and mind and strength and your neighbor as yourself."

This notion of perfection in love is different in two very important ways from the mythic faith we connect with Aldersgate. First, in the Aldersgate model, the assumption is that love is a simple attitude of heart that characterizes the Christian life from its beginnings. The Aldersgate model suggests to us that we must *start out* completely loving from the beginning of the Christian life. From such a perspective, then, the answer to the question "why am I not loving?" will always be "because I am a failure."

The ancient Christian writers who influenced Wesley most strongly—for example the author of the Macarian homilies—did not believe that deep attitudes of heart appeared automatically.[4] Love, and the integration that comes with it, comes a little at a time through a long process of practice, prayer, training, and, especially, God's grace. They stressed that nobody can expect to love God or neighbor very much in the beginning of the Christian life—and the beginning of the Christian life can last years! Ever the realists, they admitted that we are typically governed by too many destructive emotions, states of mind, and habits to be able even to *see* others, let alone love them. Ambition, envy, resentment, depression, a love of power, and anxiety (among other things!), govern our lives and prevent us from doing much loving. If you add to this the inevitable way our work, our many relationships, and the daily business of our life necessarily absorb our attention, then—even at best—we are going to be complex people.

Wesley and the ancient writers would declare that if we expect we ought to be simple, loving people with uncomplex relationships to God and each other *right now,* it is no wonder we feel like failures! We have had unrealistic expectations in the first place, expectations connected with our misunderstanding of the whole point of the Christian life.

For those of us who suffer under the burden of unrealistic and theologically unsound expectations this is a word of grace: the Christian life, and the development of the Christian personality, is a long and rarely simple process through which we grow only slowly into a loving relationship with God and with each other. For those of us who are obsessive about our need to be everything at once and to do it right, listen: we have a goal, which is love. The journey to the goal, however, takes time. Growth is slow. Be easy. This sense of time and process is the first way that the true Wesleyan model of spirituality is different from the Aldersgate model.

The second way in which the notion of perfection in love characteristic of a truly Wesleyan spirituality differs from the model of Aldersgate spirituality is the place that it makes for the acknowledgement of our complexities as we struggle with them in our everyday lives and in our churches. As we have already seen, an Aldersgate model encourages us to hide our complexities (as marks of our failures) from ourselves, our brothers and sisters in our churches and, ultimately, from God. Our inability to express ourselves truly to each other and even to God is a tragedy on a corporate scale, and it may very well have something to do with why Methodists, along with the other mainline Christian denominations, are losing members.

The true Wesleyan model of spirituality *encourages* reflection on the external and internal complexities of our lives as central to Christian life. Far from encouraging us to *fear* our complexity, it helps us to regard even our most painful family situations, our most devastating doubts, our worst tragedies as food for growth in the love of God and neighbor. It encourages us to identify and understand our own history, our motivations and choices, our patterns of relating to ourselves and others, our work and our play. Wesleyan spirituality values such self-reflection not in order to wallow in our own inadequacies or feel guilty about them, but rather so that we can place the whole of our complicated lives before God and allow God to empower our transformation.

We must undertake a lot of this self-reflection on our own, but we also need each other in our journey through our complexities. There are many who are convinced, David Lowes Watson among them, that Methodism's original power lay in the organization of its members into small groups of classes and bands.[5] These small groups served many purposes, but perhaps the most fundamental was to help people be introspective and realistic about themselves and each other; to recognize, think, and work through their complexities in the company of other Christians as they moved toward the goal of Christian perfection—that is, love.

People in Wesley's groups were (at least, theorctically) honest with themselves and with each other. We desperately need some contemporary ways of being together in our churches that can function as the early Methodist class system did if we are going to be able to be present to each other, much less to God. Some prayer groups, Sunday School classes, and Christian friendships already function in this way. David Lowes Watson recommends the reinstatement of the old class system in the modified form that he calls covenant discipleship groups.[6]

Whatever the form our small church groups take, our communal worship is central to Wesleyan spirituality. It is one of our chief means of grace. We who are ministers and leaders of worship need to lay aside our own discomfort with allowing human complexity to surface in worship, in prayer, and hymns, but particularly in sermons. I recall the experience of a United Methodist minister who casually mentioned from the pulpit that he was going to miss a UMYF meeting to attend a workshop on sexual and domestic violence. The next week he had five church members in his office, at different times, seeking help for problems he had believed did not exist in his church. Such openness in sermons could encourage the ongoing presence of those people in the congregation who are tempted to drop out of church during their most difficult times.

"Aldersgate Spirituality" and Prayer

We turn our attention now to the issue of prayer and the spiritual life. According to the Aldersgate model of the spiritual life, the simple, loving heart prays spontaneously—that is, warmly—with sincere and deep feeling at the time of prayer; its words flow forth to God like water from a tap. According to Aldersgate spirituality, prayer ought to be a simple Christian reality. Working at prayer or using the words of others, whoever they may be, suggests a lack of faith, insincerity and coldness of heart.

This insistence on the spontaneous nature of true prayer is particularly strong in southern Methodism. In public worship, the expectation that prayer be spontaneous manifests itself in the congregational demand that a minister's public prayers never be written out, whether by himself/herself or by someone in our Christian tradition. I am even aware of a congregation that refuses to use the Lord's Prayer because it is not spontaneous.

In an important sense, of course, there is actually very little genuine spontaneous prayer even in these churches! Rather, public prayer follows a standard pattern: what you pray for and about as well as the order in which you pray for them is specified in advance, and everybody knows what that pattern is. Likewise, the words of the prayer typically consist of phrases everyone regards as appropriate and even necessary for public prayer, though they are out of use everywhere else in modern life—phrases like "Lord and Savior," "our many failings," "gifts and offerings," "look with favor upon," "propitiation for our sins," and so forth. There is a story that my family in Kentucky tells which humorously illustrates the non-spontaneous nature of this kind of prayer. A few years ago, my Uncle Quentin, who is also a lawyer and a politician, was called upon to offer the blessing at the family dinner which followed my Great Aunt Jenny's funeral. He stood up to pray and began, "We just want to thank you, Lord, for this joyous occasion that brings us all together. . . ." Spontaneous public prayer is rarely truly spontaneous!

Ordinarily, when we think of private prayer needing to be spontaneous we have something different in mind. First, we mean the *words* of our prayer not only need to be our *own* words, they must be the *right* words. Second, we mean that the words must express real *feeling*; which is, again, the *right* feeling.

Let's begin with the words. According to this notion of spontaneous prayer, prayer is basically talking in our own words to God. Prayer is a verbal enterprise in which we tell God things, thank God for things, or ask God for things. When we run out of things to tell God about, or thank God for, or ask God for, we stop praying. If we have none of these things to say to God, we do not pray at all. It is not unusual for students to tell me that they are experiencing terrible discouragement about prayer because there is nothing they want to say to God.

One of the chief difficulties with this verbal understanding of prayer is that it starts with an assumption that prayer is something we *do* by talking to God. Notice the irony here. Prayer is to be spontaneous, but it is a spontaneous *duty*, a responsibility to be carried out. This is a very narrow way of understanding prayer; in fact, by being defined in verbal terms it excludes many ways Christians have prayed over the centuries. As we shall see, it also excludes the model of prayer found in Wesleyan spirituality.

As for needing the *right* words: though not many people would put it in quite these terms, a lot of us believe that only "good" words belong in our prayer. Sometimes this means that there are only certain subjects suitable for prayer—prayer for others, thanksgiving, words of repentance. By implication, it can also mean that certain subjects are *not* suitable topics for prayer. For a surprising number of people, such unsuitable topics include any prayer for what they regard as their own "selfish" needs and desires. One student, for example, did not feel that his gut-wrenching struggles with the form his ministry should take was a proper subject for prayer because the world had so many troubles about which he ought to pray that were more serious than his personal and private ones.

This brings us directly to the relationship between our prayer and our feelings. According to the Aldersgate model of spirituality, we expect the words of our prayer to be an expression of our feeling for God *at the time of our prayer*, and we test the sincerity and strength of our prayer by the depth of our feeling. The stronger the feeling, the better the prayer.

Yet, as in the case of words, the Aldersgate model excludes some feelings from a proper place in prayer. Contrition, longing for someone's healing, gratitude, love for God, and, most particularly, a sense of God's presence are the proper feelings to give our prayer substance and reality. Complex feelings make us very uneasy in prayer, but we have an even more serious problem with feelings that we consider to be unambiguously "bad." Anger, particularly if it is directed not just at God but at a person—a child or spouse or parent whom we are supposed to love—convinces us that we are unfit to pray. So does sexual attraction toward someone who is off limits. We even fear letting God see our tiredness or our distractedness, much less our confusion, depression, or boredom with our lives. We think we *ought* not to pray when we are feeling this way. If we have *no* feeling, no sense of God's presence, to back up the words we say, we believe we have at best a hypocritical prayer; that is, no prayer at all.

Does this mean that we are convinced that God loves us only when we are "good," or that God will be offended or enraged if we are not "pure" when we enter God's presence—if we can't live up to the image of the "simple, trusting heart"? I do not know, but I do know that this belief that we should pray only in certain states of mind hurts us desperately.

Such a belief about God and prayer prompts some of us to lie to ourselves about what we really feel or think about things, so that we try to feel only positive things and pray only positive prayers. "Praise Jesus!" It keeps others of us continually taking our own religious pulse, checking the rightness of our frame of mind for approaching God. For some it makes God into a judge whose main occupation is to check the suitability of our mental condition at the time of our prayer. It fills most of us, some of the time, with guilt for simply being who we are, and it reenforces our discouragement with ourselves and our Christian lives. It is a destructive notion of prayer.

Fortunately, our own tradition suggests to us an alternative way of understanding prayer, in the theology and person of John Wesley. I am aware, of course, that at first and even second glance John Wesley can be a demoralizing role model. His actual, as well as his mythological, daily habit of getting up to pray and study scripture before dawn has discouraged many an over-burdened seminary student who tried to emulate him. Wesley was an obsessive-compulsive in many ways, and his early rising may have been one of these ways. Furthermore, some of what he actually says about how to pray might seem to reinforce the destructive notions of prayer we have been discussing.[7]

What Wesley has to offer us that is truly helpful, however, is his insistence on the importance of a regular, daily discipline of prayer as an essential means of grace. Wesley prayed every day. Was Wesley able to pray every day because he had a simple, trusting, loving relationship with God? Did he always sincerely want to pray? Did his prayer arise daily from a "strangely warmed heart"? Hardly! He did not believe that he had to be perfect to pray. Rather, he prayed because he expected prayer to be a "means of grace," a place to meet God and a source of what he needed to grow in love toward Christian perfection.[8] This is what we need and receive in prayer, too.

If we take Wesleyan spirituality as our model of the Christian life, then we pray every day, not because we feel that we ought to or in order to be "good people." We pray because as Christians we have taken on a shared life with God. We share who we are, and God shares who God is. But sharing who we are does not mean just our "good" selves or our attentive selves or even our feeling selves. We share who we *actually* are on a day-to-day basis. It means we bring all of ourselves to our prayer in whatever way we can for companionship, healing, and growth over a long period of time. Some of what we bring is articulated, some is in the form of confused thoughts or images we want to be able to make sense of, and some may simply be raw feelings or hopes that can hardly be expressed at all.

That we bring all of ourselves to prayer also means that we do not skip our prayers because we are in a foul or distracted mood, any more than we do not come home to meals with our family because we are angry and mean or unable to pay them much attention. Our family want us there for dinner; we belong there with God for our prayer. There is nothing that makes us unfit for God. This is good news!

It follows that, if we are allowed to be ourselves with God, then some of our prayer will be verbal and some will not. We are, after all, much more than what we say or even think. Christians over the centuries have prayed in many different ways in order to bring all of themselves into their prayer. One of the most life-giving kinds of daily prayer to people as busy as we are is what is sometimes called centering prayer. This form of prayer actually goes back in Christian history to at least the fourth century. The person praying simply sits quietly in the presence of God, expecting nothing of God, asking for nothing, being nothing in particular. I like to think of it as "kitchen table prayer," time we spend with God that is like time we spend at the kitchen table with a spouse or a good friend with whom we share our lives in other ways already. We simply sit in silence that is sometimes peaceful, sometimes distracted, but always shared.

Another primary way of praying that does not involve our talking to God verbally in our own words is praying scripture. Once again, this would be a central part of any form of prayer that is true to Wesley's own practice and prescription.[9] Wesley talks about the absolute necessity of "searching scripture" in the context of prayer. Since the fourth century the psalms have been the backbone of daily prayer for Christians all over the world. Athanasius, the great fourth century bishop, believed the psalms to be prayers given us by God specifically for this purpose—to teach us, to be a mirror for us in which we could see our own hurts, to encourage us, to allow us to express our feelings, and to heal us.[10] The psalms prayed daily still have this power. The whole of scripture, but the gospels particularly, belong as a part of daily prayer. Here we encounter both the Jesus who still shares our human life with us, and the resurrected Jesus who has the power to raise us from our own peculiar deaths. In the gospels, in Jesus' words and actions, we meet both "what the Lord requires of us" and God's promises to us. We are able to test the insights of our prayer against those requirements and promises.

Praying scripture fosters our knowledge of ourselves. At the same time, it increases our knowledge of God. All of us are deficient in our images of God. Often our images are negative or contain negative elements; for example, where God is experienced as a gigantic school principal, or a nosey and controlling parent. Many women, (and men too!) have problems caused by the weight of oppressive male metaphors of God in our tradition. I believe our growth in the love of God is directly linked with our ability to allow the expansion and transformation of our images of God. Yet we cannot simply *think* our way into transformation. God in scripture *gives* us other powerful images to change or expand the hurtful or restricted images of God we hold. Our hearts are enabled to hear these images as they come into our prayer without the struggle to "think them up."

Some people are not sure how to go about selecting scripture for daily prayer. One way, of course, is to go through the psalms in order, one psalm or portion of a psalm a day. One could go through the gospels and/or any other book of the Bible the same way. The trouble with this is that it is not keyed to the liturgical year, so that the link between the individual and the prayer of the whole church feels more tenuous than it has to. More helpful is the use of a daily lectionary. The United Methodist church has an excellent lectionary, each day's reading including two psalms, an Old Testament reading, one from an epistle and one from a gospel.[11]

One final word about establishing a discipline of daily prayer in relation to Wesley's own mythological habits. In order for *your* discipline to be workable, you need to think small. Do not decide to get up an hour earlier to pray. It will be too hard to maintain. Pick a time of day that will actually work for you, right after breakfast or in the middle of the afternoon, or whatever. Just as important, pick a length of time that you will actually be able to devote to your prayer and that will be nourishing to you. Fifteen minutes may very well be plenty. If you need more time, build up to it gradually. Allow time to talk, to pray scripture, and just to sit. Don't worry about your frame of mind; just be there. You are not trying to justify yourself by works. You are trying to be with God.

Conclusion: Plea for a "Wesleyan Spirituality"

Aldersgate spirituality has hurt us. It has fostered impossible expectations about the Christian life. It has encouraged us to believe that one becomes an uncomplex and loving Christian simply and immediately, through a conversion experience. It has inclined us to deny parts of ourselves that are very real. It has seriously weakened the fabric of our Christian communities by encouraging us to substitute niceness for genuineness in our relationships together at church. By presenting us with a limited and untraditional notion of prayer, it has separated us from a fundamental source of God's grace and growth.

Wesleyan spirituality offers us a real alternative. A Wesleyan spirituality is rooted in the conviction that being a fully loving Christian is the *goal* of the Christian life, rather than its starting point. It does not deny us our complexity in our external or internal lives. It leads us to acknowledge and understand the very parts of ourselves that we are most tempted to repudiate. It brings us to know that Christian growth belongs in community and to expect that our churches should nurture that growth, rather than hindering it. Finally, it gives us the discipline of a way of prayer that is a constant source of grace in our lives together and with God.

The Church does not exist only to serve its own members, and particularly its own leadership. Nor does it exist to reinforce the *status quo*. Yet, there are always strong forces within the church, even within ourselves, pushing it in these directions. The church is the body of Christ; it is meant to embody God's powerful and life-giving presence in the world for the healing and transformation of the world. Without God's grace it cannot be such a source of life, but unless we make ourselves *available* to God's grace through the practice of a spirituality that develops an active love of God and God's world, the church can never be what it is meant to be. The adoption of a truly Wesleyan spirituality, I believe, can enable us to be the body of Christ in the world.

Chapter 2

Aldersgate Street and the General Rules: The Form and the Power of Methodist Discipleship

David Lowes Watson

The words are familiar; but it is never untimely to be reminded of them:

> In the latter end of the year 1739 eight or ten persons came to me in London who appeared to be deeply convinced of sin, and earnestly groaning for redemption. They desired (as did two or three more the next day) that I would spend some time with them in prayer, and advise them how to flee from the wrath to come, which they saw continually hanging over their heads. That we might have more time for this great work I appointed a day when they might all come together, which from thenceforward they did every week, namely, on Thursday, in the evening. To these, and as many more as desired to join with them (for their number increased daily), I gave those advices from time to time which I judged most needful for them; and we always concluded our meeting with prayer suited to their several necessities.
>
> This was the rise of the United Society, first at London, and then in other places. Such a Society is no other than 'a company of men "having the form, and seeking the power of godliness", united in order to pray together, to receive the word of exhortation, and to watch over one another in love, that they may help each other work out their salvation'.

These are the opening paragraphs from the first edition of a small penny pamphlet, prepared by John Wesley in February of 1743, and titled "The Nature, Design and General Rules of the United Societies, in London, Bristol, Kingswood, and Newcastle upon Tyne."[1] We may smile today at the seemingly endless sets of rules which Wesley drew up for the connectional polity of early Methodism, and even wince a little when we read their particulars, as in the "Rules for the Bands."[2] But one thing is clear. They were the basis for everything by which Methodism was known during its formative years. If we neglect to tradition them alongside the religious experience by which we have more usually come to measure our identity, we seriously misunderstand our heritage. In particular, we risk assigning to Aldersgate Street a disproportionate significance.

It is our underlying premise that it is precisely such an assignation on the part of some, and a correlatively disproportionate reaction on the part of others, which are at the root of much of the polarization of our church today—a polarization we hesitate to acknowledge, still less address, but which is all too apparent to journalists of the caliber and perception of a Bill Moyers.[3]

Before examining the particular set of rules in this penny pamphlet, and their widespread usage in early Methodism, it will be helpful to trace some of the steps which led to their publication. As we shall note, the rules are simple and straightforward to the point of inhibiting what some would regard as the freedom of our discipleship. Indeed, current attempts in the church to re-appropriate their directives are often countered with indifference and even disdain. Those involved in such efforts must often negotiate charges of laying a "guilt trip" on people, or imposing impossible criteria which only engender a permanent sense of failure, or of wishing to control people's lives to an unreasonable degree. Most sobering, however, is the objection of those who wish to amend the classical disciplines of the church on the grounds of modern custom—as if convenience were a norm of Christian discipleship. As one seasoned educator put it when offered the opportunity of daily worship as a means of grace, "No-one does *that* any more!"

It is comforting, though hardly encouraging, to find that Wesley encountered precisely the same objections to the specificity of his various sets of rules. To the General Rules, those which were most generally enforced and most widely distributed, the objections came less from those who willingly accepted them as the condition of society membership than from those who found them theologically offensive. The criticism was the same one which led to the permanent attribution of the name "Methodist" to the movement: the charge of works-righteousness. Methodists were "methodical" because they were short on grace.

The theological origins of the General Rules can readily be discerned in Wesley's *Journal* for the years immediately preceding their initial distribution. In this regard, we should remember that the *Journal* was edited by Wesley for publication, and something which he himself viewed as an appropriate record of his ministry. Noteworthy in his narrative, therefore, is that however certain *we* might be of what happened to him on the night of May 24th, 1738, he himself was much less sure. On almost every page for the following year, he seems at pains to make us aware that his spiritual journey and his theological instincts were in a constant tension.

Take, for example, his visit to Herrnhut in the summer of 1738. With the liberated objectivity of a graduated apprentice, he begins to take his spiritual mentors to task, and to question some of the very criteria which led him to that critical juncture in his pilgrimage.[4] Even more on his return, the entries for October of 1738 abound with uncertainties, primarily over the extent to which the assurance of faith was concomitant with justification.[5] We read of his "great perplexity" over what it means to be "weak in the faith,"[6] and, in a letter to his brother Samuel, he writes of that which he regarded as his own "measure of faith" as opposed to the "*plerophory* of faith experienced by others."[7] In the *Journal* for October 29, 1738, we find him "doubtful of [his] own state," and as he wonders whether he should wait in "silence and retirement" for an assurance of the kingdom of God, he alights in his testament on the words that "by works faith [is] made perfect."[8] Significantly, he wants us to know that.

Even more significantly, on November 12th of that same year he records that he "began more narrowly to inquire what the doctrine of the Church of England is concerning the much-controverted point of justification by faith."[9] Shortly thereafter he published an extract from the Homilies of the Church of England, titled "The Doctrine of Salvation, Faith and Good Works," a pamphlet which went through twelve editions in his lifetime.[10] And the following year he published an edited version of two treatises by the early English Lutheran scholar, Robert Barnes, on justification by faith, and on free will.[11]

The question with which Wesley was wrestling was as old as the English Reformation, and the real reason why England resisted the teachings of the continental Reformers, the mutual antipathy of Luther and Henry VIII notwithstanding. Generally speaking, it can be described as the issue of faith and works; though it has been given more technical investigation by William Cannon as the implicit distinction between objective and subjective justification,[12] by Harald Lindström as the distinction between justification and sanctification,[13] by Albert Outler as the question of formal or meritorious atonement,[14] and by

Martin Schmidt as the reciprocity of justification and the witness of the Spirit.[15] But however we identify it, the heart of the question remains the extent to which our salvation in Christ is contingent on our appropriation of it; an appropriation which, in traditioning Aldersgate Street, we have come to identify with the experience of the new birth.

In some parts of the church, we have by and large traditioned it as the need for personal conversion. In others, we have traditioned it more as the need for personal fulfillment in Christ. Yet in both instances, we have tended to mis-tradition the point which Wesley himself was at pains to clarify during these theologically formative years; namely, the extent to which the performance of good works is integral to our salvation, and neglect of the same is detrimental to or even destructive of our faith.

The issue was to emerge in varying contexts throughout his ministry. But the *Journal* makes clear that he fully recognized it at the outset: in the dispute at Fetter Lane over quietism;[16] in the objections at Bristol to his preaching of free grace;[17] and in his polemical essay, "The Principles of a Methodist," over the assurance of faith and Christian perfection.[18] Of more interest to our present discussion, however, is the effect which the theological issue had on the polity of early Methodism. For it was in the *kerygma* of field preaching and the *oikodomé* of the societies that Methodist theology was truly forged, and Methodist discipleship honed into authenticity.

If we accept Wesley's own account, it was the evolution of the class meeting which gave definitive expression to this tension of faith and works in the life of the United Societies. As we know, Wesley himself resisted the appellation "Methodist," a word which did not appear on the title page of the General Rules until after his death.[19] Yet methodical discipleship was the mark by which the members of the societies became known, and which was locked into their discipline at an early stage. February 15, 1742 was the date of the meeting in Bristol at which the financial expedient of class monies was adopted.[20] February 23, 1742–3 was the date appended to the first edition of the General Rules, by which time the class meeting was normative as the means of mutual accountability in the societies, and the class leader installed as the immediate means of supervision.[21]

With the exception of the various hymns which were added as appendices, and the occasional inclusion of the Rules for the Bands, the General Rules remained essentially the same in the many editions through which they passed during Wesley's lifetime. Frank Baker's *Union Catalogue* lists twenty-one editions up to that of 1790, including one in Welsh and one in French.[22] The majority of the editions were twelve pages in length, as was the first edition, with others ranging from nine to sixteen pages. The first edition was signed by John Wesley; the second and subsequent editions carried the signature of Charles as well.

Following the preamble, already cited, the Rules begin with the duties of the class leader, who is to see each person in his or her class at least once each week, to receive what they are willing to give toward the relief of the poor, to enquire "how their souls prosper," and to "advise, reprove, comfort or exhort as occasion may require." In turn, the leader was to be accountable to the minister and stewards of the society, reporting "any that are sick" or "walk disorderly and will not be reproved."[23]

Having thus established the importance of mutual accountability for the discipline of the societies, the Rules proceed to the particular requirements of membership. But first, there is an important statement of purpose, which directly addresses the issue of faith and works:

> There is one only condition previously required in those who desire admission into these societies, 'a desire to flee from the wrath to come, to be saved from their sins'. But wherever this is really fixed in the soul, it will be shown by its fruits. It is therefore expected of all who continue therein that they should continue to evidence their desire of salvation (by) . . . [24]

The wording has profound theological significance. Neither the immediate assurance of justifying grace nor the incipient sanctification of the new birth is a prerequisite for Methodist membership: but merely a *desire* for salvation. Wesley is drawing here on the principles by which he had refuted the claims of quietism in 1740,[25] and which he was to develop over the years into the richness of a doctrine of prevenient grace such as that which begins his sermon, "The Scripture Way of Salvation."[26]

If the distinction between justification and sanctification is a mark of Wesley's theology, no less is it his contribution to have drawn just as clear a distinction between prevenient and justifying grace. In a word, Wesley makes clear that the liberation of God's grace is not license. Rather, it is the opportunity to respond to the divine initiative in obedient discipleship, along with the freedom to reject God's grace in disobedience. It is this freedom which requires our compliance in the *ordo salutis,* whether it be through the innate work of conscience (i.e., prevenient grace), the *de facto* surrender of the new birth, the intentional submission to inward renewal, or the maturity of a consistently obedient discipleship in the perfection of *agape.*

Put differently, acceptance of God's grace, in whichever form, brings immediate obligations—the dimension of Christian discipleship which was seriously weakened by the doctrinal overloading of justification in the theology of the European Reformation. It was this which caused the English Reformers grave concern during the polemical reign of Henry VIII; and it was this same concern which impelled Wesley to research those pristine documents in the Anglican tradition following his Aldersgate Street experience. The question was not whether undue attention to good works would deny the fullness of God's grace in human salvation. It was whether lack of attention to good works would cheapen it.

Accordingly, while we find in the General Rules that the only condition for membership is a *desire* to flee from the wrath to come, a *desire* to be saved, the desire is to be authenticated by adherence to the specifics of the rules. There is no *pre*-condition for membership; but there are conditions to *remaining* in membership. Grace is posited for what it is: an invitation to respond to the divine initiative. We do not choose our salvation. We choose to accept or reject *God's* salvation.

The particulars of the Rules begin with a very practical list of things to avoid: not to profane the day of the Lord, by doing ordinary work or by buying and selling; not to buy or sell spirituous liquors, or to drink them (except in cases of extreme necessity); not to fight, quarrel, or go to law; not to use many words in buying or selling; not to smuggle, or engage in usury; not to do to others what we would not like them to do to us; and more.[27]

Equally practical are the works of mercy, the good to be done at every opportunity, in as many ways as possible to as many people as possible. Drawing on the Book of James (an epistle well used by the early English Reformers as a corrective to the latent antinomianism of a radical doctrine of justification) and alluding to the critical parables of Matthew 25, Methodists were first of all enjoined to do good to people's bodies, by giving food to the hungry, clothing to the naked, and by visiting or helping those who were sick or in prison. Only then were they to help their souls, and this "by instructing, *reproving* or exhorting all we have any intercourse with."[28] The injunctions are nothing if not direct, and their purpose is clearly that of spiritual guidance, rendering many of our contemporary non-directive counseling techniques tame indeed by comparison.

But the pivotal directive of the Rules, that which explains their overall purpose and states their central theological tenet in a striking use of English prose and spelling, is that Methodists are to "[trample] underfoot that enthusiastic doctrine of devils, that 'we are not to do good unless *our heart be free to it*.'"[29] Irrespective of assurance of faith, the inward witness, the reality of the new birth, good works were to be performed as a point of discipline, as a matter of form.

Yes, the grace of Jesus Christ will empower; and yes, the freedom of our salvation lies in the supersession of the law by the gospel of Jesus Christ. But this does not mean the negation of the law. The outworking of grace is not limited to the inward witness, but occasioned, enriched, and empowered by it.

This might well be described as a seasoning of the doctrine of justification by faith with a sizeable ingredient of common sense—the Anglican *via media* at its best. The inherent blind spot of the Protestant Reformation, as the Puritan casuists were quick to discern, was that refined theological concepts do not readily translate into tenets for practical Christian living. Faith will work by love—on a good day, maybe. For the other days, there must be habits, rules, and methods by which to live out what we know in our hearts is the way of Christ, but which we cannot expect to be accomplished for us by spiritual waves of grace, on the crests of which we ride with an effortless participation that is very close indeed to a new quietism.

The reality of Christian life in the world is that we must *work out* our salvation. Our response to the divine initiative in Jesus Christ is one of obedience, described in the Anglican tradition and by Wesley as the "works of mercy."[30] But more, the grace we need for these works of obedience, even the grace of Jesus Christ, requires additional steps on our part if we are to be open to it and receive it in the measure that we require. These steps, in the Anglican tradition, and likewise in Wesley, are known as the "works of piety," or the "means of grace"—the time-honored disciplines of the church. And accordingly they comprise the third component of the General Rules.

Termed "the ordinances of God," first to be listed is public worship, followed by the ministry of the Word, read or expounded, and the sacrament of the Lord's Supper. Then comes private prayer, searching the Scriptures, and fasting or abstinence. Significantly, the public ordinances precede those which are private, thereby lifting up the role of the church in Christian discipleship, a point which Wesley was always at pains to explicate and commend.

We can note that the same emphasis on the working out of salvation was explicit in the Minutes of the first Methodist Conference in 1744:

> Q. 11. Are works necessary to the continuance of faith?
>
> A. Without doubt; for a man may forfeit the free gift of God, either by sins of omission or commission.
>
> Q. 12. Can faith be lost, but for want of works?
>
> A. It cannot but through disobedience.[31]

Later in the same Minutes we find an added emphasis in the discussion about methods of preaching:

Q. What sermons do we find, by experience, to be attended with the greatest blessing?

A. 1. Such as are most close, convincing and searching. 2. Such as have most of Christ. 3. Such as urge the heinousness of [living in] contempt or ignorance of [God].

Q. But have not some of us been led off from practical preaching by (what was called) *preaching* Christ?

A. Indeed we have. The most effectual way of preaching Christ is to preach him in all his offices, and to declare his Law as well as his Gospel, both to believers and unbelievers.

Q. Do we now all preach strongly and closely, concerning both inward and outward holiness?

A. It would be well, if we were more frequently and more largely to insist upon it in all its branches.

Q. Do we insist enough upon practical religion in general? And in particular, on relative duties? Using the means of grace? Private prayer? Self-denial? fasting? Seriousness?

A. It seems most of us have been wanting here. Let us take care to supply this defect for the future.[32]

In other words, by 1744, the compass heading was set. Later course corrections would be minor, and largely in response to rough seas.

Given the number of editions of the Rules during Wesley's lifetime, we might infer not only that he regarded the form of Methodist discipleship to be as important as the power, but that he saw a constant need to stress this dimension of Methodist Societal life. Indeed, it may well have been the condition of the Society at Newcastle upon Tyne which energized his drawing up the Rules when he did. For in the entry dated February 20, 1743, Wesley notes in his *Journal* that he "diligently inquired who they were that did not walk according to the gospel; in consequence of which I was obliged to put away above fifty persons. There remained about eight hundred in the Society."[33] On Sunday, March 6 following, he "read over in the society the rules which all our members are to observe; and desired everyone seriously to consider whether he was willing to conform thereto or no. That this would shake many of them I knew well; and therefore, on *Monday* the 7th, I began visiting the classes again, lest that which is lame should be turned out of the way.'"[34]

The references to the Rules in the years immediately following their publication indicate their central role in the life of the societies. Assistants and helpers were enjoined to keep them, not "mend" them;[35] and there are similar injunctions to class leaders and stewards.[36] Later, at the thirteenth Conference at Bristol in 1756, Wesley notes that the fifty or so who met together read over the Rules very carefully, "but did not find any that could be spared. So we all agreed to abide by them all, and to recommend them with our might."[37] And in the questions asked of preachers at the Leeds Conference of 1766, the precursors of those in our present ritual for ordination, it is specifically asked whether they know the "Rules of the Society"—and whether they keep them.[38]

The Rules were likewise to be a means of nurturing an outward as well as an inward holiness in society members, and were used as a timely reminder of this on various occasions; as, for example, at morning expositions to the societies, and at the quarterly visitations when new class tickets were issued. Typically we read in Wesley's *Journal* for August 12th, 1747:

> I purposely delayed examining the classes [in Dublin, Ireland] till I had gone through the Rules of the Society, part of which I explained to them at large, with the reasons of them, every morning.[39]

Thus it was stipulated in the 1744 Minutes that new members of a society admitted on trial for three months should at their very first meeting be given a copy of the Rules[40] and in the *Large Minutes* Wesley makes this even more explicit by adding, "See that this be never neglected."[41] The point was re-affirmed at the 1766 Conference, and somewhat more directly:

> Q. Should we give the Rules of the Society to every one, when taken on trial?
>
> A. By all means. . . . When any person is admitted into a Society, even good-breeding requires him to conform to the rules of that Society.[42]

Later in the minutes of this same Conference, Wesley gives what might be described as a "state of the connection" assessment, in which he exhorts his assistants and helpers to use Richard Baxter's *Gildas Salvianus* in the house-to-house instruction of the society members. Once again, the Rules figure prominently:

> Go into *every house* in course, and teach *every one* therein, young and old; if they belong to us, to be Christian, inwardly and outwardly. Make every particular plain to their understanding. Fix it in their memory. Write it on their heart. In order to this, there must be *line upon line*, precept upon precept. I remember to have heard my father asking my mother, "How could you have the patience to tell that blockhead, the same thing twenty times over?" She answered, "Why if I had told him but nineteen times, I should have lost all my labour." What patience indeed, what love, what knowledge is requisite for this!
>
> Q. In what method should we instruct them?
>
> A. Read, explain, enforce, (1) The Rules of the Society . . .[43]

The public injunctions to follow the Rules are complemented in Wesley's correspondence by many private admonitions. Most especially is he concerned that his assistants should observe and enforce them in their circuits. A random sampling provides something of a roll call of early Methodist preachers: to Thomas Maxfield, cautioning that the very least of the Rules are important for the health of a Society;[44] to Joseph Thompson, reminding him that the Rules are to be enforced, never mind who "praises or blames;"[45] to Thomas Wride,[46] Joseph Benson,[47] William Church and John Watson,[48] Samuel Bardsley and Thomas Carlill,[49] and to Samuel Mitchell.[50]

Always the tenor of these letters is a gentle but firm insistence on the keeping of the Rules. Thus to Thomas Rankin, in America at the time, Wesley writes on May 19, 1775:

> We must speak the plain truth wherever we are, whether men will hear or whether they will forbear. And among our Societies we must enforce our Rules with all mildness and steadiness. At first this must appear strange to those who are as bullocks unaccustomed to the yoke. But after a time all that desire to be real Christians see the advantage of it.[51]

And to Joseph Benson on February 22, 1776:

> Dear Joseph, We must threaten no longer, but perform. In November last I told the London Society, 'Our rule is to meet a class once a week, not once in two or three. I now give you warning: I will give tickets to none in February but those that have done this.' I have stood by my words. Go you and do likewise. . . .[52]

And to Lancelot Harrison on January 16, 1780:

> My dear Brother, I perceive many in your circuit do not know our Rules. You should immediately read them in every Society, and receive no new member till he has read them. Let all know what they are about.[53]

There is the same concern in writing to Freeborn Garrettson in Nova Scotia,[54] and to Robert Carr Brackenbury in the island of Jersey—the occasion of the French edition of the Rules in 1784.[55]

It is noteworthy that these references in Wesley's correspondence occur with more frequency in the latter years of his ministry—noteworthy because, even allowing for the vicissitudes of old age, it points us to one of the reasons why the Rules have been mis-traditioned. For the fact of the matter is that direct references to the General Rules in the earlier years of the movement are relatively few in number. And when they do occur, it is with the clear implication that the society members took them to be quite normative in their daily living. The same inference can be drawn from the relatively few directives in

Wesley's writings for the conduct of class meetings—namely, that when the end is being pursued, the means are taken for granted. But when the means become the priority, it usually betokens the neglect of the end for which they were adopted in the first place.[56]

If it was Wesley's increasing concern to stress the enforcement of the Rules, we might therefore infer that he was disturbed by the lack of their observance in the societies. Nor was he alone in this concern. From a manuscript in the Baker collection at Duke University, dated 1790, we have some interesting correspondence on the condition of Methodist societies towards the end of Wesley's life.[57] Unfortunately the letters are unsigned. But they have the ring of authenticity, and two sections are worth examining in some detail:

> It is an indisputable maxim, "The tree is known by its fruits." Hence our Lord says, "If ye love me keep my commandments." In these principles the rules of the Methodist societies are formed—we are united "professing to flee from the wrath to come." This desire to be manifested by "doing no harm, doing all the good in our power, diligently attending the ordinances of God." In other words, "living righteously, soberly & godly." The duty of a class leader is to observe if his people walk by these rules. Hence it appears that a leader ought not only diligently to enquire into the state of his people's mind, but whether or not they walk by the rules of the society—that he ought to do the one as faithfully as the other. . . . Yet I cannot help imagining that this part of class meeting is not only not generally practiced, but very generally omitted—& that this omission is one principal cause of relaxation in our discipline & decay of divine life in our societies.
>
> . . . . .
>
> By enquiring whether our people walk by the rules of the society in class meeting is not meant a constant catechizing as it were, the members by the letter of the rules as they stand—this would soon become formal & obsolete. [But] you will permit me to notice a method which has been already tried. . . . When a person first visits a class on trial they are asked, "Do you know the design of our meeting together?" The rules of the society are given to them, with some such remarks as these: "If you continue to meet with us, you will observe these rules described both [the] end you ought to have in view & the conduct you are expected to manifest. Take them home with you—consider them alone, as in the sight of God. Consider with much prayer what you are about to do, & if you do not sincerely intend, with divine help, to forsake your sins, to take up your cross & follow Jesus Christ, do not increase your guilt by professing to belong to his followers. . . . [But] if you conclude that your union [with us] will help you, & are sincerely purposing to walk by these rules, we shall rejoice to receive you.[58]

The correspondence merely echoes what Wesley himself had said many times: that authentic discipleship consists of working out the salvation accomplished for us through the merits of Jesus Christ. And it is precisely in this regard that the General Rules afford us the opportunity to tradition Aldersgate Street in its fullness. As Joseph Nightingale, another contemporary (and less sympathetic) commentator observed, the Rules are:

> generally deserving of being adopted by all societies of professing Christians; and it is not the least that may be said in their favour, that they enjoin no peculiarities of doctrine—no dissocializing quality, arising from subscription to articles of faith, or modes of worship. Their general principles are founded on the broad, the permanent basis of rational Christianity, and practical morality.[59]

Yet a disturbing paradox emerges with some cogency as we read this little penny pamphlet which, along with their class ticket, we can assume was the property of most early Methodists. And the paradox is this: relatively few of the rules prove anachronistic today, once we make appropriate adjustments for language and social context; yet, in another sense, they are wholly anachronistic, for they have no direct equivalent in our contemporary United Methodist polity or practice.

In no small measure, of course, this is because Methodism is now a large, inclusive church. Indeed, since 1784 the Methodist Episcopal Church has been the mother church of us all. Whether we accept Troeltsch's typology for this phenomenon matters much less than the fact that United Methodism today is thereby the equivalent of the Church of England in Wesley's day—not the same, let it be quickly added, but ecclesiologically the equivalent. Accordingly, costly discipleship is given much less emphasis than the more inclusive benefits and obligations of belonging to this particular manifestation of the family of God. And properly so, given the weight of our doctrine of prevenient grace.

Precisely because of this ecclesiological transition, however, we must appropriate our Methodist tradition with care. Most especially must we endeavor to avoid that faulty historiography which accepts a tradition but mistrusts the mental processes of those who have traditioned it for us. If we interpret that moment of illumination and assurance 250 years ago as both the power and the form of our Christian discipleship, we commit just such an error. For when we examine Wesley's own accounts of the experience, and how he applied it to his own discipleship and that of his societies, we must infer that he viewed his gift of the inner witness primarily as the power of his discipleship, and therefore only half of the equation.

By contrast, the form of Christian discipleship, which he was always at pains to stress as concomitant with the power, was that which would either render grace effectual in a Christian's life, or would quench it. Put differently, the power for living out our discipleship, a power which we can only receive by grace, will always be a gift of God's Spirit. We are to expect it, seek it, pray for it, and be open to it when it comes. But we must never assume that it is the condition of our faith. It is the condition only of our justification. The condition of our faith must always be the works of obedient discipleship.

A complementary word is of course in order, namely to be reminded of the many times Wesley also enjoined upon his preachers and members the importance of the inward witness, and the need to seek, expect, and be open to the transforming power of grace in their lives. The distinction is fine between works of piety and works of mercy in which Christians engage as a response to grace, and the same works enjoined upon Christians as a substitute for grace. In this regard, Aldersgate Street is a powerful affirmation of the former, and is therefore altogether central to our heritage. It should indeed be celebrated as the mark of God's raising up the people called Methodists.

Yet our present context of cultural narcissism and neo-gnosticism should make us cautious. The Minutes of 1766 give us a timely warning:

> Q. Why are not *we* more holy? Why do not *we* live in eternity? Walk with God all the day long? Why are not we all devoted to God? Breathing the whole spirit of *Missionaries*?
>
> A. Because we are enthusiasts; looking for the end, without using the means.[60]

It is not enough to seek for the spiritual power of discipleship, exercising, more or less, a mutual proviso that we do not neglect the works of mercy and the works of piety, usually at our convenience, or when the mood takes us. There must be equal application to the task in hand, of doing the best we can to be open to grace, and following the methodical precepts so clearly and unequivocally set out in the General Rules. God will then bless us with whatever power we need, and whatever assurance is good for us.

Failure to appropriate this tradition will render us vulnerable to the peddlers of spiritual amphetamines on the one hand, and the pied pipers of presumptive utopias on the other, neither of whom are able to give us the true power of discipleship, much less its form. For the form and power of early Methodist discipleship lay in its methods: the works of mercy and the works of piety, in the doing of which our forebears confidently expected the blessings of God's grace, first to bring them the assurance of faith, and then to build them up as obedient disciples.

These methods will not be acceptable to all Methodists, of course. That is the inevitable result of being a large, inclusive *ecclesia* as opposed to a small, exclusive *ecclesiola*. And let there be no doubt about it, the General Rules did make the Methodist societies exclusive; rules enforced, as we have noted, by the quarterly issue of a class ticket. As Wesley himself observed, by this simple method no one was ever excluded from a society—they were just not kept in.[61] But the meaning was the same, as he made very clear in his conclusion to the first edition:

> These are the General Rules of our societies; all which we are taught of God to observe, even in his written Word, the only rule, and the sufficient rules both of our faith and practice. And all these we know his Spirit writes on every truly awakened heart. If there be any among us who observe them not, who habitually break any one of them, let it be made known unto them who watch over that soul, as one that must give account. We will admonish him of the error of his ways. We will bear with him for a season. But if then he repent not, he hath no more place among us. We have delivered our own souls.[62]

We should not be discouraged or disheartened by the fact that we cannot practicably apply such strictures to our congregational life today. These words were for "methodical" disciples, members of small, disciplined societies. Today, we are a national, enculturated church, with a different identity; and therefore, let it be noted, with a rich opportunity for reforming the nation. The question is, how may we first reform the church?

Could it be that there are those in our congregations who *are* ready to be methodical, to be the "modern Methodists"? If so, then these are the ones that we most urgently need to identify, in the true sense of that word—to whom we need to give an identity! If we will call them, encourage them, and build them up in their methodical (i.e., their *Methodist)* discipleship, practicing the form and seeking the power of Godliness, they will leaven, lighten, and savor our churches; just as Wesley hoped and prayed would happen to the Church of England, and thence the nation, through the discipleship of the early Methodist societies.

This scenario assumes, of course, that we are able to recognize such discipleship for what it is—a means of grace for the church as a whole. In Wesley's day the Church of England found this indigestible. Pray God we may have stouter stomachs today, and more sensitive pastoral leadership. For we are The United *Methodist* Church, and surely we have learned *something* from our heritage, not least of which is hopefully the good sense to be open to the form and the power of an obedient discipleship in our midst.

If so, it could be our most signal contribution to the coming Reign of God.

Chapter 3

Great Expectations: Aldersgate and the Evidences of Genuine Christianity[1]

Richard P. Heitzenrater

John Wesley's familiar words describing his experience of 24 May 1738 have been for some time the basis of monumental commemorations and the focus of annual celebrations among Methodists: "I felt my heart strangely warmed. I felt I did trust in Christ, Christ alone for salvation, and an assurance was given me that he had taken away *my* sins, even *mine*, and saved *me* from the law of sin and death."[2] For much of this century, a running dispute has been carried on between some who view this event in Wesley's life as a conversion experience with singular significance as a watershed in his life and others who challenge that view for a variety of reasons.

The proponents of the "heart-warming" as conversion/ watershed point to Wesley's own comments at the time, his claim that he was *now* a Christian whereas previously he was not. They support their view of the watershed nature of the event by quoting Wesley's occasional references to a significant shift or beginning point occurring in or around 1738, and by repeating a general perception that the Methodist movement began to spread like wildfire across England in response to Wesley's new-found zeal.[3]

The opponents of the view of "Aldersgate" as conversion/watershed also use Wesley's own comments to support their views, noting that before 1738 Wesley claimed to be a Christian, that he also claimed several times after 1738 that he was not now a true believer and in at least one instance implied that he never had been. On the basis of Wesley's own comments, they discard the watershed concept and see several important developments occurring in Wesley's life and thought (and Methodist history) from 1725 onward throughout the century, some of which modify or even reject the points of view that he held in 1738.

Proponents of both sides of the controversy, however, must embrace some anomalies that cause disjunctures in their own argument. Although there are a few references in Wesley's writings that can be seen as referring to a significant personal alteration in or about 1738, these comments generally occur within a few years of the event and tend to disappear completely as the century proceeds. Most of the references refer to a shift in his theology and preaching. He does not later harken back to it as his "conversion" experience,[4] much less celebrate the day as a spiritual anniversary, nor does he represent his own personal experience as a model for others to follow. Why, if it were a watershed, would Wesley ignore this event for the last half of his life? Why was it not more determinative of the shape of his autobiographical reflections? And why, in later life, would he go so far as to qualify his own earlier published autobiographical reflections on the event and its significance?[5] On the other hand, if the event was not a watershed, why did its central feature (the experience of assurance, the witness of the Spirit) become a fixture at the heart of his preaching and theology? Why did the perceptible inspiration of the Holy Spirit become a central feature of his soteriology? And why did he continue to insist upon assurance as one of the distinguishing marks of the Methodist movement?

The answers to these questions do not emerge from a simple attempt to solve the problem of whether or not Aldersgate was a conversion experience for Wesley. For the answer to that question, based on Wesley's own testimony, is both "yes" and "no," depending on when he spoke to the question and how he then defined the concept. Moreover, the primary issue in 1738 for Wesley (both in terms of anticipation and experience) was that of *assurance*, and the direct tie between assurance and conversion, assumed by Wesley at the time, he eventually dropped in his mature theology. The more important question, then, is to ask what significance this experience of 24 May 1738 had in the overall span of Wesley's life and thought, and how Wesley viewed this experience—what were his expectations? what were his immediate reactions? what were his subsequent reflections? Wesley's own attempt to resolve questions relating to the experience of assurance, as it turns out, provides a major stimulus for his continuing theological development throughout much of his life.

In looking at these questions, we would also do well to distinguish between Wesley's spiritual pilgrimage and his theological development. We will see that while Aldersgate was a crucial step in his *spiritual* pilgrimage at the time, his expectations were not fully met by the experience, and his subsequent reflections on the event caused him to modify many of the *theological* premises upon which those expectations were based. There is, of course, an obvious and essential connection between the two: his theology quite naturally develops in conjunction with his life experiences. But one soon discovers that Wesley is often more facile at *describing* his experience than at *analyzing* it. The process of theological reflection often takes years to work through a given problem—to integrate scriptural concepts, church teachings, life experiences, spiritual inspiration, and rational reflection. His descriptions at any given time must also be seen in the light of his later reflections. And later reflections need to be understood as incorporating the hindsight that comes with continued maturation.[6]

The problem that confronted Wesley at Aldersgate was the question, How do I *know* I am a Christian? a child of God? How do I *know* that I am justified? forgiven? The issue was essentially that of *assurance*. He had been convinced as a young man that persons should be able clearly to perceive if they were in a state of salvation. His problem was, in one significant aspect, epistemological—how does one know? And given his philosophical tendencies in this matter, his approach was to look for *evidence* upon which to base his knowledge. What he was looking for, then, was the evidence that he was really a Christian.

Several variables immediately enter the problem: (1) How is "Christian" *defined*? The definition entails in part some descriptive model that exhibits such things as necessary traits, minimal qualities, requisite standards. (2) How does one *become* a Christian? An understanding of the process ("what must I do to be saved?") entails crucial definitions and weighing of essentials in the process, such as grace, faith, good works, the work of the Holy Spirit. (3) How does one *know* that he or she is a Christian? What are the grounds of any certainty that a person is a Christian? What is the evidence (internal or external) that can verify one's condition? These questions pertain to both the process of knowing and the content of that knowledge.

In all three of these areas, Wesley's views changed over the years. We cannot fully understand Aldersgate without recognizing where Wesley stood on each of these issues at that time in the light of how he got to that point and where he went from there. His spiritual and theological development up to 1738 (which in part shaped his expectations) depended upon his stance in each of these areas, and his subsequent development (which was affected in part by his evaluation of Aldersgate in the light of those expectations) shows significant modifications in each of these areas. Of particular interest is the increasingly essential role that the Holy Spirit plays in Wesley's understanding of not only how people *become* Christians but also how they *know* they are children of God. It is important to recognize that Aldersgate represents a significant conjunction of pneumatology and epistemology in his life (spiritual pilgrimage) that took many years for him to work out in his thought (theological development). It also represents a testing of his theological methodology, his manner of weighing various criteria as he attempted to use rational processes to explain scriptural truths manifest in the human experience of divine realities. His theology, centered as it is upon soteriology, is an attempt to explain the *via salutis,*[7] based in part upon his observations of that spiritual pilgrimage in his own life and the lives of others, looking for the evidences of genuine Christianity (as he understood it at any particular time).

Our attempt here will be to examine the place of Aldersgate in Wesley's development. It will focus upon *how Wesley himself understood it:* the shape of his expectations in anticipation of such an event, his description of the essential features of his experience of the event, and his retrospective views of these features in the light of his subsequent theological analyses of this step of his spiritual pilgrimage. The plain story of these developments is central to our examination. Since the Moravian influence is crucial to an understanding of events in 1738, we will focus our attention upon the narrative of the chronological development of his thinking and experience through the time of his association with the Moravians up to 1740, then summarize some of the more important developments beyond that time. We will use recently discovered sermons and correspondence from his early years, along with material from his personal diaries, to put together the story in a way that has not previously been told.[8]

The Quest for Certainty

The central issue for Wesley in the spring of 1738 is the question, How do I *know* that I am a Christian? Another way of stating the same question is, What *assurance* (or certain evidence) do I have that I am a child of God? These questions were by no means new to Wesley. He had long felt that one should be able to know the answer to these questions with some certainty by seeing the *evidences* of genuine Christianity in the life of the believer. This approach, of course, fitted nicely into his generally empirical approach to questions of knowledge. He had quite early settled upon a Lockean approach to matters of this sort.[9] A letter to his mother Susanna reveals his inclination to apply an empirical approach to this question as early as 1725. Referring to the Lord's Supper, in the celebration of which "the Holy Ghost confers on us the graces we pray for," Wesley writes:

> Now surely these graces are not of so little force as that we can't perceive whether we have them or not: and if we dwell in Christ and Christ in us, . . . certainly we must be sensible of it. . . . If we can never have any certainty of our being in a state of salvation, good reason it is that every moment should be spent, not in joy, but fear and trembling.[10]

Wesley himself had recently exhibited an "alteration of his temper" that Susanna had noticed. She was hopeful that the change might have proceeded "from the operations of God's Holy Spirit" and that he, in response, would "make religion the business of [his] life" as "the one thing that strictly speaking is necessary." She had pressed him to use self-examination in order to increase self-knowledge, "that you may know whether you have a reasonable hope of salvation, . . . whether you are in a state of faith and repentance or not. . . . If you are, the satisfaction of knowing it will abundantly reward your pains."[11]

John also was fairly clear about the general form of evidence by which one might be assured of being in a state of salvation. As Susanna had written to him, "Our blessed Lord . . . came from heaven to save us from our sins . . . knowing we could not be happy in either world without holiness." Happiness and holiness were constantly linked as visible results of God's saving grace in the life of the believer. The goal, through grace, was Christian perfection, "sincerely endeavouring to plant each virtue in our minds that may through Christ render us pleasing to God." This holiness, centered in the virtues, was directed toward eternal goals, opened to human eyes and ears by the Lord who "opens and extends our views beyond time to eternity."[12]

With all of this John agreed, but his desire for certainty outstripped his parents' understanding of the means to such assurance. John understood faith to be a basic building block of this certainty. At that time he defined faith as "a species of belief," and belief he defined as "assent to a proposition upon rational grounds." Therefore, "without rational grounds there is therefore no belief and consequently no faith." This definition of faith was borrowed from Dr. Fiddes and grounded in his own correlation of faith and rational knowledge. Wesley assumed that "no knowledge can be where there is not certain evidence" (a variation of the empirical maxim that "there is nothing in the mind that is not in the senses") and that the divine testimony was "the most reasonable of all evidence whatever."[13] The present and future prospects of certainty with regard to salvation he explained in the following manner, providing both the rationale and the evidence:

> That we can never be so certain of the pardon of our sins as to be assured they will never rise up against us, I firmly believe. . . . But I am persuaded we may know if we are *now* in a state of salvation, since that is expressly promised in the Holy Scriptures to our sincere endeavors, and we are surely able to judge of our own sincerity.[14]

Samuel and Susanna soon disabused John of what they viewed as an inadequate notion of faith. Susanna provided two long discussions on the manner in which "all faith is an assent, but all assent is not faith."[15] Samuel, with typical pungency, pointed out the dangers of John's position in one cryptic sentence and tagged on a word of advice: "He that believes *without* or *against* reason is half a Papist or enthusiast; he that would mete revelation by his own shallow reason is either half a deist or an heretic. O my dear, steer clear between this Scylla and Charybdis."[16]

John capitulated in the matter: "I am therefore at length come over entirely to your opinion, that saving faith (including practice) is an assent to what God has revealed, because he has revealed it, and not because the truth of it may be evinced by reason."[17] The response of his mother/spiritual director was typical: "I am much more pleased and thankful because I have observed sometime that the Holy Jesus (to whom the whole manage of our salvation is committed) seems to have taken the conduct of your soul into his own hand, in that he has given you a true notion of saving faith, and, I hope, an experimental knowledge of repentance. . . . Dear Jacky, I hope you are a good Christian."[18]

Wesley's view of a "good Christian" up to this point had been largely determined by his childhood training in the Epworth rectory. As he later pointed out, he had early learned that the Christian is one who has received the saving grace of God. His early understanding of the means of attaining salvation was typical for the Church of England: a balance of faith and works, following the scriptural injunctions to believe, hope, and love, using the means of grace.[19] During his years at Charterhouse School where, beyond the immediate constraints of his parents his outward sins tended to proliferate, he relied for his hope of salvation upon a threefold approach: not being so bad as others; having a fondness for religion; going to church, saying his prayers, etc.[20] The evidence for such hope and the signs of genuine Christianity therefore depended upon external measures: a Christian is one saved from sin, therefore a Christian avoids sin and does good whenever possible, and upon failure to do so, relies upon repentance.[21]

A New View of Religion—Holiness of Heart

The changes that took place in Wesley's life and thought in 1725 were caused by a shift in his definition of salvation. His view that salvation amounted to freedom from sin (which the Christian exhibited by the grace of God through *outward* goodness and upon failure turned to God's mercy in proper repentance) was enlarged to include the striving for *inward* holiness. Wesley began to view true religion as seated in the heart: "God's law extends to all thoughts as well as words and actions."[22] Wesley found many helpful tutors in this regard in the books he read: from Jeremy Taylor he learned the importance of purity of intention; from William Law and Henry Scougal the necessity of a proper inclination of the soul; from Thomas à Kempis the way of appropriating the mind of Christ; from Robert Nelson a practical method of meditating on the virtues for each day of the week.

He now set upon a new life in earnest, watched against all sin *and* aimed at inward holiness. This development, which his mother had noticed and encouraged as part of his new determination to prepare for holy orders, manifested itself in several ways which Wesley himself began to chart. Meditation became the means of implanting the virtues; lists of rules and resolutions provided some measure of their presence; self-examination was the means of testing their effects. But a reliable measure of inward intentions and virtues was more difficult than spotting the absence of outward sins. A daily diary provided the ledger upon which the hourly dispositions of the mind and soul could be recorded. Sincerity became the measure of one's progress toward perfection, trying to imitate the life of Christ, having his mind and walking as he walked.[23]

The result of Wesley's endeavors in this regard was that he considered himself at the time to be a good Christian, in terms of his definition of what a Christian is, how one becomes a Christian, and how one knows that one is a Christian.[24] It is interesting to note in passing that Wesley in later life will confirm that this is the point at which he resolved to become a *real* Christian.[25] In 1725 he was not hesitant to use the term "servant of God" to describe the Christian, a term which he will eventually come back to and recognize as useful in describing a valid Christian.[26]

Wesley's conviction of the necessity of inward holiness was heightened by his study of William Law's writings in 1728–29, which convinced him even further of the "exceeding height and breadth and depth of the law of God," inward and outward. Wesley describes the impact of this insight: "The light flowed in so mightily upon my soul, that everything appeared in a new view." Wesley felt even more strongly then that he would be accepted by Christ and that he was "even then in a state of salvation."[27] At age twenty-seven, he "strove against all sin," used "all the means of grace at all opportunities," and "omitted no occasion of doing good" (another good summary of his later *General Rules*). He was convinced, however, that all this must be aimed at inward holiness, the restoration of the image of God in the life of the believer.[28]

Faith and Knowledge

The problem was still the question, How does he *know* if he is a Christian? Wesley's fascination with epistemological questions is evident in three writings he produced at the end of 1730—two sermons, and an abridgment of Peter Browne's *The Procedure, Method, and Limits of Human Understanding*. In the first of these sermons (on John 13:7, "What I do thou knowest not now") Wesley points out the possibilities and problems of our attempts to know God, speaking of the Christian's perception of the sovereignty of grace, knowing *that* God works in human lives without being able to explain either *how* God works in a person the life of grace or *why* some attain to such heights of virtue and happiness. At this point, Wesley grants that God reveals enough to undergird our faith *that* God's ways are wise and good and gracious (which allows us to *believe* and give assent to this) but acknowledges that we do not have the sensible perception of God or his truth that would allow us to know these things for *certain*. Likewise, the springs of spiritual life are ultimately unsearchable—*that* the Spirit works in us, "experience, and reason, and Scripture convince every sincere inquirer; but *how* he worketh this in us, who shall tell?"[29] The reason God clouds our vision of him is to lead us to humility ("conscious of how little we can know of him, we may be the more intent upon knowing ourselves") that we might "walk by faith, not by sight."[30]

In the second writing (sermon on Genesis 1:27, "In the Image of God") Wesley contrasts human nature in the perfection of creation and the debilities of the Fall. Created in God's image, Adam could know everything "according to its real nature; truth and evidence went hand in hand; he was a stranger to error and doubt."[31] The first step of sinful humanity toward a recovery of the image of God is humility, self-knowledge; if we cannot know God fully, at least we can know ourselves. A just sense of our condition will result in our understanding being enlightened: we must know that we are all originally foolish and vicious; then we know the necessity and the divine efficacy of our religion.[32]

Wesley's abridgment of Browne the following month broadened his perspective somewhat not only on the matter of "where knowledge ends and faith begins" but also on "where they meet again and inseparably combine for enlarging our understanding vastly beyond its native sphere, for opening to the mind an immense scene of things otherwise imperceptible."[33] Browne reiterates the basic empiricist proposition: our senses are the only source of those ideas upon which all our knowledge is founded. He goes on to describe the various kinds of knowledge and evidence, distinguishing between knowledge and faith and between different types of certainty (illustrated by scientific and moral certainty). While pointing out that sensible evidence is the ground not of faith but of knowledge, Browne goes on to say that "evangelical faith" is an act of the will beyond assent to evidential religious propositions and is based to some extent upon things that are immediately comprehended. Browne uses a definition of evangelical faith that will become central to Wesley's eventual understanding of how knowledge and faith combine in matters of religious certainty: "the 'evidence of things not seen' [Heb. 11:1] or the assent of the understanding to the truth and existence of things inconceivable, upon certain and evident proof of their reality in their symbols and representatives."[34] In his abridgment, Wesley omits this specific reference, but does refer to this "evidence which is peculiar to a quite different sort of knowledge" than knowledge of "matters merely human."[35]

Sincerity as Evidence and Hope

One major question in all this, of course, is, What is this evidence by which one can discern progress toward inward holiness or be assured of a proper status with God? Inward holiness is more difficult to sense with certainty and much harder to measure than outward holiness. In counseling a friend at this time (1731) regarding the interplay of faith and doubt, Wesley stressed one typical Anglican response to the dilemma, a reliance upon sincerity. In the process of explaining, he used a metaphor of sense perception (i.e., sight) that was becoming common to him and would provide a useful image throughout his life: by "faith . . . 'the eyes of her understanding can be enlightened to see what is the hope of our calling,' to know that our hope is sincerity, not perfection; not to do well, but to do our best."[36] One's sincerity, then, provided whatever measure of hope or assurance there might be of salvation. The virtue was in the attempt; the assurance was manifest in the sincerity of the attempter.

A few months later, Wesley expanded upon the idea of "doing our best" in a gloss to his abridgment of Robert Nelson's work, *The Great Duty of Frequenting the Christian Sacrifice*.[37] One of Wesley's answers to objections against what he called "constant communion" was that man is bound to obey the commands of God "as often as he can." To explain this point, Wesley argued that since the Fall, man is no longer required to exercise perfect obedience to every command of God (the stipulations of the old covenant), but rather to follow the "new covenant" that was made with fallen man and to "perform it as well as he can." Rather than the original agreement, "Do this and live," mankind is now bound by the second, "Try to do this, and live."[38] The sincere attempt would be recognized by God, who would acknowledge one's good intentions.[39] The dilemma of assurance was not completely resolved, of course, by this approach. Sincerity might be an appropriate (perhaps even the best) measure of an inward reality, but how could anyone ever be certain, ever rest assured, that they were indeed doing the best they could? In fact, Wesley's own attempts to measure his progress in this regard by keeping track of his spiritual pulse by means of a diary seemed only to frustrate this approach by revealing the opposite—the closer he kept track of himself, the more he became aware of his shortcomings, doubted his sincerity, and feared lest he should fall short of the mark of his calling.

Nevertheless, the conviction that true happiness came from an inward holiness was firmly planted in Wesley by the late 1720s. In 1733 he graphically characterized this inward focus as "the circumcision of the heart" in his first major sermon on Christian perfection. That Wesley and Oxford Methodism were essentially concerned with inward religion (not works-righteousness) and focused on a virtue ethic (more than an obligation ethic) has not been generally recognized by those who would try to see Wesley's life before 1738 as being in dark contrast to the light that follows 1738.[40] In this sermon, which sets the course for a lifelong emphasis on Christian perfection as love of God and neighbor—"having the mind which was in Christ Jesus"[41]— Wesley strikes a note that disarms those who see the Oxford Methodists as trusting in their own works: "the distinguishing mark of a true follower of Christ, of one who is in a state of acceptance with God, is not either outward circumcision or baptism, or any other outward form, but a right state of soul, a mind and spirit renewed after the image of him that created it."[42]

In this context, Wesley speaks of the necessity of faith as "a sure light of them that are in darkness." It must be a *strong* faith, however.[43] Such a view implies variations of faith in degrees and raises (but does not answer) the implicit question, How strong does faith have to be in order for one truly to be a Christian?[44] Faith implies new sight: to the one who thus believes, "the eyes of his understanding being enlightened, he sees what is his calling," including an assent to that important truth, "Jesus Christ came into the world to save sinners; he bore our sins in his own body on the tree; he is the propitiation for our sins; and not for ours only, but also for the sins of the whole world."[45] This proclamation of the belief in *Christus pro nobis* (Christ died for us) is eventually the ground of his experience of *Christus pro me.*[46]

Measuring a right state of soul and testing a renewed spirit, however, presented a challenge. Wesley at this point states that the marks by which one can judge his state of acceptance are the presence of a humility that brings with it a conviction of corruption, an honest attempt to walk by faith in the light of eternity, and the assurance given by "the witness of the Spirit with his spirit that he is a child of God."[47] The rules of the Oxford Methodists served the same purpose as the rules of later Methodism—a means by which one could test the external evidences of an inward inclination of the soul and the active presence of the virtues (especially the central virtue, love), which were the genuine fruits or evidence of real religion.[48]

The One Thing Needful

Wesley's conviction that holiness of heart was the focus of true religion was heightened by his contact with the mystics after 1732, who nearly convinced him that outward works were useless in the pursuit of inward holiness, which they defined as "union of the soul with God." Writings by and about Mmes. Bourignon and Guyon, Cardinal Fénelon, Pierre Poiret, and Monsr. de Renty, as well as direct contact with William Law (who by 1732 had come under the influence of Boehmist mysticism himself), encouraged his attempts to overcome his growing obsession with rules of holy living.[49] If the goal of the Christian was union with the divine being, the first step toward this goal was "purgation," the expulsion of "the world, the flesh, and the devil" from all thoughts and actions. All temporal concerns were seen as impediments to the process of transcending this world and becoming one with the divine. Rules and disciplines of life thus simply increased the fascination with the world in the attempt to overcome its power. He recognized that the mystics presented yet another "entirely new view of religion," especially in their total rejection of temporal concerns; even the rejection of "the world" should not be used as evidence of progress, lest even in this negative fashion the world become a point of focus.[50]

The mystics advised that "love was all"; this motif is reflected in Wesley's sermon at the time in which he sees the love of God as the "one thing needful" to perfect human happiness. Love is the fulfilling of the law, the end of every commandment of Christ, the first principle of all religion.[51] This "singularity of attention" is Wesley's fascination at this time, though it comes out in a variety of ways. "The one thing needful" in a sermon of the same title the following year is the recovery of the image of God, whereby one is restored to health, liberty, and holiness through redemption, new birth, and sanctification. This desideratum is not just an important concern, the *chief* thing needful; it is the *one* thing needful.[52] Another sermon on "If Thine Eye Be Single" reiterates this same theme: the Christian must have a singular intention, "to please God," or in other words, "to improve in holiness, in the love of God and thy neighbor."[53]

Wesley's Oxford Methodist friend Benjamin Ingham exhibited the same resolve in a diary notation about this time. He balanced his personal intentions with a recognition of the need for grace: "I am resolved, God's grace assisting me, to make the salvation of my soul my chief and only concern, but never to depend upon my own strength because I can do nothing without God's assistance."[54] Wesley himself gave similar advice to George Whitefield just a few weeks later, when asked by George whether weakness of body and spiritual despair should excuse one from the disciplines of Christian living. Wesley advised him to maintain the observance of external practices as much as possible, but "not to depend on them in the least."[55] Wesley was still prone to look for evidence, however, and considered the virtues to be good evidence of that love that was the manifestation of faith.[56]

The tension here between the life of discipline, which Wesley had long since adopted, and the dispensation from all such obligations, which the mystics so strongly advocated, put Wesley in a real quandary. How was he to know if he was pursuing the proper path to God? It did not take him long to discover that he was in a state of confusion in this regard. He found himself fluctuating between obedience and disobedience, continually doubting whether he was right or wrong and never out of perplexities and entanglements.[57] The dilemma presented by the mystics could not be resolved satisfactorily by his usual test of "sincerity," though he did suggest that traditional answer to his own query in his diary:

> Question: How steer between scrupulosity as to particular instances of self-denial, and self-indulgence?
>
> Answer: *Fac quod in te est, et Deus aderit bonae tuae voluntati.*[58]

Resting one's hope in one's sincerity is little consolation to a person who, on the one hand, is pressing on toward perfection and yet, on the other hand, is struggling to develop a sense of humility that recognizes that his or her own efforts must be distrusted.[59] Can sincerity be an adequate measure of certainty when perfection is the goal, "doing your best" is the watchword, humility is a necessity, and good works are taken away as evidence? What sort of certainty could be expected from sincerity under these circumstances?

The mystics had not only taken away good works as an outward measure (a tempting indicator even to predestinarians), but also left Wesley in the predicament of having no reliable form of assurance to fall back upon. Among the options he considered were those of becoming preoccupied with suffering as the mark of a true Christian (Guyon, Bourignon, etc.) and of relying upon a solifidianism that stressed faith alone instead of sincerity as the prerequisite (and the evidence) of inward holiness. At this point, however, Wesley's understanding of faith provided very little if any sensible evidence—"things that are eternal are not seen, but only through a glass darkly." He could quote "we walk by faith, and not by sight," but the faith of which he spoke at this point was a nearly blind faith.[60] And every moment of doubt immediately placed faith in jeopardy. About this time, John's father had, on his deathbed, suggested to him another manner of assurance that would soon supersede the others in John's experience: "the inward witness, son, the inward witness; that is the proof, the strongest proof of Christianity." Wesley later admitted that "at the time, I understood him not."[61]

Faith, Doubt, and Fear

The dilemma of having no solid grounds or evidence for assurance of salvation produced much of the anxiety that Wesley felt upon the eve of his departure for Georgia in 1735. Having been "tossed by various winds of doctrine," he was ready to find a right faith, which would then open the way to a right practice. Confusion had caused uncertainty; doubt had challenged faith. He hoped "to learn the true sense of the gospel of Christ by preaching it to the heathens." In the pristine setting of the New World, he felt the uncorrupted natives would "know of every doctrine I preach, whether it be of God." Wesley's own insecurity at that point was great enough to cause him even to doubt his state of salvation; to John Burton he wrote that his chief motive for embarking to Georgia was the hope of saving his own soul.[62]

The Atlantic crossing, however, added yet another source of anxiety to his quest for assurance. To his *doubt* would be added *fear*, which confirmed the insecurity of his faith. Wesley faced God in the depths of the ocean, and the first storms showed that he had no faith, for he was "unwilling to die."[63] In contrast, the German pietists on board the *Simmonds* exhibited not only humility and meekness, but also fearlessness in the face of death. On 25 January, these German Moravians continued their services without intermission while the sea raged, the mainsail was split, and the water poured over the decks "as if the great deep had already swallowed us up." His fear contrasted sharply with the Moravians' confidence. The hour of trial had given him clear evidence of the difference between those that fear God and those who do not. It was a momentous occasion: "This was the most glorious day which I have hitherto seen." He would adopt the Moravians as his tutors in the faith.[64]

The sermons Wesley wrote on shipboard begin to show an increasing acknowledgment of the Holy Spirit in his understanding of the spiritual pilgrimage. The sermon on "A Single Intention" continues his theme of singularity: "Your one end is to please and love God." But a new dynamic begins to be more evident: "His Holy Spirit shall dwell in you and shine more and more upon your souls unto the perfect day; . . . he shall establish your souls with so lively a hope as already lays hold on the prize of your high calling, and shall fill you with peace, and joy, and love."[65] These fruits of the Spirit will come to play an important role as evidence of the internal state, revealing the beginning of a shift from an emphasis on sincerity to a reliance upon the witness of the Holy Spirit and the concomitant evidence.

The following month, Wesley wrote another sermon on love, using a phrase he had often quoted from Romans 5:5, "the love of God shed abroad in our hearts," but now adding the final phrase, "by the Holy Ghost given unto us."[66] The development of a more vital doctrine of the Holy Spirit (pneumatology) in Wesley's thought was to have important consequences for his epistemology, especially regarding the question of assurance, how one might *know* that one is a Christian.

The question of assurance was pressed home to Wesley in Georgia by August Gottlieb Spangenberg, whose advice Wesley had sought.

Spangenberg first asked him: "Do you know yourself? Have you the witness within yourself? Does the Spirit of God bear witness with your spirit that you are a child of God?" Wesley's silence was met by further questions: "Do you know Jesus Christ? . . . Do you know he has saved you? . . . Do you know [this for] yourself?" Wesley's weak answers to these questions led Spangenberg to give Wesley several directions to follow.[67] When Spangenberg described to Wesley the fruits of faith, Wesley later recalled responding, "If this be so, I have *no* faith." To which the German tutor responded, *"Habes fidem, sed exiguam"* ("You have faith, but insufficient [faith]").[68] What he needed was *more* faith, a stronger faith.

On the trip back to England in December and January of 1737–38, Wesley's lack of faith became evident to him again in his fears and doubts, confirming in his mind the dangerous state of his soul. The imminent danger of death made him very uneasy, and he was strongly convinced that the cause of his uneasiness was unbelief.[69] At this point, he saw unbelief as being the result of either a want of faith or a want of right tempers.[70] He was definitely beginning to swing toward the Moravian view of *sola fide*. In a moment of self-examination on shipboard he wrote: "By the most infallible of proofs, inward feeling, I am convinced . . . of unbelief; having no such faith in Christ as will prevent my heart from being troubled, which it would not be, if I believed in God, and rightly believed also in him." True faith would eliminate doubt. The evidence upon which assurance would be based included not only the presence of positive fruits, including faith and certain virtues, but also the elimination of all contrary and troubling indications. A continuing confession of several other shortcomings is followed by Wesley's plea: "Lord, save, or I perish! Save me . . . by such a faith as implies peace in life and in death; . . . by such humility as may fill my heart . . . ; by such a recollection as may cry to thee every moment . . . ; by steadiness, seriousness, [honesty], sobriety of spirit."[71] His conviction of unbelief relied upon inward feeling. His understanding of the cure for his doubt and fear was also inward: "the one thing needful," a true, living faith.[72]

A New Gospel and Heightened Expectations

Wesley's close friends could not agree with his assessment of unbelief. Thomas Broughton, an Oxford Methodist, could not imagine that John, "who had done and suffered such things," did not have faith. Charles felt such talk from John was mischievous. A blunt exchange with them in the spring of 1738 had a positive result in John's perception: "It did please God then to kindle a fire which I trust shall never be extinguished."[73] But the sure evidence of such a confident faith was not yet constantly present in Wesley's life, and the presence of doubt and fear continually placed his small degree of confidence in jeopardy [question]. The proof of belief would have to be as sure as the proof of unbelief—inner feeling. Wesley had begun a manner of speaking that was clear to him: I feel, therefore I know—it is inwardly evident to me in my own experience.[74] This was a new twist on his desire for evidence as a basis of knowledge, a variation on the empirical method that relied on less than traditional empirical evidence and more on direct inner knowledge. This inner knowledge was, nevertheless, expressed in terms of sensation, feeling.

Within this developing framework, Peter Böhler had a fairly easy time during the early months of 1738 convincing Wesley that *true* faith eliminated all doubt. Wesley's reflections at the end of his journal account of the voyage back to England in January 1738 betray the hindsight of his later encounters with the Moravians in England, which confirmed him in two important points: (1) "I knew not that I was *wholly void of this faith*, and thought *I had not enough* of it."[75] This implies that there are *no degrees of faith*. (2) "I want [lack] that faith which none can have without *knowing* that he hath it . . . ; for whosoever hath it is 'freed from sin' . . . is freed from fear . . . and is freed from doubt."[76] Thus true faith is always accompanied by assurance and evidenced by freedom from sin, fear, and doubt, three fruits which inseparably attend assurance and attest to a proper faith.

Upon hearing Böhler outline his view of faith, Wesley remarked that he was amazed and "looked upon this as a new gospel."[77] Once again, Wesley faced another "new view" of religion and the prospect of redefining his conception of true Christianity. The consequences were clear: if Böhler was right that assurance necessarily accompanies true faith, then it was clear that Wesley (who was not free from doubt and fear, much less sin) did not have true faith and was therefore not a real Christian. On 5 March 1738, Wesley became convinced of the necessity of this faith alone for salvation (*sola fide*) and of his own state of unbelief. He began preaching salvation by faith the following day.[78] In Georgia, Wesley had been impressed by the Moravians as a contemporary exhibit of apostolic Christianity[79] and now accepted the validity of their theological presuppositions as well. Only one thing prevented him from being able (with them) to claim with confidence his own status as a child of God, and that was the lack of an experience of assurance that would eliminate sin, doubt, and fear and thereby bring true holiness and happiness through love, peace, and joy in the Holy Ghost.[80]

Salvation in a Moment

Wesley now dropped his objections to Böhler's comments on the nature of faith and assurance, understood by Wesley within the framework of the definition in the *Homilies*: "a sure trust and confidence in God." Böhler highlighted the radically experiential aspect of this concept in terms of *Christus pro me*: "that through the merits of Christ *my* sins are forgiven and I am reconciled to the favor of God."[81] Faith was not simply a matter of agreeing with this belief, a rational assent to propositional truths; faith entailed a personal experience of divine forgiveness, confirmed by the witness of the Holy Spirit and made evident in a life without sin.

Böhler also convinced Wesley that this true faith "converts at once." John was introduced to the idea of instantaneous conversion on April 22 and became convinced of it the following day by the testimony of several "living witnesses that God *can* . . . give that faith whereof cometh salvation in a moment."[82] Thus, the experience that Wesley was expecting and for which he was hoping and praying was to be an experience of faith, inevitably attended by an assurance of pardon, which would necessarily result in freedom from sin, doubt, and fear, and be accompanied by a full measure of peace, joy, and confidence—all this in a moment, and altogether understood as conversion, the moment at which he would become a real, genuine Christian.[83]

Experience and Evidence

The pressure upon John became even greater on Whitsunday, 21 May 1738, when, after hearing a sermon on "They were all filled with the Holy Ghost," he received the "surprising news"that his younger brother Charles "had found rest to his soul." Charles Wesley's experience of assurance in the Moravian manner served to confirm John even further in his own expectations.[84] Therefore, what happened on 24 May 1738 in the meeting of "a society in Aldersgate Street" was naturally understood by him at the time in the light of those expectations. He testified on the spot to those about him what he felt in his heart. He felt a trust in Christ alone for salvation (essential to the definition of faith as sure trust and confidence), and at that instant he did receive an assurance that Christ had taken away *his* sins and saved *him* from the law of sin and death.[85] He was now a Christian and could claim that a week previous he had not been.[86]

Wesley celebrated the exuberance of the moment with an immediate testimony to those present; later that evening the celebration continued in Charles's rooms with the singing of a hymn.[87] The real test, however, of the authenticity of this experience was to be found, not in terms of whether or not he felt his heart "strangely warmed,"[88] but whether or not the expected and necessary fruits of faith and assurance (as he was taught by the Moravians to expect) would be in evidence: freedom from sin, doubt, and fear, and the fullness of peace, confidence, and joy in the Holy Ghost (otherwise called "holiness and happiness").

Questions began to develop almost immediately, raised by Wesley's quest for positive evidence or the problem of evidence to the contrary. The "enemy" soon suggested that what he had experienced could not be faith: "for where is thy joy?" He was at least comforted by the awareness that, although still buffeted with temptations, he had the sense that he was now "always conqueror."[89] The following day, Wesley's empiricism got the better of him: "If thou dost believe, why is there not a more sensible change?" Again, comfort came in the form of a measure of "peace with God." The matter of fears (which he had been taught to equate with unbelief) was pushed aside for the moment by a text from St. Paul—"Without were fightings, within were fears." He resolved to go on and simply try to tread them under his feet. The same was true concerning "heaviness because of manifold temptations"—the Moravians advised not fighting them but fleeing from them.[90] Four days after Aldersgate, he was still bothered by waking "in peace, but not in joy."

During the following days, he was constantly troubled by one problem after another relating to his only partially fulfilled expectations. One area that would trouble him rather consistently was the matter of degrees of faith, which was brought vividly to his attention by simply being in the presence of Peter Böhler. Wesley perceived Böhler to be in so much higher a state than he was that he wondered if they could possibly have the same faith (that one true faith that was necessary for salvation). The clear light of such evidence caused him to fall back upon a previous assumption that there are *degrees* of faith—"Though his be strong and mine weak, yet that God hath given some degree of faith even to me, I know by its fruits."[91] Wesley could not discard the concept of degrees of faith. The evidence of his own experience, viewed in the light of Scripture, confirmed for him that although he did *not* have a constant abiding joy, he *did* at that point have constant peace and freedom from sin and therefore some measure of faith.

The issue concerning degrees of faith was highlighted by a letter he soon received from Oxford, which drew out the dichotomy of faith versus unbelief in the form Wesley had most feared: "No doubting could consist with the least degree of true faith; that whoever at any time felt any doubt or fear was not *weak in faith*, but had *no faith* at all."[92] Wesley could no longer accept this position. Against this assertion, he again posited the testimony of Scripture: 1 Corinthians 3 speaks of "babes in Christ." Certainly these had some degree of faith, though perhaps weak.

Experience and Doctrine—The Moravians in Germany

Wesley decided to visit the Moravian community in Germany to converse with "those holy men who were themselves living witnesses of the full power of faith and yet able to bear with those that are weak."[93] What he discovered, however, was that they were not all willing to tolerate Wesley's lack of full confidence and joy. On one occasion they barred him from participating in the Lord's Supper with them because it was evident to them that he was still *homo perturbatis*, a perturbed person not clearly evidencing the marks of full assurance.[94] The confusion of that occasion was compounded by his discovery that some of the Moravian views in Herrnhut differed remarkably from those of Böhler and the English Moravians on crucial points.

Nicholas von Zinzendorf, the head of the community, claimed that assurance could be separate in time from the moment of justification—one might not *know* or be assured of one's justification until long afterward. This notion countered Böhler's argument that one could not have forgiveness of sins without experiencing an immediate sensation of it. In addition to questioning the necessity of assurance as a prerequisite for claiming justification, Zinzendorf also qualified the requisite nature of other evidences of justification: peace *may* be evident, but joy is frequently *not* present.[95] For Wesley, this view of salvation seemed closer to his earlier experience and understanding of Scripture: a view that would allow for degrees of faith and sequential development, a view that might allow for a more satisfactory analysis of his own experience as well.

The German Moravians made several distinctions that Wesley would find crucial: distinguishing between justification and assurance (both theologically and chronologically), between faith and assurance, and between the beginning and the fullness of salvation. Wesley noticed especially four sermons by Christian David, who repeatedly spoke of "those who are 'weak in faith,' who are justified but have not yet a new, clean heart; who have received forgiveness through the blood of Christ but have not received the indwelling of the Holy Ghost."[96] Since his discussions with Böhler in the spring, Wesley had spoken generally in terms of "salvation by faith," as in his sermon of that title. From this point, Wesley begins to use the more precise concept of "justification" much more frequently.

While he was in Germany, Wesley met and interviewed several persons who could testify that their experience matched their doctrines. Wesley wrote careful notes on these interviews and later published them in his *Journal* as evidence of the true doctrines of the Moravian Church in order to clear the Moravians from any aspersion arising from the teachings of the English brethren. Among those he questioned was Arvid Gradin, whose personal account of "the full assurance of faith" was (as he later noted) "the first account I ever heard from any living man, of what I had before learned myself from the oracles of God and had been praying for (with the little company of my friends) and expecting for several years."[97]

The conflict between the German and English Moravian positions represented the nub of the problem for Wesley at this point. He had been taught by the English Moravians of the necessity of an experience of the type Böhler described, with its absolute requirements and necessary evidences and allowing for no doubt or fear. Wesley's confusion in his attempt to understand his own experience in the light of those expectations was caused in part by the difficulties inherent in the Moravian position. The English Moravians had, in Lutheran fashion, collapsed sanctification into justification and, in Pietist fashion, extended forgiveness of sins (imputed righteousness) into freedom from sin (infused righteousness). This approach resulted in the expectation of a sinless perfection (including a full measure of the fruits of the Spirit) as the necessary mark or evidence of salvation (genuine conversion).[98]

This tendency to equate faith with assurance and correlate sanctification with justification did not match Wesley's own theological background: he was trying to understand (and experience) a Lutheran theology in the context of his own Anglican and Arminian assumptions. The English Moravians looked for marks of salvation that Wesley would more naturally understand (within his own tradition) as evidence of sanctification.[99] They were propounding a view that essentially equated conversion with perfection, an understanding of salvation as sanctification that Wesley was never able to accept fully, even in the light of his own experience under Moravian tutelage. But it took Wesley several years to work out not only the finer distinctions between justification and sanctification, but also the various nuances of his own doctrines of faith and Christian perfection. For a while, though, he maintained his ties with the Moravians and tried to work out his spiritual quandary and theological problems in fellowship with them.

Working Out Your Own Salvation; Assurance and Faith

Back in England after his trip to Germany, Wesley began immediately to work on clearing up several matters of confusion in his own mind and experience: the nature and necessity of assurance, the problems of doubt and fear, the question of degrees of faith and assurance, the meaning of freedom from sin, the distinction between beginning and full salvation, and the role of good works and the means of grace. As he continued personally to press home several questions in his own mind in these areas over the next two years, he began to qualify many of his views and found himself increasingly in conflict with the Moravians. It is interesting to note that during the several months that Wesley was working on these issues (in growing conflict with the Moravians), although he personally dealt quietly with the questions of degrees of faith, the presence of doubt, and using the means of grace, he continued publicly by and large to preach the necessity of full assurance of faith and actual freedom from sin as the true ground of a Christian's happiness.[100] These questions all had a bearing on Wesley's attempt to understand what had happened in May 1738.

In the midst of Wesley's attempts to work out these questions in the autumn of 1738, two other important developments helped shed some light on his developing ideas. First, he read Jonathan Edwards's "surprising" narrative of the conversions in New England.[101] In this work he could plainly see the influence of the Holy Spirit in the revivals in New England. This reading confirmed for him the significance of the spiritual dynamic in the story and the pneumatological dimension in the theological explanation; it set the stage for his understanding of the movement of the Spirit among the people.

Second, Wesley rediscovered the *Homilies* on that "much controverted point of justification by faith."[102] In the homilies on salvation, faith, and good works (numbers 3, 4, and 5), Wesley discovered (within the authoritative doctrinal statements of his own tradition) the sum of what he had been putting together on his own and the answer to some of the problems raised by the Moravians. Although he could not then sense how close he would eventually come to reiterating the doctrine of the Church of England, he immediately recognized that the answer to most of his theological problems with the English Moravians were contained in those homilies, of which he hastened to publish an extract.[103]

These discoveries did not immediately solve either his spiritual or his theological problems. The last few months of 1738 were a period of intense self-scrutiny and questioning for Wesley.

Self-examination and the Fruits of the Spirit

Wesley was put in a quandary by the Moravians *requiring* the plerophory (fullness) of faith (assurance) evidenced by the *full* measure of fruits thereof (love, joy, peace) as the *necessary* expectation of the *true* (i.e., the only "real") Christian. Questions were raised by his own experience (and the experience of others), his own church's tradition, and Scripture. Nevertheless he continued to accept the Moravian position throughout his own struggle with its definition of the genuine Christian (and the evidence thereof). The tension can be seen clearly in several memoranda of self-examination Wesley wrote between October 1738 and January 1739. The first came shortly after reaching Oxford in October, in consequence of being disturbed by a letter he received:[104]

> Considering my own state more deeply . . . what then occurred to me was as follows: "Examine yourselves, whether ye be in the faith." Now the surest test whereby we can examine ourselves, whether we be indeed in the faith, is that given by St. Paul: "If any man be in Christ, he is a new creature: old things are passed away; behold, all things are become new." First, his judgments are new: his judgment of *himself*, of *happiness*, of *holiness*. . . . Secondly, his designs are new. . . . Thirdly, his desires are new. . . . Fourthly, his conversation is new. . . . Fifthly, his actions are new.[105]

With regard to holiness, Wesley judges that he is indeed a new creature, based on the evidence: "He no longer judges it to be an *outward* thing—to consist either in doing no harm, in doing good, or in using the ordinances of God."[106] He equates holiness with "the life of God in the soul; the image of God fresh stamped on the heart; an entire renewal of the mind in every temper and thought, after the likeness of Him that created it." On the second point, his designs being new, Wesley also considers himself to be a new creature. On the third point, his desires being new, he dares not claim success, but sees that God has begun (though not finished) the work. As to his conversation and actions, he also is able to measure the evidence positively.

But there is one final criterion against which he falls short. On the matter of the "fruits of the Spirit," Wesley's evidence is somewhat disheartening: he does find some measure of peace, long-suffering, gentleness, meekness, temperance; yet in other areas he is definitely lacking but still full of hope and with some confidence that he is a child of God:

> I cannot find in myself the love of God, or of Christ. . . . I have not that joy in the Holy Ghost; no settled, lasting joy. Nor have I such a peace as excludes the possibility either of fear or doubt. . . . Yet upon the whole, although I have not yet that joy in the Holy Ghost, nor the full assurance of faith, much less am I, in the full sense of the words, "in Christ a new creature"; I nevertheless trust that I have a measure of faith, and am "accepted in the Beloved"; I trust . . . that I am "reconciled to God" through his Son.[107]

The absolute demands of the Moravians were beginning to crumble in Wesley's mind. He was beginning to accept the idea that there were degrees of both faith and assurance. And he began to sense that full assurance of faith (which he now felt he had never experienced) was not necessary to the new birth, but a "measure of faith" was adequate for reconciliation through Christ.

In the matter of assurance, Wesley began to distinguish further between assurance and faith as two distinct realities. The Moravians had related these so closely as practically to correlate them. Wesley's own post-Aldersgate experiences continued to raise variations of the question of degrees of faith first posed in conversation with Spangenberg in Georgia—whether one could speak of weak faith and strong faith, and whether faith could admit any doubt or fear. As long as faith was equated with full assurance (as in the Böhler/English Moravian understanding), doubts and fears plainly indicated a lack of faith, which was to say, no true faith at all but rather the sin of unbelief. But faith must surely be able in many cases to subsist with doubt and fear.[108]

Wesley recognized that "some measure of this faith" had resulted in "peace and trust in God through Christ" in his own life. And he also was convinced that freedom from sin, which he had claimed since 24 May, surely must be understood as freedom from the *reign* of sin rather than from the *remains* of sin. And although he now realized that he had yet to experience what he had seen many others receive, full assurance through the witness of the Spirit (evidenced by the fruits of the Spirit), he could see himself and others in his condition as being Christians, even though in an "imperfect sense."[109]

Wesley also distinguished between the assurance of *faith* and assurance of *salvation*. The former, a conviction of present pardon, he still felt was important and perhaps necessary as a normal expectation for the Christian, but the latter, based on the expectation of perseverance and the promise of final salvation, was rare and not necessarily to be expected, much less required. The "plerophory of faith," he pointed out to Arthur Bedford, is "nothing more nor less than hope: a conviction, wrought in us by the Holy Ghost, that we have a measure of the true faith in Christ, and that as he is already made justification unto us, so *if* we continue to watch and strive and pray, he will gradually become 'our sanctification here, and our full redemption hereafter.'"[110] He goes on to point out that "this assurance . . . is given to some in a smaller, to others in a larger degree." Assurance, then, for Wesley was also a matter of degrees and not to be confused with final perseverance; assurance was a daily confidence (more or less) that one is a child of God. The real possibility of backsliding never left Wesley's frame of thinking.[111]

On 29 October, Wesley noted that he was again "doubtful of my own state," especially concerning faith. Some relief, in keeping with developing inclinations, was provided by his method of bibliomancy, for he opened his Bible upon James's description of Abraham (in 2:22): "Seest thou not how faith wrought together with his works? And by works was faith made perfect."[112]

Whatever comfort he might obtain from such self-examination, however, was tested by his friends, especially those associated with the Moravians. Charles Delamotte, who had accompanied him to Georgia but was now back in England and under Moravian influence, told Wesley in November that Wesley was now better off than when he was in Savannah because Wesley now recognized that he was wrong in Georgia. But, Delamotte went on, "You are not right yet; you know that you was then blind, but you do not see now." Delamotte tried to convince Wesley that he was still trusting in his own works and did not believe in Christ; that his freedom from sin was only a temporary suspension of it, not a deliverance from it; and that his peace was not a true peace—"if death were to approach, you would find all your fears return."[113]

In December 1738, Wesley wrote some notes[114] that provide a sequel to the memorandum of October 14, in which he measures himself on some of the same evidences as before. As for happiness, "I still hanker after creature-happiness," which he explains in terms that are again reminiscent of his sentiments in 1726—"I have more pleasure in eating and drinking, and in the company of those I love, than I have in God."[115] He refers to the degree of his progress with a scriptural phrase that is telling and will become a familiar metaphor: "The eyes of my understanding are not yet fully opened."[116] On the second point, as to the design of his life, his eye is not yet single. And on the third point, his desires are not all new; his affections in general are mixed between spiritual and natural.[117]

Shortly after another experience of the power of God (during a lovefeast on 1 January 1739), Wesley again took an opportunity for writing notes of self-reflection. This memo, however, reveals more serious self-critical doubt on the questions of love, peace, and joy; in it, he holds himself up to the strict definition of Christian that admits no degrees of perfection in measuring the evidence:[118]

> My friends affirm I am mad, because I said I was not a Christian a year ago.[119] I affirm I am not a Christian now. . . . That I am not a Christian at this day I as assuredly know as that Jesus is the Christ. For a Christian is one who has the fruits of the Spirit of Christ, which (to mention no more) are love, peace, joy.[120] But these I have not. I have not any love of God. . . . I feel this moment I do not love God; which therefore I know because I feel it. . . . Again, joy in the Holy Ghost I have not. . . . Yet again, I have not "the peace of God." . . . From hence I conclude . . . , though I have given, and do give, all my goods to feed the poor, I am not a Christian. Though I have endured hardship, though I have in all things denied myself and taken up my cross, I am not a Christian. . . . My works are nothing, my sufferings are nothing; I have not the fruits of the Spirit of Christ. Though I have constantly used all the means of grace for twenty years, I am not a Christian.[121]

Wesley seems again to assume the necessity of full assurance of faith, which not only excludes all doubt and fear concerning present salvation but also excludes all sin as shown by the full presence of peace, love, and joy as the fruits of the Spirit. Wesley now understands the explicit role of the Holy Spirit as central, both as a source of self-knowledge (direct internal evidence—witness of the Spirit, the basis for claiming assurance) and as a source of the fruits (indirect external evidence—fruits of the Spirit, the basis for confirming assurance). The genuine Christian is the perfect Christian, and Wesley is not hesitant during this period to define the character of a Methodist (i.e., a "genuine Christian") in these same terms, namely, as one "who has the love of God shed abroad in his heart by the Holy Spirit."[122]

Although Wesley is beginning at times to allow for some qualitative distinctions and levels within the definition of Christian, the general sense of his preaching is that the "altogether Christian" is the "real" Christian and the "almost" Christian is not really a Christian at all. To put it differently (in terms Wesley was not yet using), the hard question still is whether the only "true" Christian is the fully sanctified Christian. Wesley still has not worked out the full implications of his ideas in this regard nor the careful use of his terminology.[123]

In January 1739, he makes a crucial distinction between being born again "in the lower sense" and in "the full sense of the word." What he describes, without using the terminology, is the difference between justification and sanctification: remission of sins as distinguished from a thorough, inward change by the love of God shed abroad in the heart.[124] The implication is that the latter, being born again in the higher sense, is the genuine Christian. But it is significant that Wesley is beginning again to allow for gradations ("the lower sense") rather than to hold a simple either/or position. His mature theology will come to rest upon the "both/and" of justification and sanctification, which he is here only beginning to sense and develop.

The Witness of the Spirit—Living Arguments

Wesley nevertheless continued to preach the central significance of the "witness of the Spirit" in the societies at London and Oxford. In fact, he developed an increased measure of confidence in its truth through what he will come to call "living arguments." The work of the Spirit was beginning to be evident in the lives of his hearers. He mentions several women in particular who responded to the work of the Spirit in consequence of his preaching at Oxford. In December 1738, one at St. Thomas's Workhouse was delivered from her raving madness, and another woman at Mr. Fox's society "received a witness that she was a child of God."[125] In March 1739, Mrs. Compton, who was "above measure enraged at this new way and zealous in opposing it," was further inflamed by Wesley's arguments, but when he began praying with her, she soon experienced the witness of the Spirit and cried out, "Now I know I am forgiven for Christ's sake."[126]

Spiritual inspiration of this sort, however, brought controversy. Wesley was not simply credulous in every case but was inclined to "try the spirits" in the scriptural manner, testing "to see whether they be of God." In January 1739 he visited a meeting led by one of the "French prophets." But after over two hours of observation, he felt the evidence was inconclusive and pointed out that "anyone of a good understanding and well-versed in the Scriptures" might have said the same things and the motions could easily have been "hysterical or artificial."[127] His advice in such situations was that "they were not to judge of the spirit whereby anyone spoke either by appearances, or by common report, or by their own inward feelings . . . all these were, in themselves, of a doubtful, disputable nature . . . and were therefore not simply to be relied on . . . but to be tried by a farther rule to be brought to the only certain test—the Law and the Testimony."[128] This advice would become increasingly more important as Wesley continued to emphasize the work of the Holy Spirit in the lives of true believers while trying at the same time to determine whether the outward signs were authentic, how the inward signs could be discerned, and just what these both signified. These questions were all soon to be magnified as the Methodist movement began to leave the society room and took to the streets and fields.

This New Period of My Life

Wesley's growing tendency to develop some confidence in his views by the response to his preaching soon gained a tremendous boost. At the beginning of April 1739, Wesley began field preaching. It was not his idea. Whitefield had set the example on Sunday morning, 1 April, at the Bowling Green in Bristol. That evening at the Nicholas Street society, Wesley expounded on the Sermon on the Mount. This "pretty remarkable precedent of field-preaching" was not lost on him. The following day Wesley "submitted to be more vile" and "proclaimed in the highways the glad tidings of salvation" to about three thousand people gathered around a little eminence in the Brickyard at the edge of town.[129]

Wesley's hesitance to begin such a ministry was soon swept aside by the remarkable response to his preaching. His own journal account of this outdoor preaching occasion at Bristol reveals the significance of this development by referring to "this new period of my life."[130] Even preaching to small groups in the past had encouraged John in the quandaries of his own spiritual pilgrimage and had served to confirm the truth of the gospel he was preaching.[131] Now he was preaching to thousands and seeing a marvelous work of God in their midst. The story of Wesley's quest for assurance takes an unexpected turn—it becomes less singularly personal as he begins to sense the work of the Holy Spirit in the midst of the people, a phenomenon not unlike what he had read about in Jonathan Edwards' writings.

After preaching to a little society in Bristol on Sunday evening, 2 April, he spoke Monday afternoon to three or four thousand on the text, "The Spirit of the Lord is upon me because he hath anointed me to preach the gospel to the poor."[132] On eight occasions during the following fortnight, he spoke to large groups ranging from one to six thousand people in the Bristol area, a total attendance of some twenty-five thousand. On 29 April alone, he preached outdoors in three places to a total of fourteen thousand people, married four persons, preached to a full church at Clifton, held a society meeting at Mrs. England's, followed by a lovefeast in Baldwin Street. He closes his account of the day in his *Journal* with the remark, "Oh how has God renewed my strength! who used ten years ago to be so faint and weary with preaching twice in one day!"[133] Equally significant, however, is his remark that, during his sermon at the Bowling Green on "Free Grace," "one who had long continued in sin . . . received a full, clear sense of His pardoning love and power to sin no more."

Such confirmations of God's action bolstered his own faith to a great extent. His busy days, indeed, may have given him little time to worry about his own condition, but his continuing concern for his own spiritual condition in the midst of his "success" in preaching is evident in a comment to James Hutton and the society at Fetter Lane: "Dear brethren, pray that when I have preached to others, I may not myself be a castaway!"[134] Wesley was still at this time claiming publicly that the full assurance of faith is the true ground of a Christian's present happiness. On 28 April, his sermon on "Free Grace," which was his first major attack on predestination (and effectively declared his independence from Whitefield), reiterated his conviction that assurance of faith excludes all doubt and fear.[135] Aiming directly at Whitefield's Calvinism, Wesley also continued his assault upon its corollary, antinomianism, pointing out that predestination cuts off any zeal for good works.[136] This Arminian view, clearly stated and strongly held, would provide the snag that would start unraveling his relationship with the Moravians as well as the Calvinists.[137]

Wesley also continued to see evidence of the Holy Spirit working in the lives of the people, now on a somewhat larger scale. And many more were offended by the cries of those on whom the power of God came.[138] In a letter to his brother Samuel, in response to his question "How can these things be?" and his cautions not to regard outward signs of remission of sins, John wrote:

> You deny that God does now work these effects; at least, that he works them in such a manner. I affirm both, because I have heard those facts with my ears and have seen them with my eyes. I have seen (as far as it can be seen) very many persons changed in a moment from the spirit of horror, fear, and despair, to the spirit of hope, joy, and peace. . . . These are matters of fact, whereof I have been, and almost daily am, an eye- or ear-witness. . . . These are my living arguments for what I assert.[139]

Inevitably, this matter caused disruptions and divisions among the societies in Bristol and London.[140] Most controversial were the *outward signs* that accompanied the *inward work* of the Spirit. Although Wesley was hoping that everyone would "suffer God to carry on His own work in the way that pleaseth Him,"[141] he also wanted to provide some guidelines for interpreting and understanding the movement of the Spirit among the people. To the Methodists in Bristol, he suggested that when "appearances, common report, or inward feelings" resulted in controversy, the spirit whereby anyone spoke or acted should be tried by "the only certain test—the Law and the Testimony."[142] The inward work of the Spirit itself really held Wesley's attention, however, and his longtime inclination was that it could in some way be verified through certain evidence.

On 22 May 1739, John preached on "Awake, Thou that Sleepest" (Ephesians 5:14).[143] The published text of Charles's sermon on the same topic presents an intriguing metaphor that may have significance for the Wesleyan anthropological assumptions that underlie both soteriology and epistemology. Grace does not destroy or overcome nature, which is diseased and distorted, but rather perfects (awakens, restores, heals) it to its original image and design. This is no minor transformation, however. The disease of sin results in the person's being effectively dead unto God. And being thus dead in sin, natural man has not "senses exercised to discern spiritual good and evil" (Heb. 5:14)—having eyes, yet he sees not; he hath ears, and hears not (Mark 8:18); he has no spiritual senses, no inlets of spiritual knowledge.[144]

How can such a one be awakened and know that he is alive to God? "Faith is the life of the soul," and the Spirit of God is sufficient evidence, the *elenchos pneumatos* (divine consciousness, evidence), the witness of God that is "greater than ten thousand human witnesses."[145] The claim that one could sense the indwelling of the Holy Spirit, which was not only "the common privilege of all believers," but also "the criterion of a real Christian," led to charges of enthusiasm. Wesley, however, was attempting to develop a way to explain how one senses this divine revelation in a manner analogous to other sense perceptions that might be verified.[146] The Wesleys were quick to claim that by holding such a view of "perceptible inspiration," they taught nothing contrary to the doctrines of the Church.[147]

Wesley and the Church of England: Distinctive Emphases

By the autumn of 1739, Wesley was preaching to thousands of people every Sunday in London.[148] Contrary to his critics, who saw him as an enthusiast and fanatic, Wesley claimed that he was simply preaching "the fundamental doctrines of the Church" as clearly laid down in the Articles, Homilies, and Book of Common Prayer.[149] He further proclaimed that Methodism, although everywhere spoken against, was simply "the true old Christianity."[150] It was propagating, in Wesley's view, the true Church of England doctrine. For a clerical friend, he outlined the difference between what generally passes for Christianity in the Church of England (among those who in fact did not adhere to its doctrines) and what he himself was preaching:

> 1. They speak of justification either as the same thing with sanctification or as something consequent upon it. . . .
>
> 2. They speak of our own holiness, or good works, as the cause of our justification. . . .
>
> 3. They speak of good works as a condition of justification, necessarily previous to it. . . .
>
> 4. They speak of sanctification, or holiness, as if it were an outward thing. . . .[151]
>
> 5. They speak of the new birth as an outward thing, as if it were no more than baptism, or at most a change from outward wickedness to outward goodness.[152]

His own views are easily distinguished from these, as he points out in each case: justification is *distinct* from and antecedent to sanctification, *Christ's* active righteousness and passive righteousness are the cause of our justification, the condition of justification is faith *alone* without works,[153] sanctification is an *inward* renewal of the heart, and the new birth is an *inward* change of our inmost nature resulting in new tempers of the soul.[154] Having sorted these points out in his own mind with regard to his own tradition, Wesley was now ready to clarify the other side of his position with respect to the Moravians, especially regarding *sola fide*: he certainly did not accept the implication that such a doctrine implied discarding the means of grace. This practical point of contention would provide the issue over which Wesley finally broke with the Moravians.

Subverting the Souls of the Justified; Crisis in the Societies

Wesley soon began to notice that requiring full assurance of faith as a necessary mark of the Christian (as the Moravians did) threw many into idle reasonings, doubt, and fear, and even led some to cast away their faith. The question of true faith had practical implications that were not lost on Wesley. He began to challenge those who claimed not only that *weak faith* is unbelief, but also that only true believers (having received the full assurance of faith) should use the means of grace, in particular, receive the Sacrament. Some of the Moravians were saying that no person who does not truly believe should use any of the means of grace (sacraments, prayer, etc.). Although Wesley was certainly not yet willing to say that "good works" were necessary prior to justification, he was sure that some activity was appropriate on the part of the person desiring salvation.[155]

The Fetter Lane society began to experience problems again as the autumn of 1739 approached. On September 9, Wesley discovered that a want of love was the general complaint; during the next few days he pressed the members to love each other and to keep close to the Church and to all the ordinances of God. John and Charles went to Oxford at the beginning of October to discover that only a few had not "forsaken the assembling themselves together." John also had occasion to examine the "shattered condition" of the work at the University, where Methodism had begun. Even the remnants of their program had nearly disappeared—no one visiting the prisons, no one visiting the workhouses, the school (formerly helping about twenty poor children at a time) on the point of breaking up for lack of students or teachers. The society in the town was not much better, having been "torn asunder and scattered abroad." After a quick tour to Wales and the West Country, during which he confronted several controversial situations associated with his preaching and extraordinary exercises that attended it, Wesley returned to London to discover the society there in disarray.

Wesley's crisis with the Moravians intensified in October 1739 after Philip Henry Molther appeared among the Moravians in London. Molther's "quietism" sharpened the differentiating issues between Wesley and the English Moravians. As a result of Molther's teachings, which in effect required full assurance as a prerequisite for receiving the Sacrament, many of the Fetter Lane group were thrown into turmoil.[156] They continued to believe that any fear or doubt indicated that they had no assurance and therefore no faith at all. This assumption was not new. But Molther added a new twist: such persons should cease from all outward works and "be still." Many, including Spangenberg, were won over to this position, which simply extended the basic approach of Böhler that faith in Christ was the only means of salvation. Wesley now began to see clearly the drastic consequences of such a view, the challenge that it represented to his emphasis on Christian discipline and using the means of grace, before as well as after justification. He also began to see clearly that the Moravians were proclaiming a view of the "way of salvation" (*via salutis*) that, Wesley said, "I cannot reconcile to the Law and the Testimony."[157] For Wesley, their view represented a perverse form of antinomianism that put the requirements for justification too high and at the same time took away the normal channels of divine assistance, the means of God's grace.

Wesley had special difficulties with many of the new ideas that were spreading despair in the Fetter Lane society, especially the claim that the ordinances (the Lord's Supper, in particular) are not means of grace—that the only means of grace is Christ. Wesley began to counter Molther's teachings with what he saw as a better method of trying the spirits, that is through "true stillness"—"patient waiting upon God, by lowliness, meekness, and resignation, in all the ways of his holy law and the works of his commandments."[158] Susanna Wesley may have supplied one of the best arguments against the Moravian position. In spite of their attempts to persuade her that she had no faith, Susanna seems to have convincingly testified that she had recently experienced assurance of forgiveness while receiving the Sacrament.[159]

For the better part of a week, Wesley tried to heal the wounds in the society. But by the second week of November, he and some of his friends began to meet separately in the old Foundery in Moorfields.[160] This split was the beginning of their final separation with the Moravians. On the last day of 1739, after continual controversy over these points, Wesley wrote down the differences between himself and the English Moravians at that point. He begins to outline Molther's views as follows:

> 1. There are no degrees of faith and that no man has any degree of it before all things in him are become new, before he has the full assurance of faith, the abiding witness of the Spirit, or the clear perception that Christ dwelleth in him.
>
> 2. Accordingly you believe there is no justifying faith or state of justification short of this.[161]

In 1738, these ideas (expressed at that point by Peter Böhler) had furnished the rationale for and urgency behind Wesley's desire for (and expectations of) an experience of assurance, which he finally had at Aldersgate. These ideas also supported the framework of his attempts to explain that experience for some time thereafter. His own position on these matters was now clear at the end of 1739: there *are* degrees of faith, and there is a degree of justifying faith short of (and antecedent to) full assurance. And now he saw some of the additional problematical consequences which the Moravian position entailed. He continued to spell out Molther's views:

> That gift of God which many receive . . . —viz. "a sure confidence of the love of God to them"—was not justifying faith. And that the joy and love attending it were from animal spirits, from nature, or imagination; not "joy in the Holy Ghost" and the real "love of God shed abroad in their hearts."
>
> As to the way to attain it is to wait for Christ, and be still—that is, not to use (what we term) the means of grace; not to go to church; not to communicate; not to fast; not to use so much private prayer; not to read the Scripture; . . . not to do temporal good; nor to attempt doing spiritual good.[162]

Wesley disagreed with these positions, especially when the implication is that nothing is valid unless it agrees with Molther's own personal judgment of whether or not it is valid.[163] In an almost sarcastic use of Molther's own terminology, Wesley outlined his own understanding of the way to attain faith: "to wait for Christ and be still"; that is, "in using all the means of grace" (which he proceeds to list in great detail).[164]

By the end of 1739, then, Wesley had in effect come to the point of disentangling himself theologically from the English Moravians who had been his spiritual tutors for the previous two or three years. The next few months saw Wesley completely disavow the English Moravians as holding views with which both the Church of England and the true Moravian Church disagreed.[165] After another long interview with Molther at the end of April 1740, the Fetter Lane society was irreparably split. On 11 June 1740, Wesley visited the Fetter Lane society and, as he said, plainly told the "poor, confused, shattered society wherein they had erred from the faith—they could not receive my saying. However, I am clear from the blood of these men."[166] During the following month, Wesley was banned from preaching at Fetter Lane, and a week later he and a small group of Methodists moved their meetings entirely to the Foundery in a final separation from the Moravians.

Summary of Situation in 1739

By the spring of 1739, Wesley had begun in some small ways to soften the sharp dichotomy that the Moravians seemed to draw between the Christian and the non-Christian, while still defending his claim that he himself was only beginning to move across the gap. In a letter to a friend, he pointed out that two years earlier, he had "told all on the ship, all at Savannah, all at Frederica, and that over and over, in express terms, 'I am not a Christian; I only follow after, if haply I may attain it.'" He is at this point, however, beginning to appreciate the struggle of those who are searching but who have not yet received the witness of the Spirit. Rather than denigrate their efforts, as the Moravians seemed to do, Wesley tried to encourage those who had "a desire to be a Christian."[167] At the same time, he was beginning to distinguish between "young converts" and those who had "already attained or were already perfect," comparable to his distinction between those born again in a "lower" and a "higher" sense.[168] This insight continues a very significant theological development. Wesley was clearly differentiating between justification and sanctification and becoming more positively inclined to value the experience of the "almost" Christians (those without full assurance, i.e., not fully sanctified), a crucial step in his growing independence from the English Moravian perspective.

Explaining his principles of actions in pursuing his own desire to be a Christian, Wesley said that he had long acted on the conviction "that whatever I judge conducive thereto, that I am bound to do; wherever I judge I can best answer this end, thither it is my duty to go."[169] But such constant "doing" and "going" bothered the Moravians, who continued to press hard on the matter of *sola fide*, increasingly requiring the witness of the spirit to the virtual exclusion of the means of grace. Wesley was willing to grant the necessity of *sola fide* but was not ready to give up the means of grace or other works of piety and mercy, all of which he viewed as central to the Christian life and helpful even in pursuing the desire to be a Christian (crucial to sanctification, important to justification). Wesley was also willing to grant the importance of the witness of the Spirit as an assurance of faith but was beginning to distinguish between assurance of pardon (justification) and assurance of perfection (sanctification), while still generally associating the "witness of the Spirit" with the latter.

The English Moravians had tried to convince him that assurance of redemption was accompanied by freedom from sin (entire sanctification, in Wesley's terminology) as well as freedom from doubt and fear. But he was coming to realize that the "young convert" should not expect to be perfect; that a person, though justified, was yet a sinner.[170] And, contrary to the Moravian view, one who has not received the plerophory of faith and assurance (a sign of complete freedom from sin, fear, and doubt) should not despair of not having any faith whatsoever and certainly should not cease using the means of grace.

The relationship between the inward and outward signs of spiritual experience also continued to widen the breach between Wesley and the Moravians. Generally, Wesley continued to distinguish between the indications of "religion commonly understood" (outward: avoiding evil, doing good, using the means of grace) and those of "real religion" (inward: righteousness, peace, and joy in the Holy Ghost) but felt the two must be integrally related in the life of the believer.[171] *Outward* indications of Christian deportment must be accompanied by an *inward* experience of a living faith, which is "a sure trust and confidence in God that, by the merits of Christ, his sins are forgiven and he reconciled to the favour of God,"[172] and its inward evidence, "the love of God shed abroad in the heart, the peace of God which passeth all understanding, and joy in the Holy Ghost."[173] These are some of the inward "fruits of the spirit" that must be *felt* wherever they are. Without these very "*sensible* operations," we cannot *know* that one is born of the Spirit.[174]

The tensions inherent in this definition of faith from the *Homilies* when understood from a Moravian perspective posed considerable difficulties for Wesley. If faith was understood as a necessary prerequisite condition for justification, then faith was "a sure trust which a man hath that Christ hath loved him and died for him."[175] This faith was a trust that God has acted in Christ to redeem him (the atonement) and that his sins *will be* forgiven. This faith accompanies repentance and is a necessary condition for justification. On the other hand, if (as the Moravians said) faith also entailed assurance, then the phrase from the *Homilies* would have a quite different sense—a "confidence in God that, by the merits of Christ, his sins *are* forgiven and he *is* reconciled to the favor of God." This faith is an assurance that Christ has, in fact, redeemed him and that his sins *have been* forgiven. This faith of assurance is accompanied by an evident sense of pardon at the least (if not a fuller sense of freedom from all sin), and the personalized *Christus pro me* becomes one's motto.

In 1739, Wesley was coming to realize that these different definitions of faith, both of which might be read into the phrasing of the *Homilies* definition, represent at least two and perhaps even three different stages in the spiritual pilgrimage. And faith in each of these instances would be evidenced in a different manner, some harder than others to perceive. This developing understanding represents a direct challenge to the Moravian's unitary concept of faith. Another fairly obvious question that begins to emerge from this distinction is, How can faith, a prerequisite for divine forgiveness, also be the subsequent evidence of it?[176]

At this point, the definition of the "real" Christian for Wesley turns on the issue of whether the true child of God can be justified without being sanctified (forgiven of sin and able not to sin, or freed from sin and not able to sin? converted or perfected?). The *German* Moravians had suggested that such was the case. The matter of relying upon both outward and inward signs further sharpened the issue—what are they signs of? conversion? perfection? By late 1739, Wesley had begun to see that the external visible evidence of good works generally applies to sanctification (a real change but not necessarily entire; an internal change with external evidence), while justification (a relative change, also internal) is harder to verify by external evidence, especially in others. Wesley felt an increasing need to develop a way to explain the sensation of divine evidence for justification: spiritual senses to discern the operations of the Spirit.[177]

In this context, the Wesleys began using the definition of faith in Hebrews 11—faith is the "evidence of things unseen."[178] Generally, this phrase was used to refer to the witness of the Spirit in the sense of assurance; but if faith is also preliminary to justification, the evidence is more difficult to perceive. In either case, this divine evidence was not perceived by the unbeliever. It was presented only to the spiritual senses—the eyes of the believer were opened, the ears of faith could hear.

Further Developments, 1740 and Beyond

By 1740, then, Wesley had severed his association with the Moravians, unable to accept their position on several key issues. He does not agree that there are no degrees of faith, that there is no justification without full assurance of faith, that persons should not use the means of grace until they have received full assurance, and that good works are not part of faith. He has begun to realize that the *definition* of a Christian is more complicated than the either/or explanation presented by the Moravians, which required full assurance of faith, complete freedom from sin, doubt, and fear, and a perfect manifestation of love, peace, and joy. He is beginning to distinguish between justification and sanctification (and soon entire sanctification) as significantly distinct steps in the *via salutis* and thereby to allow that there is opportunity for growth within a range of Christian experience from infant to mature.[179]

His understanding of the process by which a person *becomes* a Christian has also undergone some development beyond the simple teaching of Böhler (exaggerated by Molther) that only a proper faith alone, without works, would instantaneously bring conversion to a new state of sinless perfection. He is expressing some ambiguity regarding the nature of real religion, holiness, which he is inclined to think necessarily includes good works.

The ground of Wesley's certainty of salvation, how believers *know* they are Christians, is still basically the witness of the Spirit, which the Moravians had taught him, but he is beginning to develop that doctrine in different directions. He not only allows for degrees of assurance and exceptions to the normal expectations that all will experience it, but is beginning to disentangle the correlation of assurance with both faith and sanctification so as to allow also for repentant faith and assurance of justification. And Wesley's attempt to explain the doctrine in scriptural terms has resulted in hints at the notion of spiritual senses.

In each of these areas, Wesley refines his views even further during the 1740s and beyond, in many cases falling back upon ideas and methods that he had been using since his Oxford days. Surveying the change should not cause us to lose sight of the continuity, as Wesley continued to press many of his themes from the early days at Oxford—Christian perfection, prevenient grace, repentance, sincerity, doing one's best, avoiding evil, the importance of the virtues—though now within a more vital spiritual context and a more dynamic theological rationale, and with an increasingly evangelistic and pastoral concern.[180]

Although early in the 1740s Wesley draws a very sharp distinction between the "almost Christian" and the "altogether Christian"[181] (with only the latter being a true Christian), by the conference of 1745 he is aware that such preaching is not fully adequate. He realizes that the Methodist preachers must take care not to depreciate justification "in order to exalt the state of full sanctification."[182] The question even came up as to whether or not the Methodists had changed their doctrine in this regard, no longer preaching "as we did at first?" Wesley pointed out that at first they had preached mostly to unbelievers and therefore spoke almost entirely of forgiveness of sins. But now, recognizing that in many of their listeners a "foundation is already laid," they can exhort to go on to perfection. This distinction,

Wesley says, "we did not see so clearly at first."[183] Wesley now begins to distinguish between being saved from the guilt of sin and being saved from the power of sin.[184] This distinction will become more useful to him as he continues to develop the distinction between justification and sanctification more fully. He will later add a third step, being saved from the root of sin, which is essential to entire sanctification.[185]

Wesley also extends the idea of being saved from the guilt and power of sin into another biblical comparison—having not only the *form* but the *power* of godliness.[186] In the early sermons such as "The Almost Christian," Wesley used this comparison to distinguish between the would-be and the real Christian. As time goes on, however, he is less prone to denigrate those who exhibit simply the *form* of godliness. In 1741, the "almost Christians," who are no better than honest heathens, are described as having only the form of godliness—trying to be honest, avoiding evil, and using the means of grace.[187] In 1744, when he published *The Nature, Design, and General Rules of the United Societies*, Wesley chose this phrase to describe a Methodist society—"a company of men 'having the form and seeking the power of godliness.'"[188] The rules themselves were the three guidelines that he tended to use so often in the late 1730s to denigrate a false view of real religion: avoiding evil, doing good, and using the means of grace. And the persons who qualified for continuing membership in the societies were given class tickets, which were as good a recommendation, said Wesley in 1749, as if he had written thereon, "I believe the bearer hereof to be one that fears God and works righteousness."[189] By 1768, Wesley applies this phrase to those Christians who have received assurance: "I believe a consciousness of being in the favour of God . . . is the common privilege of Christians fearing God and working righteousness."[190] By 1785, he openly uses this phrase to refer to the "real Christians," those who are contained within the inner circle of God's providence.[191] In 1787, Wesley explains the distinctions among the faithful a bit further by describing what he calls "two orders of Christians": (1) those who do many good works, abstain from gross evils, and attend the ordinances of God; and (2) those who spared no pains to arrive at the summit of Christian holiness. He goes on to say, "From long experience and observation I am inclined to think that whoever finds redemption in the blood of Jesus, whoever is justified, has then the choice of walking in the higher or the lower path."[192]

All of these categories undergo significant modifications in the maturing Wesley. In 1744, one who is seen by Wesley as a "*servant* of God" ("one who sincerely obeys him out of *fear*") is "a Jew, inwardly," e.g., still under the Jewish dispensation. However, a "*child* of God" is one who sincerely obeys him out of *love*.[193] Whereas in the late 1730s, Wesley had viewed "half-Christians" in terms of their *lack* of being fully Christian, by the 1780s, they are viewed with more hope in terms of their being *at least* "nominal" Christians. By that time,Wesley applied this latter phrase ("fearing God," associated with those who only have the form of godliness) in a positive sense to those who *at least* have the faith of a servant and are seeking the faith of a son.

Deprecation of the person who has the "faith of a servant," who "fears God," who has "the form of godliness," begins to disappear in later years as the emphasis turns to encouraging those who are in a state that falls short of the fullness of faith. Thus, in 1788 he can say,

> Whoever has attained this, the faith of a servant, . . . "feareth God and worketh righteousness," in consequence of which he is in a degree (as the Apostle observes), "accepted with him." . . . Even one who has gone thus far in religion, who obeys God out of fear, is not in any wise to be despised, seeing "the fear of the Lord is the beginning of wisdom." Nevertheless he should be exhorted not to stop there; not to rest till he attains the adoption of sons; till he obeys out of love, which is the privilege of all the *children* of God.[194]

This rather remarkable development seems to emerge from a maturing pastoral sensitivity as well as a more sophisticated theological perspective. By this time, Wesley can look back on his life and remark with candor,

> Indeed nearly fifty years ago, when the preachers commonly called Methodists began to preach that grand scriptural doctrine, salvation by faith, they were not sufficiently apprised of the difference between a servant and a child of God. They did not clearly understand that even one "who feared God, and worketh righteousness, is accepted of him."[195]

Most remarkable of all was Wesley's radical turnabout on the matter of assurance, which the Moravians had said was essential to the Christian. Once Wesley had seen the damage such teaching had done in the community of believers and had begun to dismantle this seemingly monolithic doctrine into its various parts, it became a much more effective element in the dynamic of his theology. Assurance was related to both justification and sanctification but no longer equated with faith or required as an essential experience.[196] Once again, looking back from the 1780s, he would be able to remark in all honesty to his friend Melville Horne,

> When fifty years ago my brother Charles and I, in the simplicity of our hearts, told the good people of England that unless they *knew*

their sins were forgiven they were under the wrath and curse of God, I marvel, Melville, they did not stone us![197]

The definition of faith itself also undergoes an interesting development during this period. Besides formulating the distinction between the faith of a servant and of a child of God, Wesley also begins to shift away from the definition of faith in the *Homilies* ("a sure trust and confidence") to the definition in Hebrews 11:1—"the evidence of things not seen."[198] He initially understood this definition of faith essentially as the witness of the Spirit, frequently explained in the terminology of Romans 8:16—"The Spirit itself beareth witness with our spirit that we are children of God."[199]

Wesley relies upon his empirical inclinations to develop this idea of "spiritual senses," eventually including not only the sense of sight and hearing (eyes and ears that see and hear divine evidence), but also the sense of taste and feel.[200] In this fashion, Wesley combines an empiricist approach with an intuitionist sense to provide a description of how the "new creature in Christ" has a transformed capacity for knowing and understanding spiritual truth that is more than simply "analogous" to sense perception.[201] This epistemological perspective was another reflection of Wesley's constant attempt to relate the inner and outer aspects of religion in a rather precarious balance that tried to emphasize both vital spiritual experience and responsible Christian living while avoiding the pitfalls of subjective enthusiasm on the one hand or legalistic moralism on the other. This development and the manner of his combining human experience with revelation of spiritual truths were the culmination of his search for human certainty within a lively pneumatology in the process of working out his own salvation.

Conclusion

Wesley's Aldersgate experience on 24 May 1738 was a significant step in his spiritual pilgrimage. It was a step that Wesley had been led to expect and for which he had been carefully prepared by his English Moravian friends. Their basic teachings on the matter were:

(1) Faith alone is necessary to salvation.

(2) Good works (of piety or mercy) are not required before salvation and in fact are not possible.

(3) There are no degrees of faith; there is only one proper faith; a weak faith is no faith but rather unbelief.

(4) A proper faith will immediately bring with it an assurance of faith which will be unmistakably known.

(5) The assurance of faith will bring freedom from sin, doubt, and fear.

(6) Assurance will be accompanied by perfect love, peace, and joy in the Holy Ghost.

(7) Without this assurance, one is not a Christian.

(8) Assurance brings perseverance unto final salvation.

The urgency of Wesley's situation was prompted by the seventh proposition in this list, along with two corollaries to propositions five and six: (1) Any doubt or fear indicates an absence of faith and assurance; (2) A lack of perfect love, peace, and joy indicates an absence of faith and assurance. Under these requirements, Wesley was becoming convinced in 1737 and early 1738 that he was not a Christian. To anxiety was added frustration, since Wesley saw his use of the means of grace (going to church, reading the Bible, taking the Sacrament, prayer, fasting, etc.) as ineffectual because he had not received assurance (no good works before salvation).

Wesley's experience of assurance on 24 May did not, however, solve all his problems. Within the Moravian understanding, he expected thenceforth to have a freedom from sin, doubt, and fear, that would be accompanied by perfect love, peace, and joy. Such was not the case. For several months, Wesley's periodic self-examinations came to the same conclusion: since he has not the fruits of the Spirit and still manifests doubt and fear, he is still not a true Christian.

Within two years, however, Wesley had noted several basic problems in the Moravian position and altered his own thinking accordingly. His differences with the Moravians were basic enough that he left the fellowship of the society he had co-founded with Peter Böhler. By the summer of 1740, he disagreed with every Moravian proposition listed above except the first. His main challenges were based on the following propositions of his own: (1) there are degrees of faith; (2) there are degrees of assurance; (3) the means of grace should be encouraged prior to assurance; (4) justification does not necessarily result in assurance; (5) assurance of justification does not necessarily bring complete freedom from doubt or fear; (6) assurance of justification does not necessarily bring full love, peace, and joy; (7) assurance is not of final salvation.

Two key developments in Wesley's own theology during this period were his recognizing the distinction between justification and sanctification, disentangling faith and assurance, and his qualifying the subjective norm of experience by appeals to the Scripture, the teachings of the Church (primitive and contemporary), and reason. Having made the break with the Moravians, he could then continue to develop his understanding of salvation by faith according to these norms and in the light of his own experience. He could further clarify his ideas on justification and sanctification, Christian perfection, faith, assurance, the witness of the Spirit, good works, eschatology, and other matters essential to the Christian life.

Through all the subsequent developments, two ideas from 1738 continued to find a central place in Wesley's theology even though he modified their explanation: salvation by faith alone and the witness of the Spirit. These were both the result of Wesley's having felt the power of the Holy Spirit in his life on that spring evening in London; his subsequent attempts to understand the theological dynamics and implications of that experience were crucial to the development of a Wesleyan theology. Wesley's affirmation of justification by faith, expectation of assurance, and the possibility of perfection became hallmarks of his theology. But these crucial concepts (learned, borrowed, observed, experienced) were necessarily altered by Wesley so as to fit within an understanding of justification and sanctification that was quite different from the Moravian theological framework [soteriology] that he had assumed in 1738.

In this light, we can say that Aldersgate is especially significant for Wesley in two ways. (1) It is the point in his spiritual pilgrimage at which he experiences the power of the Holy Spirit and at which his theology is confronted by a dynamic pneumatology. From that point on, the Holy Spirit has a central role in Wesley's definition of the "true Christian," his understanding of how one becomes a Christian, and his explanation of how one knows he or she is a Christian. (2) It is also the point from which Wesley's theology begins to develop its own characteristic shape, a cast distinguished from the Moravian view by some of its basic doctrines and distinguished from the popular Church of England view by its characteristic constellation of emphases.

Theology, for Wesley, was primarily an explanation of the *via salutis*. For him, theological reflection is inexorably tied to the spiritual pilgrimage, and both are dynamic and developmental. In this sense, Aldersgate certainly was not an inconsequential event in Wesley's life. It is best viewed, however, within the context of a man trying both to live "the scripture way of salvation" and to explain it as well. His experience often outran his understanding. Four days after Aldersgate, he was claiming that he had previously not been a Christian. According to the Moravian assumptions under which he was operating at the time, that was a true perspective. It is significant, however, that every subsequent comment of that sort (even within weeks of the experience) can be understood within Wesley's later theology as saying, "I was previously not (or am not now) a fully sanctified Christian."[202] His later distinctions between two orders of Christians, between the faith of a servant and of a child of God, between the young convert and the mature Christian, between faith and assurance (and allowing for various degrees of both), are all the result of his finally differentiating between justification and sanctification as theologically and experientially distinguishable steps on the spiritual pilgrimage. And crucial to the whole shape of his theology is the assumption that Christians can expect the privilege of knowing that they are children of God through the divine evidence of the witness of his Spirit with their spirits.

Aldersgate was for Wesley a significant step in his spiritual pilgrimage wherein he experienced an assurance of faith. It is clear that in 1738 he defined that experience of the witness of the Spirit as his conversion because he then accepted the Moravian theological framework for anticipating and explaining such instantaneous experiences. It is equally clear that he subsequently rejected many of the equations built into that Moravian theology, including the necessary correlation of faith with assurance, of assurance with salvation, of salvation with conversion, of sanctification with justification, of justification with sinless perfection, of doubt with sin. He continued, however, to stress the possibility of assurance of justification through the witness of the Holy Spirit (with modified expectations as to its necessary fruits and consequences) as a privilege to be desired by all Christians and to be known (evident) through the spiritual senses.

The irony of Aldersgate, however, is that its theological significance rests in Wesley's eventual modification of nearly every aspect of his perception and explanation of the event at the time. The Moravians had led him to great expectations that his own experience and reflection did not confirm as an appropriate or adequate understanding either of true Christianity or of what happened to him that evening. It is not surprising, in this light, that Wesley himself did not hearken back to Aldersgate as a model experience to be universalized. Rather, his subsequent attempts to explain that evening in the context of his continuing spiritual pilgrimage led to significant theological developments that eventually helped shape his own mature understanding and explanation of the scripture way of salvation.

Chapter 4

The Importance of Experience for Faith

Theodore H. Runyon

The 250th anniversary of Aldersgate has occasioned several formal celebrations. It has also provoked vigorous debate! In particular, there have been incisive critiques of the "standard" interpretation of Aldersgate as Wesley's "conversion experience" and as the crucial founding event of the Methodist movement. The critics have argued that the standard reading is an ill-fitting imposition of 19th century "conversionist" ideology upon both the details of Wesley's biography and his theological understanding of the Christian life. While Wesley's immediate post-Aldersgate reflections had a "conversionist" tone, the standard reading fails to take seriously enough Wesley's later qualifications of these early reflections. Therefore, the standard reading may subvert Wesley's mature insights about the nurture of "holiness of heart and life" by focussing Christian existence too exclusively upon a dramatic religious "experience."[1]

I share some of the misgivings about the standard interpretation of Aldersgate that these critics have raised. However, I am not entirely happy with their alternative. They seem all too ready to abandon Aldersgate, or the place of experience, in their reconception of Wesley's spiritual biography and his theology. I believe that it is more appropriate to ask *why* Aldersgate did not accomplish for Wesley what he expected it to and, more importantly, what clues this gives us to Wesley's mature insights into the role of *experience* in Christian life and theology.

Briefly put, my argument will be that Aldersgate did make an important and abiding contribution to Wesley's understanding of the role of experience in Christian life, but it was a contribution that was modified and corrected by his overall perspective. As the mature Wesley looked back on Aldersgate, he saw (as Rex Matthews has also suggested[2]) that his understanding of the event was at that time too confused by the Moravian interpretation of experience; therefore, the mature Wesley distanced himself from that interpretation in favor of a more complex view composed of elements in his theology developed before and expanded after Aldersgate.

How did the mature Wesley's understanding of experience differ from that of the Moravians—at least that of those with whom he had contact in London in 1738, particularly Böhler and Molther? I believe that they tended to understand experience primarily as "feeling", whereas Wesley ultimately understood religious experience as an epistemological event between the Divine and the human participant which involved four interrelated factors:

(1) The Divine source of religious experience who makes impressions on the spiritual senses of the human being.
(2) The *telos* of religious experience: the intention of the source, the purpose and goal for the human being.
(3) The transformation brought about through religious experience.
(4) The feelings that accompany religious experience.

In the remainder of this essay I will develop each of these factors in Wesley's understanding of religious experience, and then suggest how this understanding became the crucible within which Wesley tested the event of Aldersgate and the interpretations of that event being recommended to him.

The Divine Source of Religious Experience

We begin with the first point: the Divine source, which is both the cause and content of experience.

Wesley was in some ways at the cutting edge of developments in his day that made experience a much more important category in religion than it had been up to that point. In the 18th century, experience became a legitimate source of knowledge independent of the authority of tradition and reason. It is important to remember that Wesley pre-dates the 19th century, for we habitually view the term "experience" through 19th-century glasses, when it was reshaped by subjectivism and Romanticism. For us, therefore, "experience" tends to describe a range of feelings *within* the subject. Although the subjective element was by no means absent for Wesley, it is important to realize that for the 18th century "experience" was first and foremost "evidence," i.e., impressions made on the physical senses by the external world, giving the mind which receives those sense impressions access to reality and knowledge of the way things "really are." This epistemology was developed by the philosopher John Locke, in order to clear the way for the experimentally-derived findings of the newly emerging natural sciences to be taken seriously as genuine knowledge of reality.

Prior to Locke, the sources of knowledge were tradition and reason. The authority of tradition had long been recognized because it included revelation and that ancient wisdom which carried the warrant of age and universal acceptance. The authority of reason as a source and criterion of knowledge had been established more recently by René Descartes. He sought to free knowledge from the exclusive authority of tradition by construing reason as a divinely given principle that contained within its innate ideas the rudiments of all true knowledge. By implication, human reason was competent to make judgments concerning the reasonableness of all claims, including religious claims, and to judge between competing authorities.

Locke realized that, if the new knowledge of the world emerging from the observations and experiments of the natural sciences of his day was to be taken seriously, the previous superior position of both reason and tradition would have to be questioned. Scientists could not allow themselves to be hemmed in by either tradition or by the structures of the mind and reason, for these could too easily prejudge results and prevent the facts from manifesting themselves. Therefore, Locke had to deny Descartes' theory of innate ideas. Rather than deriving knowledge of reality from reason, the mind was construed in the more passive role of receiving, ordering, and reflecting upon the information provided it by the senses. The initiative for providing accurate information had to be accorded to the objects under investigation. Whoever would learn the truth must be open to whatever information sense data provided. This was the birth of empiricism, the epistemological orientation that has fostered the scientific advances of the last two centuries and produced the modern age.

For those of us who tend to think of Wesley as a conservative, it is instructive to see that he was at the forefront of those applying this new epistemological revolution to religion. Wesley is usually called a Lockean in his epistemology. Actually, an early and determinative influence may have been Peter Browne rather than John Locke himself. Wesley hand-copied one hundred pages of Browne's *Procedures, Extent and Limits of the Human Understanding* while still a student at Oxford, and later reprinted these excerpts as an appendix to his own *Natural Philosophy, The Wisdom of God in Creation.*[3] Since Browne was himself a modified Lockean, the influence of Locke on Wesley is, in any case, clear. Further evidence of Wesley's regard for at least some aspects of Locke's thought is seen in his prescription of Locke's *Essay Concerning Human Understanding* for the curriculum of Kingswood School, and his printing of excerpts from Locke in the *Arminian Magazine*.[4]

Of course, Wesley's interest in Locke's position was not primarily for the sake of the natural sciences. Rather, he was drawn to the denial of innate ideas as a necessary corollary to the doctrine of Original Sin. It underscored the utter helplessness of the creature to save himself or herself apart from the renewing activity of the Creator. As Barth was to do two centuries later, Wesley denied any innate natural knowledge of God. Against Descartes and the Deists, he insisted:

> If indeed God had stamped (as some have maintained) an idea of himself on every human soul, we must certainly have understood something of (his attributes); . . . but the truth is, no man ever did, or does now find any such idea stamped upon his soul. The little we know of God . . . we do not gather from an inward impression, but gradually acquire from without.[5]

And, taking a position in some ways more radical than Locke himself, Wesley could affirm that "there is nothing in the understanding that was not first perceived by some of the senses. All the knowledge which we naturally have is originally derived from our senses."[6]

Yet, it is precisely here that we encounter Wesley's decisive modification of Locke. Agreeing that the physical senses are incapable of discerning the things of God, Wesley posits "spiritual senses" which operate in close analogy to the physical senses but are attuned to the level of reality the physical senses cannot penetrate: they are "avenues to the invisible world" which the physical "eye hath not seen, neither the ear heard".[7] Of course, these spiritual senses with which every human being is endowed by the Creator have been dulled by the Fall and the habits of sin and indifference. They must be reawakened, sensitized by God's own creative Spirit of grace and truth, in order to perceive "the evidence of things not seen."

As Rex Matthews points out, Wesley was not the first to use this notion of spiritual senses.[8] Its roots lie in the biblical notion of eyes that see and ears that hear. In the third century Origen had developed a theory of spiritual perception in analogy to the five senses. But Wesley combined this with Locke's empiricism to form a religious epistemology in which the divine is both present in an experience as its content and independent of the experience as other than experience. It was precisely this ability to distinguish between the experience as having its source in God and its effects in the human being which eventually enabled Wesley to criticize what he called the "mysticism" of the Moravians.

To demonstrate this latter point, let us turn to Wesley's conversations with Peter Böhler before Aldersgate and follow the progression of events. In his *Journal* entry for 18 February 1738, Wesley recounts a conversation in Latin with Böhler in which the German confronted him with the exasperated comment, "My brother, my brother, that philosophy of yours must be purged away."[9] To what was Böhler referring? Not to Wesley's Lockean epistemology but rather to the rationalism that prevented him from being open to the experience which Böhler was recommending—an acceptance of one's justification by grace alone.

Unwittingly, the doctrine of justification by faith, and the Lutheran pietism for which it was central, were allies to the emerging empiricism of Locke, for they proclaimed a parallel method of approaching the reality of God. Locke's empiricism could, in effect, say: Do not let any rational scheme or prejudices come between your mind and the evidence that makes its imprint on your senses. Let the evidence mediated by the sense impressions speak for itself and be its own authority. Böhler's Luther could say, in effect: Don't let anything come between you and God's pure Word of grace to you—not the rationalism of theologians or of philosophers who will argue about what God can or cannot do, not human reason and its desire to dictate the form God's activity must take to meet its canons, not the human will with its desire to justify itself before God, nor the human heart and its desire to excuse itself before God. Simply be open to God's own initiative. Let God reach you directly and by mercy and love create within your heart the response of faith and trust.

In a letter dated 8 May 1738, Böhler wrote Wesley:

> I beseech you to believe in *your* Jesus Christ; but so put him in mind of his promises to poor sinners, that he may not be able to refrain from doing for you, what he hath done for so many others. O how great, how inexpressible, how unexhausted is his love! Surely he is now ready to help; and nothing can offend [or prevent] him but our unbelief.[10]

However, Wesley was not yet ready to practice the openness implicit in his Lockean epistemology. He wanted to satisfy himself first that the Lutheran interpretation of justification, and especially the Moravian notion of it as an instantaneous event that brings complete sanctification, "dominion over sin, and constant peace from a sense of forgiveness,"[11] comported with Scriptures. When he found that there was indeed evidence in Scripture that God was ready to "cleanse from all unrighteousness," he demurred that although this may have been possible in biblical times as part of that dispensation, it was not possible today. Böhler removed this last objection of Wesley by producing three Moravian witnesses,

> all of whom testified of their own personal experience that a true, living faith in Christ is inseparable from a sense of pardon for all past, and freedom from all present sins. They added with one mouth that this faith was the gift, the free gift of God, and that he would surely bestow it upon every soul who earnestly and perseveringly sought it.[12]

In light of this evidence, Wesley conceded:

> I was now thoroughly convinced. And, by the grace of God, I resolved to seek it unto the end, (1) by absolutely renouncing all dependence . . . upon *my own* works or righteousness, on which I had really grounded my hope of salvation, though I knew it not, from my youth up; (2) by adding to 'the constant use of all the' other 'means of grace,' continual prayer for this very thing, justifying, saving faith, a full reliance on the blood of Christ shed for *me*; a trust in him as *my* Christ, as *my* sole justification, sanctification, and redemption.[13]

It was in this frame of mind, and armed with the Moravian theology of instantaneous justification and sanctification, that Wesley went to the Moravian conventicle gathering in Aldersgate Street.

Someone was reading Luther's *Preface to Romans*. This *Preface* spoke directly to what Wesley had now identified as his problem: that in all of his efforts to be holy from his youth up, he had operated out of compulsion and not out of the sense of freedom which Christ brings when, by substituting himself and his sacrifice, he removes from us the necessity of meeting God's expectations in our own strength and by our own efforts. First, the reading from Luther described Wesley's present condition:[14]

> For even though you keep this law outwardly, with works, from fear of punishment or love or reward, nevertheless, you do all this without willingness, under compulsion; and you would rather do otherwise, if the law were not there. The conclusion is that at the bottom of your heart you hate the law.

Then Luther turned the screw. What the law requires, he said,

> is to do its works with pleasure and love, and to live a godly and good life of one's own accord, without the compulsion of the law. . . . Hence it comes that faith alone makes righteous and fulfills the law; out of Christ's merit.

That is, faith brings the Spirit, "and the Spirit makes the heart glad and free," as the law requires it should be. Thus good works have their source in faith.

> Faith, however, is a divine work in us. It changes us and makes us to be born anew of God. . . . Faith is a living, daring confidence in God's grace, so sure and certain that a man would stake his life on it a thousand times. This confidence in God's grace and knowledge of it makes men glad and bold and happy in dealing with God and with all his creatures.

As Luther's words described this gift of God, Wesley sensed at the core of his own being the gift being given to him. Luther's words in that moment mediated God's own Word, giving clear evidence to Wesley that God's love was reaching out to him through the actions of Christ applied specifically to him and registered on his spiritual sensorium, the heart.

Note how Lockean Wesley's description of this event is: it begins with an empirical reference (almost like a laboratory book account), "About a quarter before nine." Then follows a detailing of the circumstances, "while he was describing the change which God works in the heart through faith in Christ." Next comes the registering of the empirical evidence, "I felt my heart strangely warmed." But this is not yet the content of the experience. That follows. As Christ's love was received, it created an answering trust in Wesley's heart, "I felt I did trust in Christ alone for salvation." A relationship was established of which Christ, not Wesley's feelings, was the guarantor. "And an assurance was given me, that he had taken away *my* sins, even *mine,* and saved *me* from the law of sin and death."[15]

As we shall see in a moment, Wesley became increasingly suspicious of the Moravian understanding of the role of feelings that contributed to this Aldersgate experience. By contrast, the affirmation of justification by grace, which surfaced here, remained a central part of the message of both Wesleys. The recognition of an objective divine action of reconciliation which provided the foundation for a continuing relationship between the reconciled and God was what the mature Wesley determined to be the valid content of Aldersgate. Likewise, his chief motive and enterprise from that day forward was to make this gift of grace available to all.

Most importantly, Aldersgate convinced Wesley that "Christian experience" meant participating in an event of reconciliation that was initiated by God. As the source of the event, God remains the Other, the external referent present in the experience, but also transcendent, thus providing not only continuity to the experience but also a point of comparison with the experiences of this same God by others in

Scripture, tradition, and "conference," through which reason can critique, evaluate, and correct the understanding of any single experience. Wesley was to learn this by a painful process, as he discovered how the Moravian emphasis upon feeling tended to collapse the reality of God into the feeling itself. But, more of that later.

The Telos *of Religious Experience*

The second factor present in the mature Wesley's understanding of experience, though temporarily obscured by the Moravian influence at the time of Aldersgate, was the *telos* or goal of experience. Wesley's mature theology is thoroughly teleological. It assumed that Christian experience is rightly understood only when it is set within the context of God's renewal of the whole fallen creation. This theme was already present in Wesley's pre-Aldersgate theology. The framework of creation/re-creation constituted the bookends, so to speak, between which his more familiar and popular doctrines of justification and sanctification were set. Without this framework the latter doctrines lacked both orientation and goal.

Wesley did not create this teleological perspective *ex nihilo*. The theme of new creation was present in both Anglican and Puritan sources of his time, such as Henry Horn's *The Light of God Spreading Itself in All the Dark Corners of the Earth* (1653), Richard Baxter's *Universal Redemption of Mankind by the Lord Jesus* (1694), and Jeremiah White's *The Restoration of All Things* (1712). Albert Outler has argued that an even more important source was Wesley's study of the ancient Greek Fathers during his student years at Oxford.[16] Together with a fellow member of the Holy Club, John Clayton, who was a patristics scholar, Wesley had poured over the Greek texts of the new editions produced by the patristics renaissance in the latter half of the seventeenth century. Among his favorites were the homilies of Macarius the Egyptian, which Wesley edited and included in the first volume of his 50-volume *Christian Library*. According to Outler (following Werner Jaeger),[17] these homilies reflected the theology of Gregory of Nyssa, who saw the goal of the Christian life as "deification" (*theosis*). This specific term is liable to misunderstanding. Thus, as Ted Campbell notes, Wesley avoided it in his edition of the Macarian homilies, preferring instead the term "perfection."[18] Following the ancient Greek Fathers, such "perfection" was a part of human nature in creation, but was distorted and obscured by the fall. It was made available anew through the incarnation and saving work of Christ. It must shine forth once again as human beings are restored to the true image, to that kinship and fellowship with the divine that constitute true humanity. This is the goal toward which the Christian life is directed, and therefore is the purpose which all religious experiences exist to serve.

The Moravians' understanding of salvation lacked this cosmic framework. They operated out of a rather limited interpretation of Luther's forensic understanding of justification and sanctification, an understanding which Wesley had found convincing shortly before Aldersgate but about which he soon developed severe doubts. His objections led to a final break with the Fetter Lane society in 1740, and the beginning of the United Society at the Foundery in 1741. The reasons for the break become clear in Wesley's Latin conversation with Zinzendorf in 1741. Wesley says the two chief issues which separated them were "the goal of our faith in this life, i.e., Christian perfection" and the use of "the means of grace."[19] The Moravians held to a forensic understanding of both justification and sanctification. This is what they had in mind when they assured Wesley before Aldersgate that through the merits of Christ he would be made completely righteous and have total victory over sin. What they meant was that in the eyes of God he would be clothed in Christ's righteousness, which is total, sufficient to cover any sin. When Wesley confessed that temptations and doubts still beset him, they concluded that he must lack genuine faith because faith was by definition recumbency in Christ. Christ is always sufficient to cover for us, *if* we truly trust him. There were therefore no "degrees of faith." One either trusted in him, or one did not. Trust in Christ was thus the beginning and end of faith. This trust did not lead to and serve another end, such as the renewal of the creature. From the Moravian standpoint that would be to substitute another goal for Christ alone.

In their conversation, Zinzendorf accused Wesley of espousing "inherent perfection," actual holiness in the human being. Zinzendorf insisted that in ourselves we remain vile sinners. Only in Christ are we accepted by God as holy. Wesley countered that the purpose of Christ's mission in the world was to renew the creature. "It is Christ's own Spirit that works in true Christians to achieve their perfection."

"I know of no such thing as inherent perfection in this life," responded Zinzendorf. "This is the error of errors. I pursue it everywhere with fire and sword! I stamp it under foot! I give it over to destruction! Christ is our only perfection".[20] Thus the Moravian position, in its eagerness to honor Christ alone, denied to Christ a recreative function in the world. His only purpose was to gather the faithful (those who trusted in him to cover their sins) for heaven. Had Wesley not separated from the Moravians, the Methodist emphasis upon the renewal of this world would have been forfeited. To be sure, some of the Herrnhut Moravians, such as Christian David, took a position closer to Wesley's. But in the London societies the view of Molther, Böhler, and Zinzendorf prevailed.

The Transformation Wrought by Religious Experience

Closely related to the goal of experience is a third factor, the *means*. If the goal, as Wesley said in his sermon on "The New Creation,"[21] is a new heaven and a new earth, the way toward that goal must involve the transformation of the present order of things. *Transformation* is, therefore, the third ingredient in Wesley's mature doctrine of experience. Transformation was not essential to the Moravian position. For them the essential point was not to hope for change but to rely steadfastly upon the One who justifies the sinner whether the sinner changes or not. Because holiness is not the holiness of the believer but the holiness of Christ applied to the believer, Zinzendorf observed, "from the moment one is justified, he is entirely sanctified. Thereafter till death he is neither more holy nor less holy. . . . The event of sanctification and justification is completed in an instant. Thereafter, it neither increases or decreases."[22] Salvation is understood as a status that one has before God. Since that status is given by God, it is not subject to change but remains as steadfast as God.

From Wesley's standpoint, this lack of change does not honor God. On the contrary, it places a roadblock in the way of what God is attempting to accomplish through Christ and the power of the Spirit at work in the world. For him salvation is understood as a re-creative process, the restoration of the image of God in humanity. It is therefore "imparted righteousness" as well as "imputed righteousness." God's love granted to us in our justification is extended *through* us to others in the continuing process of sanctification. The transformation of persons is therefore necessarily the transformation of their relationships and the society around them as "love shines forth in action."[23] Faith is not an end in itself, therefore, but the necessary means toward the increase of love. Faith is the relationship that frees us to love more perfectly. And of the increase of such love there shall be no end.

In reality, Wesley's most fundamental commitments stood in significant tension with Moravian theology. Wesley himself grew more and more aware of this as he made his pilgrimage to Herrnhut after Aldersgate, and was disillusioned with Moravian theology at its source. He could not ignore the fact that there were fundamental differences between his understanding of experience and that of the Moravians.

The Feelings that Accompany Religious Experience

These differences become even more pronounced when we turn to the fourth and final point of comparison, the understanding of *feeling*. The Moravians' openness to the evidence of feeling was initially attractive to Wesley. It seemed to correspond to his own attention to the spiritual senses as mediators of God's reality. This left him vulnerable to the suggestion of the Moravians that certain feelings were necessary as signs of faith, and that the lack of those feelings was a sure indication of a lack of faith. Peter Böhler promised him "peace from a sense of forgiveness," and Wesley assumed that no one could have the "sense of forgiveness and not *feel* it."[24] However, he confessed that at times he did not feel it; and therefore he could only conclude that he did not possess true faith.

With Aldersgate, he fully expected this problem would be resolved. He found that it was not—particularly because, in the meantime, he had made a commitment to the Moravian proposition that the feelings themselves are the only true and dependable indicator. Philipp Molther had assured him "that whoever at any time felt any doubt or fear . . . had *no faith* at all."[25] His despair intensified, and his doubts were exacerbated by the notion that any trace of doubt indicated a complete lack of faith. No wonder that Wesley, seven months after Aldersgate, confessed:

> I am not a Christian. . . . For a Christian is one who has the fruits of the Spirit of Christ, which . . . are love, peace, joy. But these I have not. . . . I *feel* this moment I do not love God; which therefore I *know* because I *feel* it. There is no word more proper, more clear or more strong.[26]

Wesley had been persuaded by Moravian theology and saw no way beyond it, until he was shocked into a recognition of the larger issues and implications by the quietism of some of the London Moravians and their rejection of the means of grace. Those who were in direct contact with Christ through their feelings had no need for further means of grace. Moreover, prior to this experience any use of the means of grace tempted the seeker to rely on the means rather than on Christ. Wesley was forced to recognize that the advocates of the "stillness" doctrine had, in effect, absolutized their own feelings and merged them with Christ. They longed for an unmediated faith, not the incarnational faith essential to Christianity. As a result, their experience was not of a biblically-defined source external to themselves *mediated* through feelings. Rather, they were collapsing that source into their feelings and making feeling the final authority. That is what Wesley called pejoratively "mysticism," the loss of the *other* in experience. He wrote a friend:

> I think the rock on which I had nearest made shipwreck of the faith was the writings of the Mystics; under which term I comprehend all and only those who slight any of the means of grace.[27]

And in his *Journal*, he added:

> All the other enemies of Christianity are triflers; the Mystics are the most dangerous of its enemies. They stab it in its vitals, and its most serious professors are most likely to fall by them.[28]

Perhaps we can best explain what was involved if we observe that Wesley was a *sacramental* Christian. This has nothing to do with sacramental*ism*. It simply means that the relationship to God is a *mediated* one in which finite means are used by the Spirit to communicate transcendent reality. The supreme paradigm is, of course, the incarnation, the Word become flesh and blood. Feeling was a sacrament for Wesley. The divine intention is received through finite human feelings, through sensations that transmits a message of trans-empirical importance, sensations that communicate grace.

Now, there are two ways that the effectiveness of a sacrament can be destroyed: by making it of no importance, or by making it of absolute importance. When it is made of no importance it is approached with no expectation, and as a result no communication of the transcendent is possible. There are no eyes to see, no ears to hear. This is the typical rationalist and liberal Protestant error. But a sacrament can also be destroyed by raising it to absolute importance, where it replaces that which it symbolizes rather than standing in relative relationship to it and mediating it. This was the traditional Roman Catholic error in transubstantiation and Corpus Christi adorations. The Moravians managed to commit both errors. They said the means of grace were of no account, and therefore dissuaded persons whom Wesley thought could be helped by availing themselves of the means of grace. At the same time, they made feelings absolute, so that there was no appeal beyond them to their source. As a result feelings were no longer viewed as finite mediations but as the functional equivalent of God. They were no longer sacraments but the Absolute itself.

After Wesley separated from the Moravians, he put feelings in perspective by interrelating them with the other three factors in experience: the divine source, the teleological context, and the transformational effect. Writing to Ann Loxdale (12 April 1782), he commented,

> It is undoubtedly our privilege to 'rejoice evermore,' with a calm, still, heartfelt joy. Nevertheless this is seldom long at one stay. Many circumstances may cause it to ebb and flow. This, therefore, is not the essence of religion, which is no other than humble, gentle, patient love.[29]

To Joseph Benson he wrote (21 May 1781), "That some consciousness of our being in favour with God is joined with Christian faith I cannot doubt; but it is not the essence of it. A consciousness of pardon cannot be the condition of pardon."[30] The transforming work of God is primary; our feelings provide a secondary and dependent recognition of divine action. The testimony of the Spirit of God "must needs, in the very nature of things, be antecedent to the testimony of our own spirit . . . 'We love Him, because He first loved us'."[31]

Wesley backed away therefore from the authority he had earlier accorded to feelings, under the influence of the Moravians. He came to view them as correctable by other aspects of experience. Looking back at that Moravian period with rueful humor he wrote,

> When fifty years ago my brother Charles and I, in the simplicity of our hearts, told the good people of England that unless they *knew* [could feel] their sins forgiven, they were under the wrath and curse of God, I marvel . . . they did not stone us! The Methodists, I hope, know better now; we preach assurance as we always did, as a common privilege of the children of God, but we do not enforce it under the pain of damnation denounced on all who enjoy it not.[32]

The Importance and Ambiguity of Aldersgate

In contrast to those who would discard Aldersgate, therefore, I suggest that we should recognize its importance and its ambiguity. The developments surrounding Aldersgate, both for John and Charles, were of decisive importance for Methodism's further development. A radical doctrine of grace, and the personal appropriation of justification by grace, emerged as central Methodist doctrines that informed further practice. Without the contact with the Moravians Wesley might never have learned that lesson, and the Reformation side of the Methodist heritage might never have come to birth. Had Wesley not separated from the Moravians, however, Methodism could well have remained a Moravian sect without its Catholic element and the emphasis upon transformation. The genius is in the combination. Without Aldersgate, we probably would not have heard of Wesley or of Methodism. With only Aldersgate, we also probably would not have heard of Wesley or Methodism. We thank divine Providence for the combination.

It remains for us only to spell out briefly some of the practical implications for Methodism today.

(1) Aldersgate means that we need to recognize and claim the fact that Methodism has a distinctive theological contribution to make. I have suggested elsewhere that what Methodism can contribute to ecumenical discussion today is an *"orthopathy,"* which could provide a necessary but currently missing complement to *orthodoxy* and *orthopraxy*.[33] Here I have sought to spell out in more detail what orthopathy involves: a description of the essential components in experience that recognizes the important, powerful, and necessary contribution which experience has to make to the identity, mobilization, and mission of the church; and recognizes at the same time the checks and balances required if experience is to be guided into the most productive channels. In analogy to the integral and complementary relation between word and sacrament, experience needs the word of orthodoxy if it is to communicate rightly, and the deeds of orthopraxy if it is to be a means for sanctifying the world. But both words and deeds need to be filled with the divine power and impact of the motivating Spirit mediated, received, and communicated further through experience.

(2) Aldersgate means that Methodists are called to proclaim boldly the Christ who is acting *now,* in this moment, to overcome the barriers of misunderstanding and misinformation, to penetrate the chinks in the walls of habitual indifference, to reach the hearts of his people and sensitize them to ultimate reality. God is the source, but we are the means. We must not be intimidated by unbelief. Unbelief is the result of non-experience. We cannot expect persons whose spiritual senses have never been awakened to have accurate information or to be excited about what they do not know. Our calling is not to condemn this ignorance, this lack of eyes to see and ears to hear, but to be the means for overcoming it. We ask only that persons approach religious experience with the same openness they would bring to any other perception of the real world, abandoning rationalistic and emotional prejudices that would stand in the way of accurate reception. With Wesley, we encourage them to take the empirical approach, to be open to the evidence which even now is seeking to reach them.

(3) Third, a Wesleyan orthopathic approach means that we should not be satisfied until we see actual change. God's goals for us are not exhausted with warm feelings and a sense of assurance, important as these are. The faith that receives God's love is the faith that extends God's love in all its forms into all the world. "God has so mingled you

together with other [human beings] that whatever grace you have received of God may through you be communicated to others. . . . Love shines forth in action."[34] Orthodoxy and orthopathy join in orthopraxy.

(4) Finally, Aldersgate means sensitizing persons to the sacramental role feelings can play in their lives when informed by biblical, doctrinal, and (from Wesley's perspective) common sense, checks and balances. It may be helpful in this regard to make a distinction between feelings and experience. "Experience" refers to the whole range of factors that must be taken into consideration in orthopathy. But feelings are what is closest to us. Feelings focus our energies, enlist us, motivate us, and give us passion. Who will fight against injustice, prejudice, and corruption that does not have a strong *sense* of justice and outrage against injustice? Who will sacrifice for others and engage in acts of mercy that does not *feel* compassion? Who will spend long hours over a microscope or pouring through books that does not know the *feelings* of joy and satisfaction that come with discovering a new truth or finding new confirmation of an old truth? Who will work hard at great emotional cost putting a marriage back together that does not *feel* the importance of those relations to all who are touched by them?

The capacity to feel is a gift from the Creator. Therefore, its significance should not be neglected—least of all by religion.

Yes, Aldersgate has not just historical but remarkable continuing significance. This should not blind us to its ambiguity or make us uncritical of the distortions which surround it, both then and now. But we thank God for what came to birth there, and what must be reborn in Methodism today.

Chapter 5

"Strangely Warmed": The Place of Aldersgate in the Methodist Canon

Jean Miller Schmidt

Alongside the various celebrations that accompanied the 250th anniversary of Aldersgate in 1988 were several voices protesting the choice of this event to focus a commemoration of Wesley and his importance for Methodism. As one critic put it, "As the Methodist movement celebrates the 250th anniversary of Aldersgate, it is only celebrating its own willful distortion of its own history, its own apostasy from Wesleyan theology."[1]

In reality, what most of the critics of the recent celebration of Aldersgate were concerned to reject was not the event itself, but the current "standard" interpretation of Aldersgate which focuses on it as the *single* decisive turning point in Wesley's life—explanatory of his life and paradigmatic for later Methodist spirituality—rather than seeing it as one in a *series* of significant spiritual experiences, of which it was neither the first nor the last.

As the critics of the standard interpretation of Aldersgate are quick to point out, the exclusive focus on this event was not characteristic of Wesley's own account of his life and ministry. Rather, as Albert Outler has shown, the Aldersgate story as such drops out of sight in Wesley's writings after 1740, and the experience itself was followed by "further crises of equal, or nearly equal moment."[2]

If this is so, then where did the current "standard" interpretation of Aldersgate come from? When did Aldersgate come to be viewed as paradigmatic for Methodists?

Aldersgate and Wesley's Biographers

A good place to begin our investigation is with Wesley's biographers. How did they interpret the role of Aldersgate in his life? These biographies can be divided helpfully into three groups: the early biographies, the standard (19th and early 20th C.) biographies, and the more recent biographies/studies of Wesley.[3]

Early Biographies

Of the "early" biographies, three are worthy of mention here. Dr. John Whitehead was Wesley's physician, a local preacher at City Road Chapel, and one of the three men to whom Wesley had entrusted the disposition of his manuscripts in his will. Whitehead's two-volume *Life of Rev. John Wesley,* published in 1793 and 1796, was the first to be based on access to these manuscripts. In 1820, Poet Laureate Robert Southey, an Anglican convert from Unitarianism, published a two-volume *Life of Wesley* that is still regarded as the most distinguished literary monument to Wesley's stature and influence. Although Southey was critical of Wesley's theology and Methodist practices, his biography of Wesley commanded a much wider audience than those written by Methodists. Henry Moore was one of the young preachers named to the "Legal Hundred" of the Conference by Wesley, and the last surviving executor of Wesley's manuscripts. His *Life of the Rev. John Wesley* (two volumes, 1824–1825) was the last of the firsthand accounts and, in effect, had the last word over both Whitehead and Southey. How did these early biographers view Aldersgate?

Commenting on Wesley's first encounter with Peter Böhler in February 1738, John Whitehead writes: "After about ten years of painful labor, his experience convinced him, that his notions were not evangelical, that he had considered as causes, things that were only placed as the fruits of faith in the gospel economy; and therefore, that he neither possessed saving faith, nor had a right notion of it."[4] Whitehead's judgments about Aldersgate are best described as moderate, however. Significant attention is given to Wesley's setting in earnest upon a "new life" in 1725, and therefore Aldersgate is not described as a single watershed. Furthermore, Whitehead treats Aldersgate itself as part of a period of transition that extends over the whole of 1738.[5] The author points out clearly Wesley's own later reinterpretation of the events of 1738 in the errata sheets added to the

1774 edition of the *Journal*, and describes the development of his thought on degrees of faith and on assurance.[6]

It was not surprising that Southey, who was critical of Wesley's "enthusiastic doctrines," (instantaneous regeneration, assurance, perfection) should have viewed Aldersgate with skepticism. For him Aldersgate was a self-contradiction; an assurance which had not assured Wesley![7] In his extended review (250+ pages) of Southey's *Life of Wesley* (which he was directed by the Conference to write), Richard Watson accuses Southey of having failed to understand the "real" John Wesley, and raises the question whether a non-Methodist is adequately equipped to write a proper biography of the founder. Albert Outler describes these biographies (at least from this point on) as "Wesley Studies, Phase I."[8] That is, left with Wesley to themselves, Methodists proceeded to evolve the stereotypes and pious legends of Wesley their cult hero.

Henry Moore had the opportunity to correct both Whitehead and Southey. Instead, his treatment of Wesley's spiritual development was largely dependent upon, even plagiarized from, Whitehead.[9] If Moore provides anything distinctive, it is a tendency toward a more "evangelical" reading of Aldersgate. For example, after quoting Wesley's earlier description (in a letter to his mother) of faith as "assent upon rational grounds," Moore adds: "Men would be apt to think, that such an intellect, so improved, and so disposed, would be *easily* led into all 'the truth as it is in Jesus.' But the contrary will be seen in these memoirs. To bring such a mind to the simplicity of faith—to make it willing to lose its all and to find all in Christ, is indeed to move a mountain! But when brought to this, how mighty do we see that mind in operation! how steadfast and unmovable in all its actings!"[10]

Unlike Whitehead, Moore quotes in full Wesley's own *Journal* account of the Aldersgate experience, tracing his spiritual journey from the age of ten. Moore introduces it as follows: "The account which immediately follows, is of such deep importance, that I am constrained to give it entire in his own words. Mr. Wesley's actual obtaining the true faith of the Gospel, is a point of the utmost magnitude, not only with respect to himself, but to others. For it was not till after this, that God was pleased to own him in such a remarkable manner in the salvation of souls, as was evidenced in his future labours."[11] Thus, in general, Moore makes more of Aldersgate than Whitehead, referring to it (in the whole sequence of events) as Wesley's attaining the true Christian faith.[12]

Standard Biographies

Perhaps the best example of the "standard" view of Wesley is Luke Tyerman's monumental three-volume *Life and Times of the Rev. John Wesley, M.A.: Founder of the Methodists* (1870). Tyerman's work was distinguished by the sheer volume of material that he gathered, some of which had come to light since the work of Whitehead and Moore. Although his intent was to make Wesley "his own biographer,"[13] Tyerman's interpretive biases were very clear. They included a thoroughgoing Methodist triumphalism and opposition to "high church" positions of any sort.[14] It was this evangelical view which came to be the "standard" Methodist interpretation of Aldersgate.

Before Aldersgate, according to Tyerman, Wesley was "at least a servant of God and accepted of Him"; he was "almost a Christian."[15] From 1725 his whole aim had been to serve God, but it was only at Aldersgate that Wesley received consciousness of being saved through faith in Christ. "Now he *knew* he was safe, and he was *happy* as well as safe,"[16] Tyerman explains. He then quotes Peter Böhler's comments about the Wesley brothers (made to Zinzendorf): "They justify themselves; and, therefore, they always take it for granted, that they believe already, and try to prove their faith by their works, and thus so plague and torment themselves that they are at heart very miserable."[17] Tyerman adds: "These are weighty words on the simplicity of saving faith, and well deserve pondering by both the ministers and members of the church of the present day."[18] Tyerman sees the preaching of the doctrines that Wesley grasped in 1738 as the beginning of the "greatest revival of religion chronicled in the history of the church of Christ."[19] Here the standard view of Aldersgate has reached maturity!

Recent Biographies/Studies

More recent biographies/studies of Wesley have tended to question the traditional image of him, or to probe more deeply into one or another basic aspects of his thought. (Outler refers to this as "Wesley Studies, Phase II," the crux of which is "rescuing Wesley from his Methodist cocoon.")[20] One of the first challenges to the standard view of Aldersgate was raised by Father Maximin Piette, a Belgian Franciscan, in 1925. Piette sought to demonstrate the "catholic" elements in Wesley's revival and theology. Among other things, this led him to reject the traditional (negative) portrait of Wesley's spiritual life prior to Aldersgate, arguing that 1725 was his "true" conversion.[21]

The full impact of Piette's challenge to the standard view of Aldersgate was not immediately felt, because his view was swallowed up in the "great outpouring"[22] of writing occasioned by the bicentennial celebration of Wesley's Aldersgate experience in the 1930s. Three works, in particular, deserve brief mention here because of their theological depth and their attempt to set Wesley in the larger context of historic Christian thought: George Croft Cell's *The Rediscovery of John Wesley* (1935), Umphrey Lee's *John Wesley and Modern Religion* (1936), and William R. Cannon's slightly later *The Theology of John Wesley: With Special Reference to the Doctrine of Justification* (1946).

Cell was a self-conscious revisionist, attempting to present the Wesleyan revival as the rediscovery and reaffirmation of the faith of the first Reformers, Luther and Calvin. Cell claimed that, for Wesley, saving faith (which underlies the progress, no less than the beginning of Christian experience) is in its totality the gift and work of God. While admitting Piette's point that there were catholic elements in Wesley, Cell was primarily concerned to reemphasize the protestant elements; hence, his oft-quoted conclusion that Wesley's teaching was a necessary synthesis "of the Protestant ethic of grace with the Catholic ethic of holiness." Thus, Cell was inclined to retain the "standard" position that Wesley crossed his religious Rubicon in the spring of 1738.[23]

Umphrey Lee chose not to see 1738 as a singular watershed in Wesley's life that marked the end of his spiritual crisis. He noted that the crises continued, and that Wesley's theology continued to mature beyond Aldersgate. He referred both to Wesley's subsequent change of mind about the Aldersgate experience, and to his failure to mention Aldersgate in his histories of Methodism. What was crucial about Aldersgate for Wesley, in Lee's view, was his experience of the love of God which awakened an answering love.[24]

According to William Cannon, it was at Aldersgate that Wesley learned for the first time the true meaning of justification by faith. Cannon probed deeply the synergism of Wesley's thought in terms of *how* justifying grace is appropriated by human beings. "Faith as the one condition of justification is offered unto [humans] as a free gift by a gracious God," Cannon explained, "but then [we] must actively respond to that offer and reach out with the arms of true repentance to receive the gift."[25] Cannon stressed that although forgiveness is the primary fact in the beginning of religion, the Wesleyan emphasis is on perfection. Thus, in all Wesley's theology "the emphasis [is] on justification as a means to holiness, and on free human responsiveness as the condition both of pardon and acceptance and of perseverance in the way of entire sanctification."[26]

These three works (and others like them from this same period) represented a much more adequate and profound exploration of Wesley's thought than his biographers had attempted. While they did not unanimously reject the standard interpretation of Aldersgate that developed in the biographies, they at least planted the seeds of dissent that have blossomed in our day.

Aldersgate in the Practice of the Churches

So far we have focussed our attention on scholarly studies of Wesley's life and the place of Aldersgate within it. What about the *practice* of the British and American Methodist churches? What role did the Aldersgate experience play in their history? When did they begin to celebrate the anniversary of Aldersgate?

Centennial of Aldersgate?

Contrary to popular opinion, the fact is that there was *no* celebration of the one hundredth anniversary of Wesley's Aldersgate experience in 1838, either in British or in American Methodism! The centenary of Methodism was celebrated not in 183*8* (to commemorate Aldersgate), but in 183*9*, commemorating the formation of the United Societies. This fact is clear from several historical sources.

In 1838 the president of the English Conference, Thomas Jackson, was directed by the conference to prepare a volume "giving a brief, but comprehensive view of the subject to which the centenary celebration would relate." The volume was published in 1839, with the title *The Centenary of Wesleyan Methodism: A brief Sketch of the Rise, Progress, and present State of the Wesleyan Methodist Societies throughout the World.*[27] While this work included one chapter on the early life and conversion of the Wesleys, the principal focus was on the great revival of religion that began in 1739. Thus, successive chapters were devoted to: the measures adopted by the Wesleys for the revival of religion (including field preaching), the formation of societies, employment of lay preachers, an itinerant ministry, erection of separate places of worship, the publication of books, and the "adoption of a simple and impressive mode of preaching."[28] Within the work, Jackson reviewed the history of the earlier Methodist societies: at Oxford, in Savannah, at Fetter Lane, and in Bristol. He carefully distinguished between these and the first of the United Societies, formed in London toward the end of 1739.

Further details on the manner in which the centenary was celebrated in 1839 can be found in two other sources. One is a chapter on "The Centenary Celebration" in a history of Wesleyan Methodism by George Smith, the third and concluding volume of which was published in 1861. The other is a brief article on the Centenary in the *Encyclopedia of World Methodism*.[29] Both note the decision of the British Conference that 1739 (rather than 1725 or 1738) was "the most suitable period for commemoration as having originated Wesleyan Methodism."[30] In October 1838, the president of the conference, Thomas Jackson, convened a select committee of over 250 ministers and laymen in Manchester to plan for the centenary celebration. In addition to religious observances, a "pecuniary effort" was planned, out of "gratitude to God and veneration for Wesley."[31] Contributions in excess of £220,000 were disbursed for missionary and educational purposes, and for the support of retired ministers and widows. The final acts of celebration were associated with the conference in July 1839 and at simultaneous religious meetings held throughout the Connexion on October 25, 1839.

As for the Methodist Episcopal Church in the U.S. in 1838, it was preoccupied with the reform agitation which had led to the departure of the Methodist Protestants in 1828, and even more troubling, the debates over slavery that disrupted the General Conferences of 1836 and 1840. In the fourth and last volume of Nathan Bangs' *History of the Methodist Episcopal Church*, published in 1838–41, there is no mention of the anniversary of Aldersgate, but there is reference to the centenary celebration of 1839. Bangs writes: "As the first Methodist society was formed in London in the month of October, 1739, so 1839 became properly the one hundredth year of Methodism. Accordingly, our brethren in Europe and America prepared to celebrate the event with all due solemnity and religious fervor. The 25th of October was fixed upon as the day for this religious celebration."[32] After explaining the appropriateness of both religious exercises and taking collections, Bangs concludes: "The manner in which the celebration was conducted had a hallowing influence upon the Church generally, and tended very much to increase the spirit of devotion, to give more enlarged views of the divine goodness in raising up such a man as John Wesley, and in blessing the world with such a system as Methodism."[33]

Since there is also no evidence of any observance of the 150th anniversary of Aldersgate in 1888 (the American Methodists were celebrating the centennial of Episcopal Methodism in 1884), we can only conclude that celebrations of the anniversary of Aldersgate are a product of *this* century! In 1924, British Methodists celebrated "Wesley Day" on May 24 for the first time. An open air evangelistic campaign in Hyde Park marked this first observance. In subsequent years, Wesley Day was observed with special services on May 24, whether it fell on a Sunday or during the week. Viewing the Aldersgate experience as "an epochal event in Wesley's life, from which sprang successful evangelism," these Methodists desired "both to commemorate the event and to seek a renewal of the spirit of evangelism."[34] At the World Methodist Council meeting in Oxford in 1951, the function of Wesley Day was extended to (and replaced by) Aldersgate Sunday, the Sunday "falling upon or immediately preceding Wesley Day." This was endorsed by the Council as "an occasion for remembering the faith of our founders and for rededicating ourselves in universal fellowship to the spreading of scriptural holiness throughout the world."[35]

Why was there no celebration of Aldersgate one hundred years after? Was it because its evangelical significance (for Wesley and his heirs) was assumed, and what was marked as the beginning of Wesleyan Methodism was the point that distinguished Methodism from its Anglican context—the organization of the United Societies? It is difficult to know for sure, but it is a point worth pondering.

Similarly, how was the perspective on Aldersgate one hundred and fifty years later affected by American Methodist struggles over the issue of holiness in the 1880s. (This was the beginning of the "come outer" phase of the formation of separate holiness denominations.) An article in the *Methodist Review* in 1887 expressed concern about Wesley's less mature views on Christian perfection as he emerged from the "cloud of Moravian belief and error." Those less mature views were apparently being adopted by the author's contemporaries.[36]

These two illustrations may serve to remind us of how Wesley has been interpreted through the history of Methodism in the nineteenth and twentieth centuries. We have not often seen him whole, and in his own times, on his own terms (which Outler sees as the aim of "Wesley Studies: Phase III").[37]

Bicentennial of Aldersgate

With the precedent already set by "Wesley Day," there was a fully developed celebration of the bicentennial of Aldersgate in 1938. Moreover, it was a celebration dominated by the "standard" interpretation of Aldersgate that we traced in the biographies. This fact can best be demonstrated by considering a volume edited by Elmer T. Clark, entitled *What Happened at Aldersgate: Addresses in Commemoration of the Bicentennial of the Spiritual Awakening of John Wesley in Aldersgate Street, London, May 24, 1738.*[38] This work is a collection of addresses delivered at the Aldersgate Session of the General Missionary Council of the Methodist Episcopal Church, South, meeting in Savannah, Georgia, early in 1938. The theme of the meeting was "The Primacy of Personal Religious Experience in the Life and Work of Methodism" (p. 5). A quick survey of the titles of these addresses gives some sense of the way Aldersgate was seen to be paradigmatic: "Aldersgate the Basis of Social Morality," "Aldersgate the Motive Power of the Church," "The Aldersgate Evangel," "Aldersgate the Basis of Methodist Doctrine," "The Need of Aldersgate in Modern Life," "Aldersgate the Source of Missionary Passion," "Aldersgate the Power Uplifting Women," "Aldersgate and Enduement for Service," "Aldersgate and Christian Stewardship," etc., etc.

In an interesting address (was it the opening address of the meeting?), Elmer T. Clark asked "what really happened on Wednesday evening, May 24, 1738, and what was its significance"? (p. 22ff) While not wanting to insist on the term "conversion," since Wesley seldom used it, Clark asserted that "the awakening of John Wesley was a process, of which the Aldersgate incident was the high culmination." The point, for Clark, was that before Aldersgate Wesley was a failure in his work and miserable in his heart, and that after Aldersgate he was transformed. "The priest," he said, "became the prophet, the ritualist became the evangelical. The whole spirit and structure of Methodism traces back to 1738" (pp. 33, 39).

Other addresses were variations on this same theme. Edwin Lewis talked of Aldersgate as a demonstration of the central place of emotion in religion (pp. 80–1). Bishop Ralph Cushman (Methodist Episcopal Church) asked, "Is it not evident, judging from *our* fruitlessness, that we of today need an Aldersgate experience just as much as Wesley did?" (p. 94) James H. Straugh (President of the General Conference of the Methodist Protestant Church) wondered out loud about this revived interest in Aldersgate. "Is it that we really believe altars can be rebuilt, that fires again may burn and that Methodism may once more glow with renewed heat?" (p. 144) Charles Selecman urged that something more come out of these Aldersgate celebrations than "retreats, prayer meetings, and a strange warming of the heart." "Methodism, yea, Protestant Christianity, must face the blatant, sullen evils of our day with a radiant experience, a buoyant hope, and no uncertain message" (p. 152). Bishop A. Frank Smith

(Methodist Episcopal Church, South) suggested that "many of us find ourselves just where John Wesley found himself between his so-called 'Church' conversion in 1725 and his 'evangelical' conversion in 1738. We believe. Our lives will bear scrutiny. We proclaim what we are convinced is the truth. But there is no 'drive.' There is no assurance in us and no response from the people" (p. 217). Bishop U. V. W. Darlington (Methodist Episcopal Church, South) expressed the fear "that we will celebrate a great event in the life of John Wesley and then turn away from the Commemoration without having brought the living fact of Wesley's experience into the Church of our day" (p. 222).

It was just prior to the outbreak of World War II, and a time when Neo-Reformation theology had called renewed attention to Divine judgment, revelation, grace, and the nature of the church. Methodists, on the threshold of reunification, had plenty of reason to be reviewing and revaluing their own history. The works of Rattenbury, Cell, Lee, and others were raising important issues for the interpretation of that history. It is not difficult to see in these addresses and other events of 1938 a quest for identity and a hungering for the spiritual power that influenced their interpretation of Aldersgate.

The Results of the Aldersgate Paradigm

We have traced the history by which the standard interpretation of Aldersgate became the paradigm for understanding Wesley and defining normative Methodist life. What are the results of this development? Both in terms of Wesley's own faith journey, and with regard to the origins (and therefore, significance of) Methodism, the focus on Aldersgate as an isolated single event has seriously distorted our historical tradition.

Moreover, as Roberta Bondi and David Lowes Watson have demonstrated so persuasively, this historical distortion actually harms the lives of our people and our church when the simple faith of so-called "Aldersgate spirituality" becomes a model, and when we tradition the power without the form of Christian discipleship.[39]

The irony is that what Aldersgate *was* in all of its complexity is so much more adequate than what it has come to mean! I think Professor Bondi is right that "Aldersgate spirituality," as we have made it into a pattern for our own spirituality, does have the characteristics she described (a *simple* faith, free of complexity and ambiguity). And yet surely it was at Aldersgate that John Wesley's experience of being grounded in God's love freed him from his compulsive attempts at self-justification and enabled him to love God and other people in a new way. Did Aldersgate change anything? I believe Wesley *was* a new man after Aldersgate, as are all those who have experienced the forgiving, accepting, and reconciling love of God in their lives. But his faith was confirmed even more powerfully by the fruits of his preaching. (In Albert Outler's words, "he had preached faith until *others* had it, and now his own was confirmed by *theirs*!")[40] We ought to be encouraged to know that Wesley's spiritual struggles were not all resolved at Aldersgate. *His* was not the kind of "simple faith" we have come to associate with "Aldersgate spirituality."

Absolutely fundamental to Wesley's theology and practice was his conviction that to be in Christ is to be growing in love—and therefore that we need to be nurtured and challenged in small groups of fellow Christians. True Wesleyan spirituality is not a private matter, a once-for-all experience of "being saved." Instead, it has to do with Christian life as a journey, a pilgrimage, a dynamic process of perfect*ing*, of maturing faith, hope, and love. The revival, in other words, cannot be understood apart from the disciplined fellowship of the Methodist societies, organized around the concept of *social* holiness.

We must *reconsider* Aldersgate, because if we do not, we are in danger of losing too much that is central to our Methodist heritage. In the United States, especially in the nineteenth century, Methodists enjoyed one of the great success stories in the history of the expansion of Christianity. Today, perhaps we need to be more concerned about faithfulness than success. Yet we have in our tradition what a Lutheran historian and churchman once referred to as "a powerful three-part package":[41] transformed individuals, nurturing and challenging people in disciplined small groups, and the vision of a parish as large as the world.

Can we celebrate the anniversary of Aldersgate without succumbing to "Aldersgatism?" Perhaps we can, especially if we can learn to see Aldersgate in the wider perspective of what Albert Outler calls "Wesley's comprehensive vision of the Christian life: life in and from the Spirit (from repentance to justifying faith, to reconciliation, assurance, and regeneration, to sanctification); and life in and under grace as an eventful process punctuated by conversions and disciplined by the moral imperatives of personal and social holiness."[42]

That is a heritage worth celebrating! May it inform *our* Christian living as we move with trust and hope into the future.

Chapter 6

Aldersgate, the Holiness Movement, and Experiential Religion

W. Stephen Gunter

Throughout most of the twentieth century, John Wesley's "Aldersgate experience" has been a topic of discussion among the denominations of the holiness movement. These denominations are characterized by two significant emphases: (1) a preoccupation with the *structure* of the experience of sanctifying grace, and (2) a concentrated interest in personal *experience*. As one might suspect, these emphases have played a vital role in shaping the holiness movement's interpretation of Aldersgate.

Introduction to the Holiness Movement

The "holiness movement" is a formal designation referring to the various denominations that grew out of the holiness revival of the nineteenth century.[1] This revival movement may be described as an unique blend of historic pietism, American revivalism, and Wesleyan perfectionism.

It is important to remember that many of the significant personalities of the revival movement were members of the Methodist Church. As early as 1825 the Rev. Timothy Merritt, a New England Methodist minister, was enunciating a specific holiness emphasis in his *Christian Manual*.[2] In 1839 he began his own holiness journal, *Guide to Christian Perfection*. In 1837 the evangelist Charles G. Finney and Oberlin College President Asa Mahan began presenting their views on perfection in the *Oberlin Evangelist* (although Mahan was perhaps more "Methodist" in his views than Finney). During the same decade, two Methodist women, Phoebe Palmer and Sarah Lankford, gave the holiness revival movement a distinctive emphasis through their Tuesday Meetings for the Promotion of Holiness. Bishop John Newman went so far as to say that Palmer was following the example of Wesley's class meeting, creating a "nursery of Scriptural Holiness."[3]

In the Tuesday Meetings, Palmer and Lankford testified to an experience of entire sanctification that they described as a "rest of the soul." They claimed that, after a prolonged period of severe inner spiritual struggle, the believer could experience spiritual peace. This spiritual victory was the result of the believer placing "self" on the altar of sacrifice. Dieter describes Palmer's "altar theology" succinctly:

> Mrs. Palmer believed that the Scriptures taught that Christ was both the sacrifice for her sin and the altar upon which she could offer up her whole heart in consecration to God. . . . The New Testament, she said, told her that "the altar sanctifieth the gift." She declared that in the sanctifying efficacy of Christ as the Christian's altar, the exercise of faith was certain to secure to the individual an experience characterized by a freedom from any inclination which did not spring from love.[4]

The influence of the Tuesday Meetings on the developing holiness movement is reflected in the fact that they continued thirty years after Palmer's death. A publishing program and home meetings patterned after the New York Tuesday Meeting spread Mrs. Palmer's teachings throughout the country.

Methodist leaders of the revival movement were not hesitant to claim that Palmer's formulations actually represented the steps one followed into the experience that John Wesley had called "perfect love." Thus, Palmer's structuring of the sanctification experience into the four steps of entire consecration, faith, confession, and blessing became increasingly normative for the holiness revival. Such was especially the case for those streams in the revival that eventually coalesced into the holiness denominations.[5] The influence of Palmer's formulations is probably the dominant explanation for the two characteristics discernable in each of the several denominations of the holiness movement: 1) the preoccupation with the structure of the experience of sanctifying grace, and 2) the concentrated interest in personal experience.[6]

The reference to "the several denominations" that comprise the holiness movement is perhaps misleading to those who are not aware that there are more than 100 missionary societies, evangelical associations, and denominations, spanning more than 150 years, that have considered themselves part of the holiness movement. Many of these have ceased to exist as separate entities, but their successors are conscious of a specific heritage and mission: "to spread scriptural holiness." Among the groups that exert a discernible influence in this distinctive heritage are: Church of God (Anderson, Indiana), Church of the Nazarene, Churches of Christ in Christian Union, the Friends, Free Methodist Church, the Salvation Army, the Wesleyan Church, and several branches of the modern Pentecostal Movement.

While these denominations are not monolithic, they are bound together in their annual Christian Holiness Association convention by their shared mission to spread scriptural holiness. Likewise, while these groups have undergone some change with passage of time (such as their recent rediscovery of the social concern that marked their original Wesleyan heritage[7]), there is one aspect of their heritage from the nineteenth century that has always remained evident: experiential religion.

Examples of Holiness Interpretation of Aldersgate

The concern with experiential religion has been determinative of holiness interpretations of Wesley's Aldersgate experience. In almost every discussion of Aldersgate that one may find in their literature, one of two emphases appears: the *structure* of religious experience, or the *nature* of religious experience. This is true whether one is dealing with personal testimonials, essays written by pastors for publication in denominational periodicals, or formal theological position papers read at gatherings of holiness scholars.

To demonstrate this point, we have chosen five relatively recent examples, from these various categories, which are representative of the holiness interpretations of Aldersgate. In considering our analysis of these examples, the reader should keep in mind three presuppositions of the holiness movement: (1) their goal is to spread scriptural holiness; (2) they believe such holiness is available to the seeking believer in this life (i.e., they affirm entire sanctification); and (3) they construe entire sanctification as a definable crisis experience, subsequent to conversion. In this sequence there is an emphasis on the substance of holiness, but there is also a strong concern for the structure of the believer's spiritual experience.

A. C. F. McKee

The impact of the holiness tradition's emphasis on experience, combined with their presuppositions concerning entire sanctification, on their interpretations of Aldersgate is clearly evident in our first example: a testimonial entitled "Aldersgate Still Happens," published in 1979 in the *Preachers' Magazine* (a quarterly holiness periodical).[8] A. C. F. McKee relates that while he was a senior ministerial student at a Kentucky college, the philosophy professor assigned a paper to be written on a significant church leader. Though not a Methodist, McKee chose John Wesley. He worked diligently on the research and writing, fully expecting to receive the highest grade available for his essay.

To his dismay the high mark did not come, and he went to visit with the professor about the shortcomings of his assignment. The professor asked only one question, "Why did you leave out Mr. Wesley's Aldersgate experience?" In a straightforward manner the student replied, "Because I did not believe it. . . . I just don't believe people have those kinds of experiences." In an equally direct manner the professor retorted, "Well, maybe you can't [believe it], but Mr. Wesley did, and you can't understand him unless you understand his Aldersgate, and what it meant to him."

This opinion is not unusual[9] and the professor was probably correct to insist that Aldersgate should not be omitted from a biographical essay on Wesley. It is, however, the subsequent aspects of McKee's testimonial that are relevant to our inquiry. McKee testifies:

> Then in the spring of 1977—34 years after I had said, "I don't believe people have Aldersgate experiences," I had mine. . . . [In a holiness church] I listened to believers testify to victory. . . . When [others] went to the altar, I went. I prayed. They prayed with me and for me. I felt I had been saved, finally saved, completely and thoroughly. My heart was 'strangely warmed'—even mine! My Aldersgate convinced me that my salvation had been completed in sanctification—the missing ingredient.

Several things are important about McKee's testimony. While studying for the ministry, he had been told by his college professor that John Wesley's spirituality could not be adequately interpreted if Aldersgate was omitted. Then, after three decades of service in various forms of Christian ministry, he became convinced that his own spiritual experience was less than adequate to the task. He found that the missing ingredient was an Aldersgate-type experience. Since he received this experience in a holiness church (even though he was not a holiness movement minister), he interpreted it to be the crisis experience of entire sanctification. Had McKee attributed to this experience merely an increase of spiritual intensity, an inward assurance of salvation, or a renewed vision for bringing people to personal faith, he would have remained within the commonly accepted Methodist hermeneutic of Aldersgate.[10] But McKee's interpretation is much more specific. Aldersgate is equated with entire sanctification, a second definitive work of grace.

Peter Gentry

In the same issue of the *Preachers' Magazine*, an article by Peter Gentry, a British holiness pastor, helps us understand how a non-holiness minister arrived at this distinctively holiness interpretation of Aldersgate.[11] Gentry is aware that John Wesley never publicly professed receiving the experience of perfect love that he urged Methodists to pursue. Nonetheless, he confidently claims:

> I believe Wesley found entire sanctification in that memorable meeting on London's Aldersgate Street. . . . This was undoubtedly his spiritual climax, up to which everything else in his life had been leading—and from which all that followed took its direction and purpose.

If one inquires into Gentry's warrants for this interpretation of Aldersgate, it soon becomes clear that they are not primarily derived from historical analysis of the evidence related to Aldersgate, in particular, or Wesley's spiritual pilgrimage, in general. Rather, his interpretation is fostered by his *own* concern for the structure of spiritual experience, especially the definable moments of conversion and entire sanctification.

Gentry proceeds from the presupposition that Wesley was a genuine believer prior to 1738, therefore Aldersgate could not be his conversion experience. He dismisses even those who interpret 1738 as Wesley's "evangelical conversion," accusing them of abusing the term conversion: "Conversion in the theological sense is bound to be evangelical unless it be purely theoretical, and Aldersgate certainly was not [theoretical]." If John Wesley had a conversion experience prior to 1738 (presumably 1725), then—Gentry argues—it is incumbent upon the modern interpreter to define theologically what actually took place at Aldersgate:

> If he indeed had a relationship with God at that time, this step [Aldersgate] would be what he afterwards taught as entire sanctification. . . . Aldersgate always emerges as the great moment. . . . When John Wesley testified, 'I felt my heart strangely warmed,' . . . this was his moment of glorious sanctification.[12]

If Gentry is aware of the fact that there is not a single mention of such an interpretation of Aldersgate in the entire Wesley corpus, he remains undaunted.

David Cubie

In an essay that is historically and theologically more sophisticated than the article by Gentry, David Cubie (professor at a holiness college) presents a carefully nuanced apologetic for a holiness interpretation of Aldersgate.[13] Cubie's task is much more difficult than Gentry's, because he wants to appeal to Wesley's own reflections on Aldersgate as an authority in developing his theological interpretation. Accordingly, he stresses the *doctrinal* significance of Aldersgate for Wesley and, particularly, its impact in convincing Wesley of the doctrine of justification by faith.[14]

Of course, the problem is that Cubie does not want to relate Aldersgate to justification, but to sanctification. Where can he find warrant for such a changed emphasis in Wesley? He argues that it is *implicit* in the development of Wesley's discussion of the "stages" and "states" in the *ordo salutis* following Aldersgate.

Cubie begins by noting Wesley's well-known concern to describe the process of the Christian life in terms of its "stages," and relates this concern to similar endeavors by Moravians, Calvinists and Anglicans in the Eighteenth Century. He then suggests that Wesley's reflection on these stages gained increased intensity following Aldersgate:

> The doctrine of stages evident in [Wesley's pre-Aldersgate sermon] "The Circumcision of the Heart" became explicit soon after Aldersgate, both in his sermon "Christian Perfection" (1741), where the stages are specified in the Johannine terms of babe, young man, and father, and in his preface to *Hymns and Sacred Poems* (1740) where they are described developmentally, with the prefacing comment, "Indeed, how God may work, we cannot tell; but the general manner [is . . .]"[15]

More importantly, Cubie argues that Wesley's understanding of the stages of Christian life underwent a significant change following Aldersgate, as he struggled with the question of how these stages related to the "states" of movement from non-Christian to Christian (i.e, fallen humanity, humanity under the law, and humanity under grace; or, the "natural man," the "servant," and the "son"):

> Wesley's developed doctrine of states and stages is *apparently* (emphasis mine) an attempt to explain Aldersgate. The questions he *seems* (emphasis mine) to be asking are: "How does this great evangelical experience fit within the overall order of salvation?" "What was my relationship to God before Aldersgate?" "In what state of grace were my parents and my devout Anglican friends before any heard the preaching of these evangelical truths?"[16]

Cubie's essential argument is that immediately following Aldersgate Wesley assumed that his pre-Aldersgate life was that of a "servant," which was a non-Christian state. Accordingly, Aldersgate was construed as his birth as a "babe" in the Christian life. However, the mature Wesley came to equate the "faith of a servant" with the first stage of Christian life itself—i.e., that of a babe. In this case—though Wesley does not explicitly make the point—his "conversion" must have preceded Aldersgate. Thus, Cubie claims (from the perspective of his "mature Wesley"): "Whatever may have been Wesley's experience with God in childhood and youth, it is evident that the years 1725 and 1726 contain his moment or period of mature choice for Christ."[17]

But, if Wesley was "converted" in 1725–26, what was the significance of Aldersgate? Cubic argues that it was not a choice to *begin* the Christian life, but a commitment to a *higher* Christian life: "Aldersgate was a perfectionist experience; that is, Wesley . . . in reaction against the prevailing tendency to identify Christians by sacrament, creed, or allegiance, set the standards of who is a Christian at a level of perfection."[18]

More importantly, Cubie views Aldersgate as more than a desire for a higher Christian life, he sees it as the *attainment* on this higher life. His holiness hermeneutic leads him to conclude, "Aldersgate was a further *stage* (emphasis mine) in the Christian life rather than the moment of evangelical conversion." Of course, this claim is followed immediately by the admission, "Wesley's own statement may suggest otherwise but does so because his order of salvation differs from modern evangelical terminology, including that of the holiness movement."[19] Nonetheless, Cubie believes he has shown that:

> Wesley's own Christian life prior to Aldersgate was fully in harmony with the holiness understanding regarding the pre-Pentecost Christian. Thus Aldersgate, if placed descriptively in the context of the modern holiness movement, was . . . a moment of cleansing [i.e., entire sanctification] and preparation for a life of service.[20]

One could question Cubie's basic strategy of relating issues surrounding the order of salvation to Wesley's Aldersgate experience, since Wesley does not explicitly do so himself. However, there is a more troubling question: why, even though Cubie himself notes that Wesley nearly always had a trinity of stages in his order of salvation, does Cubie essentially reduce this to two stages? It would appear that we are seeing here the same "holiness hermeneutic" of Aldersgate as in Gentry's article.

Both Cubie and Gentry are aware that Aldersgate has been recognized as one, if not *the* most significant event in the spiritual pilgrimage of John Wesley, and both are anxious to preserve the Aldersgate experience as a significant factor in holiness theology. Thus, they identify it with a second crisis experience in Wesley's spiritual journey. What Gentry does not seem to discern, and Cubie chooses to play down, is the fact that such an insistence on a two-fold structure is inherited from the nineteenth century.[21] It is anachronistic to read such nineteenth-century concerns back into the eighteenth century. Obviously, their reason for doing this is to preserve the distinctive Wesleyan holiness message, but interpreting Wesley's Aldersgate experience in a manner totally different than Wesley himself, or his immediate successors, may not be the best means to accomplish this goal.

Rob Staples

Lest one gain the impression that there have been no dissenting voices to the "second-blessing" holiness hermeneutic of Aldersgate, the voice of Rob Staples (professor at a holiness seminary) needs to be heard. In his 1963 doctoral dissertation Staples proposed a reinterpretation of John Wesley's doctrine of perfection, with resulting differences in the interpretation of Aldersgate.[22]

Staples is fully cognizant of the holiness movement's tendency to place a premium emphasis on the structure of religious experience, and he knows how Aldersgate has usually been made to fit into this structure as a "second blessing." Staples disagrees with the typical interpretation:

> In 1725 Wesley committed himself to the Christian goal, but this goal was not realized fully until Aldersgate. Wesley's "conversion" should not be bifurcated. 1725 and 1738 are not two separate events but two phases of one event. But only at the consummation of the event in 1738 did it truly become an "evangelical conversion."[23]

Staples understands this to mean that Wesley found that for which he had been

> seeking so diligently and so despairingly. . . . He was seeking, first, an assurance of personal salvation, and, secondly, Christian perfection. To have the first, he believed, was to have the second. Aldersgate, then, was Wesley's "evangelical conversion." It was also his "entire sanctification." The second is included in, and is a part of, the first.[24]

Staples, then, departs from the majority who insist on a strictly bifurcated structure of the *ordo salutis* between the poles of 1725 and 1738. Accordingly he insists that the search for Wesley's "second blessing" in the post-Aldersgate period [or in any period] is an artificial and illegitimate search:

> The assurance of pardon and Christian perfection—the "love of God and man" producing "all inward and outward holiness"—are not two separate experiences or stages in the Christian life. They are related as cause is to effect. Holiness springs from a conviction of the pardoning love of God. And this is what Wesley experienced at Aldersgate.[25]

Staples summarizes in one succinct paragraph why he chose to depart from the holiness denominations' traditional interpretation:

> The questions concerning . . . Wesley's religious experience are best solved by our proposed interpretation of Christian perfection as a dialogical relation. Most of these questions arise out of a presupposed interpretation of Christian perfection as an individual possession. Since the latter concept is tied to a schematization of states and stages, it becomes necessary, under this interpretation, to explain everything in terms of this teleological schematization. But if entire sanctification be seen not as the inauguration of an ideally continuous and uninterrupted state, but as an ever-possible, ever-fleeting, and ever-renewable I-Thou relation in the existential present, then Wesley's religious experience becomes clearly understandable. This explains why he never testified explicitly to have attained to a state of perfection. His own experience taught him that Christian perfection was not a "continuous state." But he also knew that he had experienced "moments" of what he called Christian perfection, first at Aldersgate and many times thereafter.[26]

Clearly, Staples has departed from the two-stage structure that has typically characterized the holiness movement's interpretation of Aldersgate as the significant moment in Wesley's spiritual journey; but in so doing he has collapsed the structure of experiential religion that has characterized the holiness revival movement and its denominations for over 150 years. This collapsing of the "sacred structure" has met with no small amount of opposition; for the fear is great that the doctrine of holiness itself is at stake. Staples responds to this fear by pointing out that the substance of holiness as an experiential doctrine should not be equated with the structure of the experience whereby the believer realizes the existential reality of holiness. Staples is correct in pointing this out, but in the almost thirty years since his "reinterpretation of perfection" and reappraisal of Aldersgate, only a few in the holiness movement have been willing to take his path.

Herbert McGonigle

A perspective that mediates between the positions of Gentry and Staples is articulated by Herbert McGonigle, principal of a holiness theological school in Great Britain.[27] In May 1988, while most of the Wesleyan community was looking exclusively at John Wesley's Aldersgate experience, McGonigle chose to look at the religious experience of Charles Wesley as well.

Whereas John Wesley was convinced of the validity of "instantaneous conversion," Charles was extremely skeptical. During the days preceding Pentecost Sunday, Charles was being nursed through a severe illness in the home of John Bray, a member of a religious society to which Charles belonged. These days proved to be a time of serious spiritual introspection for Charles. McGonigle notes, "May 21, 1738, was Whitsunday, and Charles began his *Journal* entry for that day with the words: 'I wakened in hope and expectation of His coming.'"[28] On that day, a guest in the Bray household, Mrs. Turner, (because of a vision she had) spoke the following words so audibly that they were heard by Charles Wesley in another part of the house: "'In the name of Jesus of Nazareth, arise, and believe and thou shalt be healed of all thy infirmities.' . . . Charles Wesley heard the words, and they spoke faith to his soul."[29]

Related to these events of Whitsunday 1738, and his brother's admonition to embrace instantaneous conversion, Charles wrote, "I felt opposition and reluctance to believe; yet still the Spirit of God strove with my own and the evil spirit, till by degrees he chased away the darkness of my unbelief."[30] McGonigle's assessment is, "His spiritual experience on May 21 was just as revolutionary and had as many far-reaching repercussions as John's was [sic] three days later . . . ," and this forces one to ask the question, "How significant were these two events of May 21 and 24 . . . ? What did they each mean to the man concerned in them?"[31]

McGonigle chooses to interpret the 1738 events as neither "conversion" nor "entire sanctification" experiences but as experiences that brought the warm certainty of spiritual assurance. He grounds this interpretation in John Wesley's specific words that night: "I *felt* my heart strangely warmed . . . I *felt* I did trust in Christ . . . and an *assurance* (emphasis McGonigle's) was given me."[32]

Conclusion

The five interpretations of Aldersgate that we have surveyed reveal that there is a lack of uniformity among holiness readings of this event. However, they also demonstrate an underlying unity in their stress on the importance of experiential religion. The emphasis on the structure of religious experience and the definition of that experience is impossible to overlook. Both of these aspects are related to two definite works of grace: conversion and entire sanctification. These spiritual experiences are viewed, in four of the articles, as "moments" on a continuum, and Aldersgate is, in three of the essays, the second moment—i.e., entire sanctification.

We would suggest that the typical holiness conclusion that Aldersgate was Wesley's sanctification experience is precisely the product of allowing their emphasis on structure to dominate the discussion. If it is necessary to locate the moment of perfection in Wesley's life, then there is no more well-known event than Aldersgate.

By contrast, neither Wesley nor his contemporaries found it necessary to allow structure to subordinate an emphasis on the substance of holiness; even though, as Cubie reminds us, Wesley was very interested in states and stages of the believer's pilgrimage.

Not until the middle of the nineteenth century does structure begin to dominate the discussion of the doctrine of Christian perfection. We may conclude then, that the emphasis on structure that leads to interpreting Aldersgate as Wesley's moment of perfection is "Wesleyan" only in a secondary sense. The nineteenth-century revival movement was very taken with the need to define structure and experience. If the twentieth-century holiness movement insists on continuing these emphases, it needs to be done without "resorting" to Aldersgate. The historical warrants for continuing to present Aldersgate as a "prooftext" for second-blessing holiness are simply not available. The holiness movement needs to chart a new course in its continuing exploration of the all-important questions of experiential religion and heart holiness.

Chapter 7

ALDERSGATE: A TRADITION HISTORY

Randy L. Maddox

The 1988 commemoration of the 250th anniversary of the event of Aldersgate may well be remembered more for the renewed vigor it brought to debate about the meaning of this event than for any of its celebrations. One of our aims in this essay is to show why such debate was inevitable. Another aim is to highlight the dynamics of this debate and suggest some of its implications for understanding the place of Aldersgate in Wesley's life and in later Wesleyan traditions.

The Need for Tradition-Historical Investigation

It is no secret that the Aldersgate event has been interpreted in a variety of ways by Wesley scholars and those in the various traditions descended from Wesley's ministry. Indeed, Frederick Maser has developed a typology of these various readings that divides them into five main categories: (1) Those who accept the Aldersgate experience as an important watershed or conversion in Wesley's life (Maser lists five varying specific descriptions of the nature of this watershed); (2) Those who deny that Aldersgate was a conversion experience, assigning that experience to some earlier date, while still recognizing Aldersgate's importance as a religious crisis in Wesley's life; (3) Those who deny that Aldersgate had any enduring significance for Wesley's life—emphasizing, instead, some earlier date (usually 1725) as his conversion; (4) Those who stress the gradual nature of Wesley's spiritual development and see Aldersgate as simply one step in a steady process of growth; and (5) Those who believe that Aldersgate is one of many "conversions" in Wesley's life.[1]

How could a single event spawn such a variety of interpretations? One obvious possibility is that the information which Wesley's later interpreters have to work with is inconclusive. A quick reading of participants in the debate about the meaning of Aldersgate reveals that they spend much of their time dealing with the ambiguities of Wesley's references to the event. These ambiguities have received extensive scholarly attention in recent years and the major textual dilemmas are now fairly clear.[2]

First: On the one hand, Wesley's initial account of Aldersgate in his *Journal* presented it as a dramatic transition to a consistent Christian life, in explicit contrast with the perceived shortcomings of his earlier practice. On the other hand, Wesley added footnotes to the 1774 and 1775 editions of the *Journal* which significantly qualified this contrast. Moreover, the accounts in the full *Journal* cast doubt upon both Wesley's initial pessimistic reading of his life before Aldersgate and his initial optimistic claims about the results of the event.

Again: On the one hand, Wesley reprinted the extract of the *Journal* containing the Aldersgate account five times during his life. On the other hand, he almost never again mentioned Aldersgate explicitly in his *Journal* or other published works.[3]

Finally: On the one hand, Wesley made frequent chronological references that highlight 1738 as significant both to his own life and to the Methodist revival. On the other hand, these references are all quite general and may have referred to the beginning of open-air preaching or the organization of the first society rather than to the event of Aldersgate.

In drawing our attention to these textual dilemmas, Wesley scholars have shown why there has been room for a debate about the significance of Aldersgate in the Wesleyan traditions. Indeed, the ambiguities are such that this debate cannot be settled on textual grounds alone. The consideration of other relevant aspects of the issue would appear to be necessary.

The increased hermeneutical sensitivity of the last few decades confirms this need for considering other aspects of the issue. Contemporary hermeneutic philosophy has made us keenly aware that the act of interpretation is influenced by the cultural/historical assumptions of the interpreter's context as much as by the object of interpretation and its context.[4] This suggests that the differing interpretations of Aldersgate should be analyzed not only in the light of textual ambiguities but also from the perspective of the history of shifting theological concerns within the later Wesleyan traditions. The need for this second type of analysis has been mentioned a couple of times in the discussion of Aldersgate (e.g., McIntosh 1969; and Snow 1963), but no extended treatment has been forthcoming. Hence, our initial foray into this promising field.

Historical Shifts in the Interpretation of Aldersgate

The purpose of a tradition-historical study is to increase an interpretive community's awareness of shifts or developments in the history of its understanding of a classic text (or event). Central to such a study is the attempt to correlate shifting interpretations with broader changes in the self-understanding of the community. Thus, our task is to investigate correlations between changes in the general theological self-understanding of the Wesleyan traditions and their shifting interpretations of Aldersgate.

1791–1850: Aldersgate as Personal Conversion Event

In the first half-century following Wesley's death, Methodism was an adolescent movement seeking to find its own feet. During this time, it generally honored Wesley more as its founder than as its theological mentor or norm.[5] Thus, the major literary productions of this period were funeral eulogies and triumphalistic biographies, rather than theological studies. When these early works mention Aldersgate, they generally portray it as Wesley's "conversion." Thereby, they were primarily re-presenting Wesley's own early evaluation, for they depended heavily on the early volumes of his *Journal* for their account.[6] Indicative of such dependence, these works typically do not clarify what they meant by "conversion." If they evidence any distinctive concern, it was to defend Wesley from charges of enthusiasm by stressing that it was a transition to which he was brought by calm rational and scriptural considerations.[7] In other words, they portrayed Aldersgate more as Wesley's *personal* conversion *event* than as an *exemplary* conversion *experience*.

The suggestion that, during this time period, Aldersgate was regarded more as an intriguing event in Wesley's life than as a normative model for subsequent Methodist piety is lent further support by the Methodist centennial celebrations of 1839. The event that British Methodists chose to commemorate as most crucial to their founding was the establishment of the first Society in 1739. This choice sparked a mild protest from Thomas Jackson (1838), who argued that the centenary of Aldersgate would have been more appropriate. Nonetheless, both the centennial and sesquicentennial of Aldersgate passed without formal commemoration.[8] While defended as Wesley's "conversion," it had not yet been adopted as the defining metaphor of Methodist belief and practice.

1850–1870: Initial Questions About Aldersgate as "Conversion"

In the absence of a stated definition, one is left with the impression that the previous biographies assumed some version of Wesley's *Dictionary* definition of conversion: "a thorough change of heart and life from sin to holiness."[9] The problem with such a definition of what happened at Aldersgate, of course, is that it is not at all clear that this event was such a dramatic and thorough change in Wesley's life—as he admitted later himself. As such, it was only a matter of time before designations of Aldersgate as Wesley's "conversion" provoked debate. One of the earliest public debates took place in the pages of the *Wesleyan Methodist Association Magazine* in 1854. A letter from a reader (Miller 1854) argued that Wesley's early piety and good works demonstrated that he was already a Christian, so Aldersgate could not have been his conversion. The editors (Anonymous 1854) admitted that the pre-Aldersgate Wesley would have been saved if he had died, but insisted that Aldersgate was his conversion from trusting in his own righteousness to trusting in Christ for salvation. So began a continuing variety of refined definitions of Aldersgate as a "conversion."

The most striking refined definition during this period came from Robert Brown. Brown authored one of the few nineteenth-century considerations of Wesley *as a theologian*. He argued that Wesley's theology was essentially a matter of morals, drawn directly from the conscience. In keeping with this general characterization, he suggested that Aldersgate was not a total conversion but only one "from a comparatively low standard of Christian morals . . . to a high standard"![10] Given the rigorous nature of Wesley's early life, this suggestion has found few supporters. Rather, it stands as vivid evidence of how easily Aldersgate could take on the hue of the position from which it was being viewed.

1870–1900: Aldersgate as the Rejection of High-Church Bigotry

One of the most significant issues with which nineteenth-century British Methodism struggled was its relationship to the Anglican tradition from which it had come. Wesley remained an Anglican priest until his death and never tired of claiming that all of his distinctive doctrinal claims could be found in the Anglican standards of doctrine. Shortly after his death British Methodists followed the earlier example of their American counterparts and officially separated from the Church of England. Some leaders helped facilitate this decision by obscuring the most explicit evidences of Wesley's (high-church) Anglican loyalties and stressing those aspects of his life or work that favored the (low-church) dissenting traditions.[11]

The debate concerning Wesley's apparent high-church sympathies and their significance for later Methodism became increasingly reactionary with the emergence of the Oxford Movement, reaching a fever pitch in the 1870's. In this setting an alternative refinement of "conversion" in relation to Aldersgate surfaced. Those who wished to champion an evangelical (i.e., low-church) model of Methodism began to argue that Aldersgate was not a conversion from sinner to believer, but Wesley's rejection of his former high-church bigotry and intolerance, and his adoption of the true form of Christianity.[12] This reading of Aldersgate also proved to be impossible to sustain, given Wesley's life-long eucharistic practice and theology, etc.[13] Once again, the desire to provide traditional warrant for a contemporary theological agenda overrode the text.

1900–1963: Aldersgate as Partisan Theological Warrant

Wesley's early twentieth-century descendants demonstrated more theological interest in their founder than their nineteenth-century counterparts. However, this interest typically continued to be of a partisan nature; i.e., they appealed to Wesley as a "theological hero" in support of their particular theological agendas. Appeals to Wesley occurred most often in the context of debates between concurrent theological agendas. The result of this was a proliferation of contrasting redefinitions of Aldersgate, which are best organized around the agendas that championed them.

Catholic Readings: Aldersgate as a "Mystical" Conversion. One of the significant developments in early twentieth-century Wesley Studies was the emergence of Roman Catholic investigations of Wesley. In general, these scholars sought to highlight the "catholic" elements in Wesley, and some even argued that he could serve as a helpful mediator between Protestantism and Catholicism. Understandably, these studies took particular offense at Wesley's immediate post-Aldersgate disparagement of his earlier spirituality, since this early spirituality drew heavily from catholic spiritual writers (both Eastern and Roman). They insisted that Wesley's real conversion to serious religious life was long before Aldersgate—in 1725. Aldersgate was then read as simply a further step of a religious man to a higher stage of devotional practice and experience.[14] Eventually, the term "mystical conversion" was applied to this reading of Aldersgate.[15] It has been the reading of most Roman Catholic studies and of some other Wesley scholars who recognize and appreciate the catholic elements in Wesley.[16]

Liberal Readings: Aldersgate as the Validation of Experience as a Theological Source. The elevation of the role of experience in theological reflection was a prominent element of Protestant Liberalism in the early twentieth century. This emphasis was derived both from the growing dominance of the empirical model of the natural sciences and from Schleiermacher's influential *Glaubenslehre,* which tried to relate all normative theological claims to the (Romantic) human experience of absolute dependence. The underlying agenda of Liberalism was the rejection of mere subservience to traditional authorities, accepting only those theological convictions that could be grounded in or derived from experience.

The most prominent nineteenth-century Methodist theologians had largely avoided the challenges being raised for traditional theological claims by the developments in the sciences, etc. However, some adventurous theologians began to embrace these new intellectual trends in the early twentieth century and to seek a corresponding reformulation of Methodist theology. Intriguingly, they believed that they found warrant for their endeavor in the example of John Wesley. For some he was an early model of a truly empirical theology. For others he was a proto-Schleiermacher. Either way, it was argued that his major theological contribution was to elevate the place of experience in theological reflection. More importantly—for our purposes—it was suggested that the real significance of Aldersgate was that it marked the emergence of his emphasis on experience.[17] That is, Aldersgate was valued not so much for its place in Wesley's spiritual development as for its contribution to his theological method!

Neo-Orthodox Readings: Aldersgate as Conversion to Evangelical Doctrine. The neo-Orthodox movement that swept Protestant theology in the second and third decades of the twentieth century emphatically rejected the experientialism of liberal theology and called for a return to the biblical and doctrinal commitments of the Protestant Reformation. This movement found many sympathizers in Methodist circles; so many that there was talk of a "neo-Wesleyanism."[18]

Understandably, those sympathetic to neo-Orthodoxy were uncomfortable with both the Catholic and Liberal readings of Aldersgate just summarized. Indeed, they polemicized against them![19] In contrast to the Catholic reading, they argued that Aldersgate embodied Wesley's turn from his earlier "catholic" theological training to an unreserved appropriation of the Reformation *sola fide*. In contrast to the Liberal reading, they argued that the importance of Aldersgate lay not in its elevation of experience in theological method, but in its affirmation of traditional theological claims. Aldersgate was put forward as emblematic of Wesley's theological rejection of works-righteousness and his embracing of the Reformation doctrine of justification by faith.[20] If it was a conversion, it was a doctrinal conversion. As such, they could still value Wesley's religious commitment in 1725, and yet argue that he was not fully Christian until his "evangelical" conversion of 1738.[21]

Revivalist Readings: Aldersgate as the Model Conversion Experience. None of the interpretations of Aldersgate discussed so far were the majority voice in the chorus of answers offered in the first half of the twentieth century. That honor belongs to the reading of Aldersgate as Wesley's exemplary *conversion experience*. Central to this position are two claims: (1) that Aldersgate marked Wesley's *conversion* from a pre-Christian state to a Christian one (cf. the title of Smith 1930, "BC and AD in John Wesley"), and (2) that the central element of this conversion was his *experience* of the "warmed heart" (cf. Raymond 1904 on "Wesley's Religious Experience").

It is important to note that this interpretation of Aldersgate originated among and was championed by those Methodists concerned to stress evangelism or revivalism. One of the earliest clear examples of this reading was an essay by Henry Elderkin commemorating the bicentenary of Wesley's birth in a journal dedicated to renewing appreciation of great evangelists among Methodists. Elderkin referred to Aldersgate as Wesley's "second birth" and as the most important experience of his life.[22] A second early example comes from the Fellowship of the Kingdom, an evangelical movement within Methodism that urged people to seek "the transforming experience of the resources of God in Jesus Christ;" which, of course, is what Wesley was considered to have received at Aldersgate.[23]

We have suggested that this "conversionist" reading of Aldersgate became the majority position in the first half of the twentieth century. An evidence (and *cause*!) of this dominance was its appropriation by official Wesley commemorations. The earliest example was 1924, when the London Mission Committee inaugurated a yearly observance of "Wesley Day" on May 24 *with an evangelistic campaign*.[24] Obviously, such a commemoration assumes a conversionist reading of Aldersgate.

With the precedent set, it is no surprise that the bicentennial of Aldersgate was officially commemorated in 1938. Nor is it a surprise that the majority of the reflections surrounding this celebration assumed a conversionist reading of Aldersgate. For example, a major commemoration by the Methodist Episcopal Church, South focused on the theme: "The Primacy of Personal Religious Experience in the Life and Work of Methodism." It defined Aldersgate as Wesley's "experience of spiritual transformation," and most of the addresses presented viewed Aldersgate as a crisis conversion that illustrated the importance of experience.[25] Similar claims were presented at the British Methodist recognition,[26] and in a commemorative address presented to Methodists in China.[27] Likewise, the conversionist reading of Aldersgate permeated the study volumes prepared for the bicentennial of Aldersgate by the Methodist Episcopal Church—both North (Joy 1937) and South (Watkins 1937)—and, to a lesser degree, by German Methodists (Nuelsen 1938).[28]

Ironically, while Aldersgate had been neglected (in favor of other events) by official Wesley commemorations until 1938, it became the dominant event from there on. Other events were now either passed by unnoticed (such as the bicentennial of the founding of the first Society), or were given an "Aldersgate ambience." A case in point: both British and American Methodists chose to focus the 250th anniversary of Wesley's birth (1953) around the theme of evangelism. By this time, however, evangelism and Aldersgate were nearly synonymous; so Aldersgate encroached on the celebration, with some suggesting that the celebration be moved to May 24 as more appropriate to the emphasis on evangelism.[29]

Given its new-found dominance, even the 225th anniversary of Aldersgate (1963) was commemorated (particularly by American Methodists), again focussing on evangelism, and again dominated by a conversionist reading of the event. At least, those materials that were most directly connected to evangelistic settings carried on the conversionist reading. Good examples are three related books published by the Board of Evangelism (Thomas 1962, Ten Methodist Bishops 1963, and Arnett *et al.* 1964). One should also note the article by the Secretary of the Board of Evangelism (Denman 1963) and that of the Director of the Department of Preaching and Evangelism (Lacour 1963). While several other articles joined in such a conversionist reading,[30] an incipient critique of this interpretation also began to emerge. We will return to this critique later, however.

If one were to look for a classic example of this conversionist reading of Wesley's own spiritual journey, they could probably do no better than Clark 1950 or Jeffery 1960. Both of these present Wesley's life up to Aldersgate as a search for a "satisfying religious experience."

Of course, the conversionist reading did not apply just to Wesley. Rather, his conversion experience was presented as emblematic of what ours should be. To quote just one example, "The chief concern for all Methodists is not that two hundred years ago John Wesley had an experience of the warm heart, but have the Methodists in this good year of our Lord the experience; and if they have not that experience, may they get it?"[31]

Moreover, this experience was not seen as simply initiatory to the Christian life, it was presented as the *dynamic* of that life. In particular it was frequently argued that effective social service and reform (dear to many non-evangelistic Methodists of the day) were actually *derivative* of such an experience (e.g., Urwin 1938, and Yost 1938).

In other words, the first half of the twentieth century witnessed a widespread attempt to make Wesley's Aldersgate *conversion experience* definitive of Methodist identity.[32]

Holiness Readings: Aldersgate as Entire Sanctification. Justification was not the only crisis experience with which Aldersgate was identified during this time period. Some of Wesley's descendants, particularly in the holiness movement, proposed that Aldersgate was actually his *second* crisis experience—i.e., his entire sanctification.[33] According to this distinction, Aldersgate was not the time when Wesley received forgiveness of sins and began his Christian walk. It was the completion of his conversion—his purification from the "sin nature," his filling with perfect love, his attainment of Christian perfection.

The topic of entire sanctification has been the focus of considerable debate among Wesley's twentieth-century heirs. For many Methodists it is simply an *ideal* toward which we (and Wesley!) continually strive but never attain in this life. By contrast, for many in the holiness movement it is a unsurpassable *state* which can be attained instantaneously by faith, shortly after justification. There are still others who view entire sanctification as a significant *transition* within our growth in Christ-likeness. To use developmental terms, they do not see entire sanctification as the arrival at adulthood, but as the move from the passivity of spiritual infancy to the Spirit-empowered growth of Christian adolescence. As one might suspect, a careful reading of those who identify Aldersgate as Wesley's entire sanctification reveals similar distinctions. For some, Aldersgate was the "spiritual climax" of Wesley's life (Gentry 1979). For others, it was his transition from the state of a "babe in Christ" to that of a "young man" (Cubie 1989; see also Sommer 1938, p. 347; and Sommer 1953, p. 56).

Overall, the identification of Aldersgate as Wesley's entire sanctification faces serious questions. In the first place, there is the issue of which of the understandings of sanctification noted above are most true to Wesley's own views. More important is the fact that Wesley never explicitly claimed to have obtained entire sanctification—at Aldersgate or thereafter.[34] If he intended the Aldersgate event to function as a normative model of entire sanctification for his followers, surely he would have identified it as such.

Pentecostal/Charismatic Readings: Aldersgate as Wesley's "Baptism in the Holy Spirit." The next reading of Aldersgate is closely related to the holiness reading. One of the (debated!) developments in the holiness movement was the identification of entire sanctification with the "baptism of the Holy Spirit." For them this baptism was an experience, subsequent to conversion, that brought cleansing from inward sin. It required only slight alteration of such a position to construe the baptism of the Holy Spirit as an experience of new spiritual vitality and power for service, bestowed upon (previously powerless) Christians—the characteristic emphasis of the Pentecostal and Charismatic movements.[35]

While relatively rare, there have been some advocates of a Pentecostal or Charismatic model of Christian life that have identified Aldersgate as Wesley's "pentecostal" experience of the baptism of the Holy Spirit.[36] Again, the serious questions faced by this reading would be whether such a definition of "baptism of the Holy Spirit" was congruent with Wesley's own theological understanding and why Wesley never identified the event in this manner himself.[37]

Protestant "Once-Born" Readings: Aldersgate as the "Witness of the Spirit." The last significant reading of Aldersgate during this time period agrees with the previous three that the event had something to do with Wesley's spiritual *experience*. However, it differs from these previous views in that it does not perceive in Aldersgate, or Wesley's spiritual development in general, an emphasis on dramatic or instantaneous (i.e., crisis) experience. Put in the terms of William James' influential analysis of the varieties of religious experience, this reading views Wesley as a better example of a "once-born" person whose spiritual development is gradual, than of a "twice-born" person whose spiritual development is marked with major disjunctures (see especially: Bashford 1903, and Funk 1963).[38]

As a result, this reading assumed greater continuity between the pre- and post-Aldersgate Wesley than did the conversionist, holiness, and pentecostal readings. It assumed that Wesley was already truly a Christian and growing in Christ-likeness before the night of May 24, 1738. But, if this is so, then what was the significance of that night? Their answer is that Aldersgate was the time when Wesley's growing Christian life was further strengthened and clarified through the "witness of the Spirit," or gift of assurance.[39]

Such a "witness of the Spirit" may accompany one's transition into the Christian life, but (as the later Wesley came to see) it does not always do so.[40] It's distinctive contribution to Christian life is not justification *per se*, but our release from intense spiritual self-preoccupation through a *felt* assurance of God's acceptance. For one like Wesley who is thoroughly convinced of God's desire for Christians to be holy, such an assurance is crucial, because it changes our motivation in Christian life from seeking to *insure* God's acceptance to *living out of* that acceptance.

We have noted how this interpretation of Aldersgate is distinguished from the revivalist, holiness, and pentecostal readings by its rejection of an exclusively "twice-born" model of Christian life. It carries slightly different emphases than the three other views current during this time as well. Compared to the Liberal reading, its primary emphasis is on the contribution of experience to Christian life, not theological method (though Wesley's experience of assurance surely served as a warrant for later developing his doctrine of the "witness of the Spirit"). Likewise, while the possibility of assurance is consistent with the Neo-Orthodox stress on justification by grace, it is not a necessary correlate (see Luther!) and may be grounded more in theological syllogisms than in an experience of the Spirit (see Calvinist Scholasticism!) Finally, the "witness of the Spirit" is not just a general "mystical" transition to a deeper spirituality, but a specific experience of assurance that grounds spiritual life *per se*.

1963 to the Present: Questioning Partisan Readings of Aldersgate

The last three decades have witnessed a dramatic professionalization in the field of Wesley studies. A truly critical edition of Wesley's works has been undertaken (*The Bicentennial Edition*) and Wesley scholars have developed a broadened awareness of his context and an historical-critical realism about his unique stance or contribution.[41]

The most obvious result of this professionalization in relation to Aldersgate has been the rejection of many of the previous partisan readings of the event. We have noted the questions raised about some of these models in our earlier summary. Since the "conversionist" reading was the dominant one in the period leading up to the 225th anniversary in 1963, it was this reading that received the greatest amount of critical attention.

Already in 1960, Webb Garrison expressed dissatisfaction with the "myth" that Aldersgate was the central factor or single climactic hour in Wesley's spiritual quest (Garrison 1960). Several participants in the 1963 discussion added their qualifications to the conversionist reading of Aldersgate. Frank Baker carefully detailed the interpretive issues regarding Wesley's original *Journal* entries and later footnotes concerning Aldersgate, demonstrating that a strong "twice-born" reading of the event was untenable. Theophil Funk highlighted Wesley's continuing spiritual struggles *after* Aldersgate and the crucial role of the nurture of community and the means of grace in Wesley's mature understanding of Christian life. Gerald Kennedy stressed the importance of Wesley's prior disciplined life to his attainment of peace. And, Albert Outler chose to stress how Wesley held together learning and piety, countering anti-intellectualistic appropriations of Aldersgate language.

Two contributors to the 1963 discussion were particularly critical of the conversionist reading. Lawrence Snow, drawing on recent hermeneutic philosophy, claimed that the portrayal of Aldersgate as a private conversion experience was an example of reading present concerns *into* Wesley's experience. He then argued that such a reading fits, at best, only materials around 1738 and does not do justice to the full corpus of Wesley's reflection. Boyd Mather filed a similar charge that American Methodists had imposed a camp-meeting revivalist model upon Wesley's Aldersgate experience and, *it did not fit*. In particular, he argued that the typical expressions of the anniversary's evangelism thrust (with their focus on personal religious experience) lacked the very elements that the mature Wesley considered essential to awakening and forming Christian life: *discipline* and *doctrine*.

The questions raised during the 225th anniversary of Aldersgate received continuing scholarly attention in the years leading up to the most recent anniversary. One result of this is the greater awareness of the ambiguities of Wesley's references to Aldersgate noted at the beginning of this essay. Another result is a deeper appreciation of the theological nuances of the *later* Wesley. A particularly noteworthy result is the insights gained from some sophisticated psychological studies of Wesley's *life-long* spiritual development, placing Aldersgate within this context.[42]

What has been the impact of this continuing study in relation to the previous dominance of the conversionist interpretation of Aldersgate? To begin with, the emphasis of these studies has generally shifted from the discontinuities to the continuities in Wesley's religious development (see especially: McIntosh 1969, and Míguez 1983). As a result, while a few continue to view Aldersgate in conversionist terms (e.g., Maser 1978), the more common tendency is to identify Aldersgate as the time when Wesley (already a Christian) received a deeper sense of assurance, which empowered him for a life of obedience and ministry (e.g., Heitzenrater 1973, p. 8; and McIntosh 1969, p. 59).

With these developments we are brought to the 250th anniversary debate about Aldersgate surveyed in the Introduction to this volume. As was noted there, this debate shows all the signs of an interpretive revolution with the conversionist reading of Aldersgate being displaced from its previous dominance, in favor of a nuanced version of the identification of Aldersgate with Wesley's reception of the "witness of the Spirit."

Conclusion

Perhaps the most appropriate conclusion to a tradition-history study such as this is not an argument for one of the alternative readings of Aldersgate but a plea for hermeneutic responsibility. The key to a legitimate appropriation of a past text or event by a present community lies in preserving the integrity of *both* of the contexts involved—that of the original event and that of the present community. To use the terms of Hans-Georg Gadamer, a proper interpretation must "fuse these two horizons."[43]

Such a fusion requires that the two horizons be self-consciously identified in the process of their dialogue. It is not sufficient merely to engage in historical inquiry into the precedents or intricacies of Wesley's own understanding; one must also ask what such an understanding would mean today in light of our differing precedents and needs. In this process, however, we must exercise extreme caution that we do not simply impose our current agendas upon an ill-fitted historical authority. The best way to determine if a legitimate "fit" has been found is to forward a proposed interpretation into the community of interpretation and see how it survives the questions of those with differing perspectives.

We have observed several examples of this process in our preceding survey. At the moment, it appears that the most adequate reading of Aldersgate is that which focuses on the place of assurance in Christian life. Whether this reading will remain the most persuasive will depend on how well it can stand up to continuing historical study of Wesley's context and continuing theological inquiry into the current setting and needs of Wesleyan (and larger Christian) traditions.

Notes

Note: The following abbreviations for Wesley's primary works are used throughout these endnotes.

Journal (Curnock)
: *The Journal of the Rev. John Wesley, A.M.* 8 vols. Ed. Nehemiah Curnock. London: Epworth, 1909–16.

John Wesley MS
: Manuscript materials at the Colman Collection of the Methodist Archives, The John Rylands University Library, Manchester, England.

Letters (Telford)
: *The Letters of the Rev. John Wesley, A.M.* 8 vols. Ed. John Telford. London: Epworth, 1931.

MS London Diary, MS Oxford Diary
: Manuscript copies of Wesley's diary in the Methodist Archives, The John Rylands University Library, Manchester, England.

Works
: *The Bicentennial Edition of the Works of John Wesley.* Editor in Chief, Frank Baker. Nashville: Abingdon, 1984ff. (Volumes 7, 11, 25 & 26 originally appeared as the *Oxford Edition of The Works of John Wesley.* Oxford: Clarendon, 1975–83).
Vol. 1: *Sermons I.* Ed. Albert C. Outler, 1984.
Vol. 2: *Sermons II.* Ed. Albert C. Outler, 1985.
Vol. 3: *Sermons III.* Ed. Albert C. Outler, 1986.
Vol. 4: *Sermons IV.* Ed. Albert C. Outler, 1987.
Vol. 7: *A Collection of Hymns for the Use of the People Called Methodists.* Eds. Franz Hildebrandt & Oliver Beckerlegge, 1983.
Vol. 9: *The Methodist Societies I: History, Nature and Design.* Ed. Rupert E. Davies, 1989.
Vol. 11: *The Appeals to Men of Reason and Religion and Certain Related Open Letters.* Ed. Gerald R. Cragg, 1975.
Vol. 18: *Journal & Diaries, 1735–39.* Eds. W. Reginald Ward & Richard Heitzenrater, 1988.
Vol. 19: *Journal and Diaries, 1738–1743.* Eds. W. Reginald Ward and Richard P. Heitzenrater, 1990.
Vol. 25: *Letters I, 1721–39.* Ed. Frank Baker, 1980.
Vol. 26: *Letters II, 1740–55.* Ed. Frank Baker, 1982.

Works (Jackson)
: *The Works of John Wesley.* 14 vols. 3rd ed. Ed. Thomas Jackson. London: Wesleyan Methodist Book Room, 1872; reprint ed., Grand Rapids: Baker, 1979.

Introduction

1. The most important commemoration took place at St. Paul's Cathedral in London. For a description of this and related events, see *World Parish* 29.4 (1988):1–7. Further commemorations in London and Tokyo are noted in *World Parish* 30.1 (1989):4. For a collection of suggested commemorative services for United Methodist congregations, see Yrigoyen, editor 1988.

2. Lawson 1987 was the lecture given to the Wesley Fellowship. Jennings 1988 reproduces relevant sections of the focal essay of the AAR Wesley Studies section. Papers from the WTS 1988 meeting appear in Volume 24 of the *Wesleyan Theological Journal*, including Collins 1989b and Cubie 1989. The two lectures given to the Methodist Sacramental Fellowship were published as: John Newton & Donald Soper, *What I Owe to the Wesleys* (Methodist Sacramental Fellowship, 1988).

3. Those dealing with Aldersgate specifically include Voigt 1988; Wood 1988; and *Im Glauben Gewiss: Die bleibende Bedeutung der Aldersgate-Erfahrung John Wesleys*, edited by the Studiengemeinschaft für Geschichte der Evangelisch-methodistischen Kirche (Stuttgart: Christliches Verlagshaus, 1988). Two more general commemorative volumes were: Donald English, *The Meaning of the Warmed Heart* (Nashville: Discipleship Resources, 1987); and John Stacey, editor, *John Wesley: Contemporary Perspectives* (London: Epworth, 1988). One could also note a book by Robert Tuttle that grew out of a lecture given to commemorate the 250th anniversary of Aldersgate: *Mysticism in the Wesleyan Tradition* (Grand Rapids: Zondervan, 1989).

4. See Thomas S. Kuhn, *The Structure of Scientific Revolutions*, 2nd enlarged edition (University of Chicago Press, 1970). For the continuing discussion of Kuhn's work, see: Imre Lakatos & Alan Musgrave, eds., *Criticism and the Growth of Knowledge* (Cambridge University Press, 1970); and Gary Gutting, ed., *Paradigms and Revolutions* (University of Notre Dame Press, 1980).

5. Note the discussion of the growing dominance of the conversionist reading of Aldersgate in the early twentieth century in the Maddox essay in this volume.

6. It is no accident that Jeffery's account of Wesley's "Religious Quest" *ends* at Aldersgate! For Jeffery, the quest is over and everything that follows is simply application.

7. Newton and Soper, *What I Owe the Wesleys.*

8. Cf. Baker 1963, Funk 1963, Garrison 1960, Mather 1963, and Snow 1963.

9. Note, for example, how quickly Charles Yrigoyen moves beyond the acknowledgment that "some have disputed whether this 'Aldersgate Experience' of John Wesley may be called his conversion" to defining it as a critical moment in Wesley's spiritual pilgrimage when he attained a "true, living faith" (Yrigoyen 1988, p. 12). See also McKenna 1988.

10. Edwards 1963a & 1963b are reprinted unrevised in Yrigoyen, editor 1988. The introduction to Wood 1988 makes all the same points as Wood 1963, with no discussion of intervening questions raised about this interpretation.

11. Note his exclusive appeal to the "Standard Sermons" in all three pieces. While this might have some warrant in contexts debating Methodist standards of doctrine, it is a questionable limitation in the enterprise of accounting for the spiritual development of the "whole Wesley."

12. One could also mention Robert Tuttle's reading of Aldersgate (Tuttle, *Mysticism in the Wesleyan Tradition*). He approaches the event in the context of Wesley's interaction with mysticism, but emphasizes the same points: (1) that Wesley's Christian life dates back to at least 1725 (p. 55); (2) that Aldersgate had to do with receiving a sense of

assurance (p. 120); and, (3) that Wesley initially overemphasized the effects of Aldersgate and had to modify these evaluations later (p. 106).

13. See also: Manfred Marquardt, "Gewissheit und Anfechtung bei Martin Luther und John Wesley," *Theologie für die Praxis* 14.1 (1988):14–28. This theme was particularly relevant to German Methodists because of their ongoing dialogue with the Lutheran tradition and its suspicions about claims for certainty in Christian life.

14. For further information on this issue, see Randy L. Maddox, "Celebrating Wesley—When?" *Methodist History* 29 (1991).

Bondi—Aldersgate Spirituality

1. For example, Albert Outler, *John Wesley* (New York: Oxford University Press, 1964), p. 14; and the "Introduction" to this volume.

2. For Wesley's most developed presentation of his doctrine of Christian perfection see his "Plain Account of Christian Perfection," *Works* (Jackson), 11:366–445.

3. Quoted in "Plain Account," §19, *Works* (Jackson), 11:394.

4. For an available modern English translation of the Macarian homilies see George Maloney, *Intoxicated with God* (Denville, New Jersey: Dimension Books, 1978). For the spirituality of the early Christian writers as a resource for modern Christians and particularly Methodists, for whom this material is especially relevant and attractive, see Roberta Bondi, *To Love as God Loves: Conversations with the Early Church* (Philadelphia: Fortress Press, 1987).

5. See Watson's essay in this volume.

6. David Lowes Watson, *Accountable Discipleship* (Nashville, TN: Discipleship Resources, 1986).

7. Wesley, for example, stressed the need for our prayer to be sincere in such a way that we might be encouraged to believe that he was demanding that we have the right *feelings* when we pray. See, however, his note on Matthew 6:8 in his *Explanatory Notes upon the New Testament* (Reprint, Grand Rapids, MI: Zondervan, 1983): "The chief thing wanting [to us when we pray] is, a fit disposition on our part to receive [God's] grace and blessing. Consequently, one great office of prayer is, to produce such a disposition in us . . . "

8. Cf. Sermon 16, "The Means of Grace," *Works*, 1:378–97.

9. For particular stress on daily scripture reading as a means of grace, see Ibid., §§III.7–10, *Works*, 1:386–9.

10. See "A Letter to Marcellinus," in *Athanasius: The Life of St. Antony and the Letter to Marcellinus*, trans. and intro. by Robert Gregg (New York: Paulist Press, 1980), especially par. 10–12.

11. W. Douglas Mills, *A Daily Lectionary* (Nashville, Tennessee: The Upper Room, 1986).

Watson—Aldersgate and the General Rules

1. (Newcastle upon Tyne: John Gooding, 1743); reprint in *Works*, 9:69–73.

2. "Rules of the Band Societies," drawn up December 25, 1738. Subjoined to the Fourth Edition of the General Rules (London: Strahan, 1744). Reprint in *Works*, 9:77–8.

3. *God and Politics: The Kingdom Divided*, Executive Editor, Bill Moyers (New York: Public Affairs Television, Inc., 1987).

4. *Journal* (1–14 August 1738), in *Works*, 18:267–97; and *Journal* (3 Sept. 1741), in *Journal* (Curnock), 2:490–500. See also Letter to Count Zinzendorf and the Church at Herrnhut (5–8 August 1740), *Works*, 26:24–31.

5. I have explored this in more detail in "The 'Much-Controverted Point of Justification by Faith' and the Shaping of Wesley's Evangelistic Message," *Wesleyan Theological Journal* 21.1 & 2 (Spring-Fall, 1986):7–23.

6. *Journal* (9 October 1738), in *Journal* (Curnock), 2:88–9.

7. Letter to Samuel Wesley, Junior (30 October 1738), *Works*, 25:576–7.

8. *Journal* (Curnock), 2:97.

9. *Journal* (Curnock), 2:101.

10. *The Doctrine of Salvation, Faith and Good Works*. Extracted from the Homilies of the Church of England (Oxford, 1738).

11. *Two Treatises, The First on Justification by Faith only, according to the Doctrine of the Eleventh Article of the Church of England. The Second On the Sinfulness of Man's natural Will, and his utter Inability to do Works acceptable to God, until he be justify'd and born again of the Spirit of God, according to eh Doctrine of our Ninth, Tenth, Twelfth and Thirteenth Articles . . .* By John Wesley, A.M. Fellow of Lincoln College, Oxford (London: Printed and Sold by John Lewis [Printer to the Religious Societies], 1739).

12. William R. Cannon, *The Theology of John Wesley, with Special Reference to the Doctrine of Justification* (Nashville: Abingdon, 1946; repr. ed. Lanham, MD: University Press of America, 1984).

13. Harald Lindström, *Wesley and Sanctification: A Study in the Doctrine of Salvation* (Stockholm: Nya Bokförlags Aktiebolaget, 1946; repr. ed., Grand Rapids, MI: Francis Asbury Press, [1980]).

14. Albert C. Outler, "The Place of Wesley in the Christian Tradition," in *The Place of Wesley in the Christian Tradition*, edited by Kenneth E. Rowe (Metuchen, N. J.: The Scarecrow Press, 1976), pp. 11–38.

15. Martin Schmidt, *John Wesley: A Theological Biography*. 2 vols. in 3 pts. (New York: Abingdon, 1962, 1972, 1973), 1:221ff.

16. *Journal* (5 June 1740 and following), in *Journal* (Curnock), 2:349ff.

17. Letter to James Hutton and the Fetter Lane Society (30 April 1739), *Works*, 25:639–40. Cf. *Journal* (29 April 1739), in *Journal* (Curnock), 2:185–6; and "Thoughts on Salvation by Faith" (1779), *Works* (Jackson), 11:492–6.

18. *The Principles of a Methodist . . . Occasioned by a late pamphlet, entitled "A Brief History of the Principles of Methodism [by Joseph Tucker]* (Bristol: Farley, 1742). Reprint in *Works* 9:48–66.

19. Frank Baker, "The People Called Methodists: 3: Polity," in *A History of the Methodist Church in Great Britain*, Vol. 1, edited by Rupert Davies and E. Gordon Rupp (London: Epworth Press, 1965), p. 222, n. 29.

20. *Journal* (Curnock), 2:528. Cf. *Journal* (15 October 1743), in *Journal* (Curnock) 3:97; "Plain Account of the People Called Methodists," §II.3, *Works* 9:260; and "Thoughts Upon Methodism," §5, *Works* 9:528.

21. It is useful to be reminded by this example of the old and New Style calendars, that Great Britain did not adopt the Gregorian calendar until 1752. The New Style calendar had been introduced by Pope Gregory XIII in 1582 to correct an accumulated error of ten days in the old Gallein calendar. Not only had this grown to eleven days by 1752, but there was the further complication that England, since the 14th century, had observed the new year on March 25th, whereas the New Style calendar established firmly that the beginning of the year would be January 1st. Thus, in dates earlier than March 25th and prior to 1752, there are instances such as this where the year is listed according to both styles.

22. The Welsh edition was published in 1761; the French in 1784. Cf. Frank Baker, *A Union Catalog of the Publications of John and Charles Wesley* (Durham, NC: The Divinity School, Duke University, 1966).

23. "General Rules," §3, *Works* 9:70.

24. "General Rules," §4, *Works* 9:70.

25. *Journal* (22 June 1740 and following), in *Journal* (Curnock), 2:354ff.

26. Sermon 43, "Scripture Way of Salvation," §I.2, *Works*, 2:156–7.

27. "General Rules," §4, *Works* 9:70–1.

28. "General Rules," §5, *Works* 9:72.

29. Ibid.

30. See the footnote 65 by Albert Outler in *Works*, I:343.

31. *Minutes of the Methodist Conferences, from the First held in London, by The Late Rev. John Wesley, A.M. in the Year 1744*. Volume I (London: Corceux, 1812), p. 5. (Hereafter cited as *Minutes*.) Extracts reprinted in *Works* (Jackson), 8:275ff, here 277.

32. *Minutes*, p. 20.

33. *Journal* (Curnock), 3:67.

34. *Journal* (Curnock), 3:68.

35. *Minutes*, p. 15. Cf. *Works* (Jackson), 8:310.

36. *Minutes*, p. 11. See also the "Large Minutes," Q. 11, in *Works* (Jackson), 8:301; and "A Plain Account of the People Called Methodists," §X.2–3, *Works* 9:273.

37. *Journal* (26 August 1756), in *Journal* (Curnock), 4:185.

38. *Minutes*, p. 52.

39. *Journal* (Curnock), 3:313.

40. *Minutes*, p. 12.

41. "Large Minutes," Q. 14, *Works* (Jackson), 8:307.

42. *Minutes*, pp. 56–7.

43. *Minutes*, p. 68. Cf. *Works* (Jackson), 8:315.

44. (2 November 1762), *Letters* (Telford), 4:194. By this time, Wesley was heavily involved in the perfectionist controversy with Maxfield and others. See John R. Tyson, *Charles Wesley on Sanctification: A Biographical and Theological Study* (Grand Rapids, MI: Francis Asbury Press, 1986), pp. 268ff.

45. (18 July 1772), *Letters* (Telford), 5:330.

46. (12 November 1773), *Letters* (Telford), 6:54.

47. (7 November 1776), *Letters* (Telford), 6:238.

48. (13 October 1778), *Letters* (Telford), 6:324.

49. (25 January 1782), *Letters* (Telford), 7:103; and (3 April 1782), *Letters* (Telford), 7:116.

50. (14 January 1786), *Letters* (Telford), 7:313.

51. *Letters* (Telford), 6:150. See also Letter to Thomas Rankin (20 February 1762), *Letters* (Telford), 4:171; and Letter to Thomas Rankin (20 March 1762), *Letters* (Telford) 4:180.

52. *Letters* (Telford), 6:208.

53. *Letters* (Telford), 6:374.

54. (26 June 1785), *Letters* (Telford), 7:276.

55. (10 January 1784), *Letters* (Telford), 7:204.

56. I have argued this with respect to the class meeting in *The Early Methodist Class Meeting: Its Origins and Significance* (Nashville: Discipleship Resources, 1985), pp. 136f., 145ff. See also p. 182, n. 35.

57. The letters are reproduced in Ibid., pp. 215–25.

58. In Ibid., pp. 219f.

59. Joseph Nightingale, *A Portraiture of Methodism: being An Impartial View of the Rise, Progress, Doctrines, Discipline, and Manners of the Wesleyan Methodists. In a Series of Letters Addressed to a Lady* (London: Longman, Hurst, Rees, and Orme, 1807), pp. 142f.

60. *Minutes*, p. 68.

61. "Plain Account of the People Called Methodists," §IV–V, *Works* 9:265–6.

62. "General Rules," §7, *Works* (Jackson), 8:271.

Heitzenrater—Great Expectations

1. This essay previously appeared as chapter 6 in my book *Mirror and Memory: Reflections on Early Methodism* (Nashville: Abingdon, 1989). A summary of the essay appeared in *Circuit Rider* 12 (May 1988):4–6.

2. *Journal* (24 May 1738, §14), *Works*, 18:250.

3. See, e.g., Wesley's comment in 1745 that "from 1738 to this time, . . . the 'Word of God ran' as fire among the stubble." *The Principles of a Methodist Farther Explained*, VI.1, in *Works*, 9:222–23.

4. In fact, he told one critic that "conversion" was a term "which I very rarely use, because it rarely occurs in the New Testament." *A Letter to the Author of The Enthusiasm of the Methodists* (1749), in *Works*, 11:368.

5. Wesley's own editorial corrections in subsequent editions of his *Journal* and *A Plain Account of Christian Perfection* make it clear that he changed some of his earlier evaluations of his own spiritual condition during the period surrounding Aldersgate, as we shall see below.

6. This caution should apply also to Wesley's *Journal* accounts, many of which benefit from a normal four or five year delay between the last events described and the preparation of the material for publication. *Works*, 18:82. Wesley is also notoriously inaccurate as to historical details in many of his retrospective flashbacks.

7. "The way of salvation." It is no surprise that one of the finest summaries of his mature theology is his sermon entitled "The Scripture Way of Salvation" (Sermon 43, *Works*, 2:153–69).

8. See especially *Letters I* (1721–39), *Works*, vol. 25; *Oxford Diaries* (1725–35), forthcoming as *Works*, vol. 32; *Journal and Diaries I* (1735–39), *Works*, vol. 18; and Wesley's early sermons (1725–41) in *Works*, 4:201–419.

9. Several works have appeared recently that emphasize and analyze this point; see especially Richard E. Brantley, "Young Man Wesley's Lockean Connection," ch. 1 of *Locke, Wesley, and the Method of English Romanticism* (Gainesville: University of Florida Press, 1984); Frederick Dreyer, "Faith and Experience in the Thought of John Wesley," *American Historical Review* 88 (February 1983):12–30; Rex D. Matthews, "'Religion and Reason Joined': A Study in the Theology of John Wesley," Th.D. thesis, Harvard University, 1986, and "'We Walk by Faith, not by Sight': Religious Epistemology in the Later Sermons of John Wesley," paper presented to the Wesley Studies Working Group of the American Academy of Religion, 25 November 1985.

10. Letter to Susanna Wesley (18 June 1725), *Works*, 25:169–70.

11. Letter from Susanna Wesley (23 February 1725), *Works*, 25:160. "The one thing needful" will be a useful imperative for Wesley, defined in a number of ways throughout the years.

12. Letter from Susanna Wesley (8 June 1725), *Works*, 25:165–66. These comments came in the midst of a continuing discussion of Thomas à Kempis.

13. Letter to Susanna Wesley (29 July 1725), *Works*, 25:174–75; cf. 25:186–87. See Wesley's later use of this maxim in Sermon 117, "On the Discoveries of Faith." §1, and Sermon 119, "Walking by Sight and Walking by Faith," §7, *Works*, 4:29, 51; see also Rex D. Matthews, "Religious Epistemology," pp. 17–23.

14. Letter to Susanna Wesley (29 July 1725), *Works*, 25:175. This letter is an early manifestation of his opposition to the idea of "perseverance of the saints."

15. Susanna also uses familiar imagery when commenting upon zeal: "Yet after all that can be said, though prudence and charity should correct the irregular motions of our zeal, they must by no means extinguish it. But we must keep that sacred fire alive in our breasts." (18 August and 10 November 1725), *Works*, 25:179, 185.

16. Letter from Samuel Wesley, Sr. (1 September 1725), *Works*, 25:181.

17. Letter to Susanna Wesley (22 November 1725), *Works*, 25:188.

18. Letter from Susanna Wesley (30 March 1726), *Works*, 25:193–94.

19. See §§1–2 of his autobiographical reflections, 25 January 1738: " . . . having from the very beginning valued both faith, the means of grace, and good works, not on their own account, but as believing God, who had appointed them, would by them bring me in due time to the mind that was in Christ." *Works*, 18:212n.

20. *Journal* (24 May 1738, §2), in *Works*, 18:243. This formula was not necessarily distinctive with Wesley but will become familiar to later Methodists as the guidelines in the *General Rules* (1743): avoid evil, do good, attend to the ordinances of God. Wesley's respective view of his "sins" during this period is qualified by the understatement, "which I knew to be such, though they were not scandalous in the eye of the world."

21. *Journal* (24 May 1738, §3), in *Works*, 18:243.

22. Ibid., §4.

23. See letter of 8 June 1725 from Susanna Wesley, who argues that perfection is essentially internal and centered on the virtues. *Works*, 25:165–66. Wesley soon came to hold this view himself. He published this letter in the first issue of the *Arminian Magazine* in 1778, pp. 33–36. See above, n. 12. Sincerity also became a consistent theme for Wesley throughout his lifetime; see below, at nn. 39, 59, 180.

24. "So that now, doing so much and living so good a life, I doubted not but I was a good Christian." *Journal* (24 May 1738, §4), *Works*, 18:244.

25. "When it pleased God to give me a settled resolution to be not a nominal but a real Christian (being then about two and twenty years of age). . . ." Sermon 81 (1781), "In What Sense we are to Leave the World," §23, *Works*, 3:152. See also his later comment that his resolve "to dedicate all my life to God" as a result of reading Jeremy Taylor, Thomas à Kempis, and William Law, came from a recognition of "the absolute impossibility of being half a Christian," and he determined, "through his grace (the absolute necessity of which I was deeply sensible of), to be all-devoted to God." *Plain Account of Christian Perfection*, §2, *Works* (Jackson), 11:366–67. These early and late evaluations bracket a contrasting account of his condition at Oxford found in Sermon 2 (1741): "I did go thus far for many years . . . : using diligence to eschew all evil; . . . buying up every opportunity of doing all good to all men; constantly and carefully using all the public and all the private means of grace . . . [*viz.*, the *General Rules*]. Yet . . . all this time I was but 'almost a Christian'" (which, in his understanding of 1741, was none at all). *Works*, 1:136–37; and see pp. 84–86, below.

26. Wesley speaks in terms of "the happiness God has promised to his servants," which he always links with holiness and defines in terms of the Great Commandment, here in 1725 and throughout his life. Sermon 134 (1725), "Seek First the Kingdom," §4, *Works*, 4:218; see below, pp. 87–88.

27. *Journal* (24 May 1738, §5), *Works*, 18:244–45. In a correction added in 1774, Wesley himself confirms this sentiment, saying "And I believe I was"; ibid., 18:245n. Albert C. Outler views the "radical change" that occurred in Wesley at this point as "a conversion if ever there was one." *John Wesley* (New York: Oxford University Press, 1964), p. 7.

28. *Journal* (24 May 1738, §6), *Works*, 18:245.

29. Sermon 140 (1730), *Works*, 4:284–287. Wesley here lists three of his traditional authorities.

30. Ibid., 4:287–88; an early use of this text (2 Cor. 5:7) that will become central to his mature views. One of his later critics turns Wesley's own early sentiments back upon him by claiming that Methodists who claim to be wholly sanctified upon the instant of their justification show a lack of humility. See *A Letter to the Right Reverend Lord Bishop of London* (1747), §7, in *Works*, 11:338.

31. Sermon 141 (1730), *Works*, 4:294.

32. Ibid., 4:299–302.

33. *John Wesley MS V*, "The Procedure, Extent, and Limits of Human Understanding," pp. 1–2.

34. Peter Browne, *The Procedure, Extent, and Limits of Human Understanding* (London: Innys, 1729), p. 250.

35. MS "Procedure," p. 49; in the end, Wesley will ignore Browne's use of "analogy" to make the connection between the human and divine realms, that as reason perceives what the senses grasp, so faith apprehends the things of God; Wesley will draw a more direct parallel between the two, using the idea of "spiritual senses."

36. Eph. 1:18; letter to Ann Granville (3 October 1731), in *Works*, 25:318. The "seeing" metaphor has several variations with different implications: the eyes are opened, renewed, or new eyes are given; the sight is restored, renewed, enlightened, or new sight is given. See below, n. 116.

37. *John Wesley MS XX*, "The Duty of Receiving the Lord's Supper." This extract was the basis for Wesley's "sermon on the Sacrament," used heavily by the Oxford Methodists and later revised as "The Duty of Constant Communion" (Sermon 101, in *Works*, 3:427–39; see also 4:525–28 for a comparison of the manuscript and printed versions.

38. MS, "Duty," f.v. 18.

39. See below, at n. 58.

40. This tendency is encouraged, of course, by Wesley's own comments in the months following his experience in May 1738, describing his present and previous condition in the light of his perspective at that time.

41. Sermon 17, in *Works*, 1:407, 414. See Wesley's comment in his *Plain Account of Christian Perfection* fifty years later: "This was the view of religion I then had, which even then I scrupled not to term 'perfection.' This is the view I have of it now, without any material addition or diminution." *Works* (Jackson), 11:369.

42. *Works*, 1:402.

43. "Such as faith as is 'mighty through God.'" Ibid., 4:404.

44. By this time, Wesley had begun to delineate the distinction between "half-Christians" or "common" Christians, and "true" Christians, as seen in the contrast between those who simply "use God and enjoy the world" (Pascal's phrase) on one hand and those who are evangelists and martyrs on the other hand. Sermon 142 (1731), "The Wisdom of Winning Souls," *Works*, 4:310–14.

45. *Works*, 1:405.

46. In his later revision of this sermon for publication in 1748, Wesley incorporates the personal language, "loved *me*," "reconciled *me*," etc., noting that this material "is not added to the sermon formerly preached." Ibid., 1:405.

47. Ibid., 1:409–11. One must be cautious in assuming that this whole sermon, save for the one passage which Wesley explicitly acknowledges was later added, stands as it was preached in 1733. This phrase may be a later interpolation.

48. Love (of God and neighbor) is the primary virtue, evident in the presence of other virtues, which are evidenced by good works. See n. 56 below.

49. Wesley began to test his many rules, including early rising and fasting, by casting lots in order to discern God's providence in these matters. See *MS Oxford Diaries*, 5:152 (Friday, 7 February 1735), where he cast lots ("as to sleep") between 5 and 6 a.m. to see if

he might go back to bed, and between 9 and 10 a.m. ("as to eating") to see if he might have breakfast (break the Friday fast early).

50. See his autobiographical reflections in his *Journal* (25 January and 24 May 1738), *Works*, 18:213, 245–46.

51. Sermon 144 (September 1733), "The Love of God," in *Works*, 4:329–45. Love of God and neighbor (the great commandment) will be a major focus of Wesley's mature theology. The ascription at the end of this sermon reveals that the twofold basis of the Wesleyan soteriology was present in seminal form at that point: redemption by the blood of Christ, and a heart filled with love by the grace of the Holy Spirit.

52. Sermon 146, *Works*, 4:354–58. The concept of "the one thing needful" (Luke 10:42) had arisen in this discussion as early as 1725 (see above at n. 11), and would continue to be a useful concept well past 1738 with a succession of different goals seen as the "one thing."

53. Matt. 6:22, Sermon 148 ("A Single Intention"), *Works*, 4:374; Charles transcribed this sermon and referred to it as "A Single Eye."

54. Richard P. Heitzenrater, ed., *Diary of an Oxford Methodist; Benjamin Ingham, 1733–34* (Durham: Duke University Press, 1985), p. 109 (1 February 1734).

55. Whitefield, *A Short Account of God's Dealings with the Rev. Mr. Whitefield* (London: Strahan, 1740), p. 44; *MS Oxford Diaries*, 5:159–60.

56. "Love is the end of every commandment of Christ . . . ; the positive [commands] are only so many means of love, or the practice of those particular virtues which are the genuine fruits of love." Sermon 144, "The Love of God" (September 1733), *Works*, 4:332.

57. *Journal* (25 January 1738), §6, *Works*, 18:213.

58. *MS Oxford Diaries*, 5:vi; cf. Thomas à Kempis, *Imitatione Christi*, I.vii.1 (cited as from Augustine, *Sermones ad fratres in eremo*, 27), translated by Wesley in his 1735 edition of Kempis (*The Christian's Pattern*) as "Do what lieth in thy power, and God will assist thy good will." Although some solifidian opponents would characterize Wesley's position as "works-righteousness" or "trusting in his own works," the synergism that Wesley espoused was based on a view of God's grace perfecting human nature. For a discussion of the background and development of this idea, see H. A. Oberman, *The Harvest of Medieval Theology* (Cambridge: Harvard University Press, 1963), pp. 120–45.

59. See Ingham's comment that he was "resolved, God's grace assisting me, . . . never to depend upon my own strength because I can do nothing without God's assistance; therefore ever distrust thyself." *Diary* (1 February 1734), p. 109. Although some of the tension resulting from this reliance on sincerity was resolved for Wesley in 1738, he continued to reiterate the necessity of "doing one's best" within the context of human/divine synergism. See Albert C. Outler, "Methodism's Theological Heritage," in Paul M. Minus, Jr., ed., *Methodism's Distiny in an Ecumenical Age* (Nashville: Abingdon, 1969), pp. 51–63.

60. Sermon 147, "Wiser than Children of Light," *Works*, 4:367.

61. This comment by Samuel was recalled thirteen years after his death, in a letter to John Smith after Smith had suggested that, if assurance were a prerequisite for salvation (as Wesley was preaching in the early 1740s), then Wesley himself at Oxford stood in jeopardy of damnation as well as his father, who died before John started preaching this doctrine. Letter (22 March 1748), *Works*, 25:288. The dialogue with Smith was the occasion for a good deal of clarification in Wesley's thinking (accompanied by some evasive rhetoric that reveals intellectual uncertainty).

62. Letter to John Burton (10 October 1735), *Works*, 25:439.

63. *Journal* (23 November 1735, 23 January 1736), *Works*, 18:140, 142.

64. *Journal* (25 January 1736), Works, 18:143. Clifford W. Towlson is careful to point out that Wesley's becoming a pupil of the Moravians was more complicated than simply

a reaction to their demeanor during this storm. Moravian and Methodist (London: Epworth, 1957), p. 39.

65. Sermon 148, *Works*, 4:377. This sermon was begun on 29 January and finished on 4 February 1736, the day they first saw land; Georgia Diary I, in *Works*, 18:346–49.

66. Sermon 149 (1736), "On Love," *Works*, 4:385; cf. Sermon 144 (1733), "The Love of God," *Works*, 4:334.

67. *Journal* (8 February 1736), *Works*, 18:145–46.

68. Conversation recalled in a letter to Joseph Benson (11 October 1771), Letters (Telford), 5:281. Spangenberg's differing evaluation of Wesley is further noted in his own diary at the time: "I observe that grace really dwells and reigns in him." Quoted in Martin Schmidt, *John Wesley; A Theological Biography* (Nashville: Abingdon, 1962–73), 1:153.

69. In the midst of his fearfulness and unease, he found it useful to preach to others, perhaps not unlike his resolve to go to Georgia in the hope of saving his own soul, hoping at the same time to learn the "true sense of the gospel of Christ by preaching it to the heathens." Letter to John Burton (10 October 1735), *Works*, 25:439. See *Journal* (2 and 9 January 1738): "Being sorrowful and very heavy . . . in the evening, therefore, I began instructing the cabin-boy, after which I was much easier." "I had resolved, God being my helper, not only to preach it to all but to apply the Word of God to every single soul in the ship. . . . I no sooner executed this resolution than my spirit revived." *Works*, 18:207–10.

70. *Journal* (28 December 1737), *Works*, 18:207.

71. *Journal* (8 January 1738), *Works*, 18:208–9.

72. Ibid. (24 May 1738, §11), *Works*, 18:247.

73. Ibid. (25 April 1738), 18:235; notice the pietist and Moravian fire imagery.

74. This view will be clearly expressed in his memo of 4 January 1739: "I *know* because I *feel* it." *Journal, Works*, 19:30. Wesley, never able to sever completely inner and outward religion (or later the direct and indirect witness of the Holy Spirit) was also never able completely to swing fully to an intuitionist perspective which is in part what preserved him from falling into the trap of "enthusiasm." See Lycurgus M. Starkey, Jr., *The Work of the Holy Spirit* (New York: Abingdon, 1962), pp. 64–77.

75. *Journal* (24 May 1738, §11), *Works*, 18:247.

76. *Journal* (epilogue following 2 February 1738), *Works*, 18:215. Böhler gave new meaning to the phrase "sure trust and confidence" in the Homilies definition of faith by seeing it in terms of full assurance.

77. *Journal* (24 May 1738, §11), *Works*, 18:248. Wesley's logical mind was operating with two syllogisms at this point, the first element in each coming from the Moravians: (1) One cannot have forgiveness of sins and not feel it; I feel it not; therefore, I do not have forgiveness; and (2) there is no true faith without a sense of forgiveness; I feel no sense of forgiveness; therefore, I have no true faith.

78. On 5 March, he was "clearly convinced of unbelief." His inclination was to "leave off preaching," but he reports that Peter Böhler then said to him, "Preach faith till you have it, and then, because you have it, you will preach faith." *Works*, 18:35, 228; but cf. Böhler's own account, which reports that Wesley's attitude on this occasion was simply "if that is true which stands in the Bible, then I am saved." W. N. Schwarze and S. H. Gapp, "Peter Böhler and the Wesleys," *World Parish* 2 (November 1949):6. Preaching and speaking to others always seemed to make him feel better about his own problems; see on shipboard, and later. *Journal* (2 and 13 January 1738), *Works*, 18:208, 210. James Hutton recalled that "Wesley preached this Gospel everywhere as soon as he believed it and many received it. Wesley's manner and the Gospel itself . . . made much ado in the Societies." "The Beginning of The Lord's Work in England," tr. by J. N. Libbey, *Proceedings* WHS 15 (1926):185.

79. *Journal* (28 February 1736), *Works*, 18:151. Wesley was no doubt attracted to the Moravians' self-conscious attempt to recapture and preserve the traditions of Apostolic times. See Towlson, *Moravian and Methodist*, p. 32.

80. *Journal* (23 March, 22 April 1738), *Works*, 18:232–34.

81. *Certain Sermons or Homilies Appointed to Be Read in Churches in the Time of the Late Queen Elizabeth*, "Of Salvation," Pt. III; *Works*, 18:215–16, 233–34; cf. 250. One of the strongest restatements of this in the Wesley corpus is found in the comments on faith he later added to his Oxford sermon on "Circumcision of the Heart," I.7: "a confidence whereby every true believer is enable to bear witness, 'I know that my Redeemer liveth'; that I 'have an advocate with the Father,' that 'Jesus Christ the righteous is' my Lord and 'the propitiation for my sins.' I know he 'hath loved me, and given himself for me.' He 'hath reconciled me, even me to God'; and I 'have redemption through his blood, even the forgiveness of sins.'" Sermon 17, in *Works*, 1:405.

82. Böhler's Moravian friends in the first instance, followed by Mr. Hutchins of Pembroke College and Mrs. Fox in Oxford; *Journal* (23 and 26 April 1738), *Works*, 18:234–35, 576 (diary entry for 23 April, "convinced that faith converts at once"). Böhler reported that Wesley and his friends were "as though struck dumb" at the narratives of the four Moravian witnesses, and while singing a hymn, Wesley frequently dried his eyes, then asking Böhler how he should attain to such faith, saying that "if he once had *this*, he would then certainly preach about nothing other than faith." "Peter Böhler and the Wesleys," p. 8.

83. Though the Moravians would have seen no reason for any qualifying adjective—anything less than this state is not Christian at all. Having been convinced of this position, Wesley wrote to William Law twice during May 1738, criticizing his former spiritual mentor sharply (and probably unjustly) for not having advised him of his lack of a true faith in Christ. *Works*, 25:240–50.

84. "I felt a strange palpitation of heart. I said, yet feared to say, 'I believe, I believe!' . . . I found myself convinced . . . I now found myself at peace with God." Charles Wesley, *The Journal of the Rev. Charles Wesley* (London: Culley, 1910), 1:147. Thorvald Källstad, viewing John Wesley's situation in psychological terms, sees Charles's experience as further reinforcing John's own anticipations and strengthening his susceptibility to a similar experience, which Källstad interprets as a stage in the "reduction of cognitive dissonance between the Anglican and the Moravian models of faith." *John Wesley and the Bible; A Psychological Study* (Stockholm: Nya Bokförlags, 1974), pp. 234, 238. Sydney G. Dimond views these developments within what he calls "the psychology of suggestion" and "the resolution of pathogenic conflict." *Psychology of the Methodist Revival* (Nashville: Whitmore, 1926), p. 87–99.

85. See above, at nn. 74, 81; see also his subsequent refinements in the definition of the "witness of the Spirit." Albert Outler points out that "whatever psychological account one may prefer, the theological import of Aldersgate was largely *pneumatological*." "A Focus on the Holy Spirit: Spirit and Spirituality in John Wesley," *Quarterly Review* 8 (Summer 1988):9.

86. Mrs. Hutton considered him to be "turned a wild enthusiast or fanatic" because of his claims on 28 May: "Mr. John got up and told the people that five days before, he was not a Christian." Her response was: "If you was not a Christian ever since I knew you, you was a great hypocrite, for you made us all believe you was one." *Journal* (28 May 1738), *Works*, 18:252n. The point is rather obvious (as we have seen) but crucial: Wesley would not have disclaimed his Christian standing during his earlier years, nor would he be so critical of himself during that period from the perspective of later years; but the Moravian framework of his experience of 24 May 1738 led him to hold this view at that time.

87. "Towards ten, my brother was brought in triumph by a troop of our friends, and declared, 'I believe.' We sang the hymn with great joy, and parted with prayer." Charles Wesley, *Journal*, 1:153.

88. Traditional pietist and Moravian terminology associated with variety of experiences; see, e.g., 21 December 1740: "Our hearts were warmed." *Journal, Works*, 19:175. The noteworthy word in Wesley's phrase is "strangely," implying "unusually," "inexplicably," or somehow "different from other times."

89. *Journal* (24 May 1738, §§15, 16), *Works*, 18:250.

90. *Journal* (25 and 26 May 1738), *Works*, 18:251. 91. *Journal* (29 May 1738), *Works*, 18:253.

92. *Journal* (6 June 1738), *Works*, 18:254.

93. Ibid.

94. "His head had gained an ascendency over his heart." Daniel Benham, *Memoirs of James Hutton* (London: Hamilton, Adams, & Co., 1856), p. 40. The insulting rejection was apparently heightened by their willingness to allow Ingham to partake. Hutton goes on to say that Wesley "unhappily concealed and brooded over" this offence.

95. *Journal* (12 July 1738), *Works*, 18:261, where Wesley lists eight main ideas outlined by the Count and six contrasting views that had been taught by Peter Böhler. Zinzendorf's ideas were confirmed by Christian David's sermons a few days later. *Works*, 18:270–71. See his letter to brother Charles (28 June 1738), *Works*, 25:554.

96. *Journal* (10 August 1738), *Works*, 18:270. This distinction confirmed a crucial point in Wesley's own developing theology. See also his comments in the second published extract of his *Journal* (Preface), §§7–10, *Works*, 18:219–20

97. *A Plain Account of Christian Perfection*, §8, *Works* (Jackson), 8:370. See also *Journal* (11–14 August 1738), *Works*, 18:291. It is especially interesting that Wesley here in retrospect (1763) is saying in effect that he himself had not experienced this full assurance of faith at Aldersgate, even though in 1738 that is what he had been led to think he had experienced, since within the English Moravian framework there was only one type and degree of assurance.

98. Martin Schmidt questions whether Wesley really understood what Böhler had taught him, saying that Wesley interpreted what he heard in terms with which he was familiar. Schmidt's own analysis of the theological basis of Wesley's conversion also combines Pietist and Reformed ideas in a Lutheran fashion that would be problematic from an Anglican point of view. *John Wesley*, 1:238–39.

99. The English Moravian doctrine of freedom from sin also tended to overlook (or failed to develop) an important element of their own Lutheran background, the crucial concept of *simul iustus et peccator*—the Christian is at the same time justified and a sinner. Böhler records that on the evening that the Fetter Lane society had been organized (1 May 1738, three weeks before Aldersgate), Wesley "feels himself justified and is a seeking poor sinner," adding his own comment, "May the Saviour receive him on his arm and lap." "Peter Böhler and the Wesleys," p. 12.

100. "An assurance that excludes all doubt and fear," Sermon 110 (1739), "Free Grace," §14, *Works*, 3:549; "A Christian is so far perfect as not to commit sin," Sermon 40 (1741), "Christian Perfection," II.20, *Works*, 2:116. James Hutton reported that after John's return from Germany, "he and his brother were also not grounded, but still at that time they did much, and protested against the 'Inspired,' etc." "Beginning of the Lord's Work," p. 186.

101. *A Faithful Narrative of the Surprizing Work of God . . . in New England* (London: John Oswald, 1737).

102. 12 November 1738, *Journal, Works*, 19:21.

103. *The Doctrine of Salvation, Faith, and Good Works: Extracted from the Homilies of the Church of England* (Oxford: n.p., 1738). The tract was republished at least twenty times during Wesley's lifetime. When the revival started in Bristol in 1739, the Wesleys gave

away these pamphlets by the hundreds, John remarking to James Hutton that this pamphlet was "better than all our sermons put together." Letter of 8 May 1739, *Works*, 25:645.

104. The letter received on 14 October may well have been by William Delamotte (10 October), who commented on the question of assurance in response to Wesley's observations on "weak faith." *Works*, 25:567–68; see also *Journal*, *Works*, 19:16. Wesley wrote the following notes ("wr.n.") between 2 and 3 p.m.; *MS London Diary*, 1:91.

105. 14 October 1738, *Journal* (Curnock), 2:89–90.

106. Here he is reiterating his decade-long rejection of external actions (summarized by the trilogy of the later *General Rules*) as the essence of real (internal) holiness; see at nn. 18, 20, 23 above. See also *Journal* (13 September 1739), where he also denigrates the typical clergy emphasis on sanctification as "an outward thing" in terms of the threefold outward activities (*General Rules*), and instead emphasizes internal renewal and holy tempers; see also Sermon 2 (1741), "The Almost Christian," I.13, *Works*, 1:136: an honest heathen follows those three outward rules, as he did while at Oxford for so many years, but that does not make one "an altogether Christian."

107. 14 October 1738, *Journal*, *Works*, 19:18–19; see also letter to Samuel Wesley, Jr. (30 October 1738), *Works*, 25:576–77.

108. As early as 29 May 1738, Wesley had been "tempted to doubt" whether he and Böhler had the same faith; *Works*, 18:253. In early June, he was becoming settled in his mind that degrees of faith were possible; *Works*, 18:254. By October, his recollection of 24 May indicated that he himself had then received "such a sort or degree of faith as I had not till that day"; letter to Samuel Wesley, Jr. (30 October 1738), *Works*, 25:576.

109. Letter to Samuel Wesley, Jr. (30 October 1738), *Works*, 25:575–77. Although not an experience of "full" assurance, Aldersgate did represent for Wesley an assurance of pardon which provided an experiential confirmation for his developing doctrine of the witness of the Spirit. See Colin W. Williams, *John Wesley's Theology Today* (Nashville: Abingdon, 1960), p. 104–5, and cf. Arthur S. Yates, *The Doctrine of Assurance* (London: Epworth Press, 1952), p. 11. Yates refers to the "witness of the Spirit" as "a theological name for 'the heart strangely warmed.'"

110. Letter (25 September 1738), *Works*, 25:564; see also Sermon 110 (1739), "Free Grace," §16, *Works*, 3:550.

111. "Saved from the fear, though not from the possibility, of falling away from the grace of God." Sermon 1, "Salvation by Faith," II.4, *Works*, 1:122; on 27 December 1738, Wesley preached at Whitechapel on "I will heal their backsliding." *Journal*, *Works*, 19:28–29.

112. *Journal*, *Works*, 19:20.

113. Conversation of 26 or 27 November 1738, recorded by Wesley in his *MS London Diary* 1:113.

114. Indicated by the usual abbreviation "wr.n." in his diary.

115. 16 December 1738, *Journal*, *Works*, 19:27; cf. self-examination of 29 January 1726: "I have loved women and company more than God"; *MS Oxford Diaries*, 1:35.

116. The question of whether the renewal of one's nature in the image of God results in *new* eyes or *renewed* sight has interesting implications for the doctrine of the Fall and the condition of "natural man." Although Wesley does not deal with this metaphor in a consistent fashion that would indicate a well-considered approach, he does tend to opt for the "renewed" and "enlightened" eyes most often, implying a higher anthropology (and assuming a different relationship between nature and grace) than if the eyes needed to be replaced.

117. 16 December 1738, *Journal*, *Works*, 19:27–28; cf. 19:17–18.

118. In effect, requiring entire sanctification as evidence of genuine Christianity, i.e., collapsing sanctification into justification, a typical approach for the Moravian Lutherans,

as we saw above. These bouts with despair through self-questioning cannot simply be ignored or disregarded, as James Richard Joy has suggested (Joy 1937, p. 70).

119. See at n. 71 above.

120. Cf. the requirements for the "altogether Christian": love of God, love of neighbor, and a faith that works through love. Sermon 2 (1741), *Works*, 1:137–139.

121. Again the formula: avoiding evil, doing good, using the means of grace—these do not suffice to make one a Christian. *Journal, Works*, 19:29–31. Recall Charles Wesley's and Thomas Broughton's confusion on this a year before (at n. 73).

122. See *Character of a Methodist* (1742), §5, in *Works*, 9:35, where he consciously uses the model of the perfect Christian from Clement of Alexandria; see also Sermon 40 (1741), "Christian Perfection" (*Works*, 2:105–21), where he explains that a Christian is cleansed from all sin and therefore "in such a sense perfect as not to commit sin," although later he denies that he ever uses the term "sinless perfection" (*Plain Account*, §19, *Works* [Jackson], 11:396); see Sermons 13 and 14, "On Sin in Believers" and "The Repentance of Believers," *Works*, 1:314–52; Sermon 43, "The Scripture Way of Salvation," III.11, *Works*, 2:166). The correlation between Methodism and genuine Christianity is straightforward in Wesley: "These are the marks of a true Methodist. . . . If any man say, 'Why, these are only the common, fundamental principles of Christianity'—'Thou hast said.' So I mean." *Character*, §17. See also his *Plain Account of Genuine Christianity* (1749), also used to defend Methodists. *Works*, 11:527–38.

123. He was at this time beginning to refer to himself and others who had not received full assurance as being Christians in an "imperfect" sense. Letter to Samuel Wesley, Jr. (30 October 1738), *Works*, 25:577.

124. Most of those who are baptized are born again only in a "lower sense", i.e., receive the remission of their sins (some in neither sense). See 25 January 1739, *Journal, Works*, 19:32. Later, Wesley will disentangle new birth or regeneration from justification in a theological sense, stressing that it is the "gate" or "threshold" of sanctification. Sermon 45, "The New Birth," IV.3, *Works*, 2:198; Sermon 107, "On God's Vineyard," §§6–7, *Works*, 3:506–7.

125. 5 and 10 December 1738, *Journal, Works*, 19:23, 27. At that point, such responses do not generally occur when Wesley was doing some occasional preaching at parish churches, but rather when he was with the societies, in workhouses, or speaking in private. Almost a year after Aldersgate, the same phenomenon will begin to occur in a greatly expanded context as he starts "field-preaching" to large groups out-of-doors.

126. 2 March 1739, *Journal, Works*, 19:35.

127. 28 January 1739, *Journal, Works*, 19:32–33. Five months later, he provided similar advice to the women of the Fetter Lane society, among which many misunderstandings and offenses had crept in: "not to believe every spirit, but to try the spirits, whether they were of God" (1 John 4:1). 13 June 1739, *Journal, Works*, 19:69.

128. 22 June 1739, *Journal, Works*, 19:73. This reference to the Old and New Testaments reiterates his lifelong reliance upon Scripture as the primary authority for theological and spiritual questions, especially as a test for individual experience. See above, p. 59 at n. 45.

129. 2 April 1739, *Journal, Works*, 19:46.

130. 28 March 1739, *Journal, Works*, 19:38.

131. See above, nn. 69, 124, 125.

132. The journal account reports three thousand (2 April 1739), *Journal, Works*, 19:46; a letter to James Hutton (4 April 1739) reports three or four thousand; *Works*, 25:625.

133. *Journal, Works*, 19:52. According to the diary, the field preaching was at 7 and 10:30 a.m. and 4:30 p.m.

134. Letter (7 May 1739), *Works*, 25:644. John wrote regular journal letters to "the brethren" in London, reporting on his activities in Bristol. C. J. Podmore has shown rather

persuasively that the Fetter Lane society was quite thoroughly Moravian in its foundation and character and that Wesley's role in its leadership has been exaggerated. "The Fetter Lane Society, 1738," *Proceedings WHS* 46 (1988):137–40, 144–48.

135. Assurance did not necessarily imply a full assurance of our future perseverance, but does indeed imply a full assurance that all past sins are forgiven, that you are now a child of God. Sermon 110 (1739), §§14, 16, *Works,* 3:549–50. He prepared this sermon in response to pressure to preach against "the decrees" and as a result of casting lots on April 26 (result, "Preach and publish").

136. Sermon 110, §18, *Works,* 3:550–51. Harald Lindström claims that Wesley was caught up in 1738 with the doctrines of "present justification" and "present salvation" and overlooked the importance of good works (as anything other than the result of faith) until he later began emphasizing final salvation. *Wesley and Sanctification* (Nashville: Abingdon, 1946), pp. 208–9. This view ignores the controversy with the Moravians over the use of the means of grace by the repentant or seeking person; see below, at n. 155.

137. Not all German Pietists denigrated active obedience or leaned toward antinomianism. Halle and Herrnhut represented two quite different approaches, and the more energetic and active Hallensian piety of August Hermann Francke and the Salzburgers in Georgia had already impressed Wesley. In June 1739, Wesley published *Nicodemus; or, A Treatise on the Fear of Man,* an extract of a work by Francke (*MS London Diary,* 30 May-1 June 1739). See Arthur W. Nagler, Pietism and Methodism (Nashville: Smith and Lamar, 1918), pp. 153–54; and Martin Schmidt, "Wesley's Place in Church History," in Rowe, ed., *The Place of Wesley in the Christian Tradition,* pp. 87–88.

138. 30 April, 1 May, 30 July 1739, etc., *Journal, Works,* 19:52–53, 77, 82.

139. Letter to Samuel Wesley, Jr. (4 April 1739), *Works,* 25:622–23. Samuel's critical perspective had swayed Susanna to become critical of John. When she had seen his account of Aldersgate in June 1738, she approved it, and "blessed God who had brought him to so just a way of thinking." A year later, with an account from Samuel intervening, she had fears that John "had greatly erred from the faith." 13 June 1739, *Journal, Works,* 19:68.

140. 11–18 June 1739, *Journal, Works,* 19:66–72.

141. 7 July 1739, *Journal, Works,* 19:79.

142. 22 June 1739, *Journal, Works,* 19:72–73.

143. Also on 24 August 1739. Charles later preached a sermon at Oxford on the same text, 4 April 1742, which was published as Sermon 3 in John Wesley's *Sermons on Several Occasions* (1746). John had written several sermons that Charles was still preaching at this time, and although there is no evidence that John wrote this published sermon on Ephesians 2:5, one can assume for a variety of reasons that John certainly agreed with the content. See *Works,* 1:142–58.

144. Sermon 3, "Awake, Thou That Sleepest," I.3–11, *Works,* 1:145–46.

145. Sermon 3, I.3–11, *Works,* 1:146. John begins using "divine evidence or conviction" (Heb. 11:1) at least by 24 August 1744 (Sermon 4, "Scriptural Christianity," *Works,* 1:161)

146. In 1746, Wesley would equate "the inspiration of the Holy Ghost" with assurance and "the revelation of Christ in us." Minutes (13 May 1746), *Works* (Jackson), 8:290.

147. Sermon 3, *Works,* 1:155. The question of "perceptible inspiration" also led to controversies surrounding the "extraordinary gifts of the Spirit," a topic which John Wesley usually tried to channel into discussions of the "ordinary gifts of the Spirit." See Sermon 4, "Scriptural Christianity," §5, *Works,* 1:151.

148. By his own account, Wesley preached to ten thousand on 2 September, to thirty thousand on 9 September, to thirty thousand on 16 September, and to thirty thousand on 23 September; the diary reports him preaching to twenty-seven thousand on 30 September. *Journal, Works,* 19:92–100.

149. 13 September 1739, *Journal, Works,* 19:96. This became a consistent argument for Wesley as part of his continual claim that the Methodists were not separating from the Church of England.

150. 16 September 1739, *Journal, Works,* 19:97. See also *Character of a Methodist,* §17, *Works,* 9:41, and n. 122 above.

151. Wesley explains this point by yet another reference to religion in terms of the outline of the *General Rules*: "as if it consisted chiefly, if not wholly in . . . : the doing no harm; the doing good; . . . the using the means of grace." See above, n. 106.

152. 13 September 1739, *Journal, Works,* 19:97.

153. His sermon on "Salvation by Faith" (1738) had said, "We speak of a faith which is necessarily inclusive of all good works and all holiness." A critic writing to the *Gentleman's Magazine* pointed out the inherent contradiction of this position with his *sola fide* views, so that in subsequent editions, Wesley changed the wording to read "faith which is necessarily productive of all good works and all holiness." See *Elusive Mr. Wesley,* 1:91. But Josiah Tucker, an Anglican priest and critic from Bristol, wrote to him in November 1739 after hearing him preach: "I must confess, sir, that the discourse you made that day, wherein you pressed your hearers in the closest manner . . . not to stop at *faith* ONLY, but to add to it *all virtues* and to show forth their *faith* by every kind of *good works,* convinced me of the great wrong done you by a public report, common in people's mouths, that you preach *faith* without *works.*" *Journal, Works,* 19:113. Wesley spent much of the rest of his life trying to explain a view of "faith alone" that also necessarily entailed good works "in some sense"; e.g., *A Farther Appeal to Men of Reason and Religion* (1745), II.11, *Works,* 11:117; Sermon 43 (1765), "The Scripture Way of Salvation," III.2, III.13, *Works,* 2:162–63, 167.

154. This language of "tempers" hearkens back to the meditative piety of his Oxford days and will come highly visible in his common vocabulary again in the 1780s. *E.g.*, real religion as "holy tempers" or "right tempers," 24 March and 11 December 1785, *Journal* (Curnock), 7:59, 130; see also Sermon 107 (1787), "On God's Vineyard," I.9: "Who then is a Christian? . . . He in whom is that whole mind, all those holy tempers, which were also in Christ Jesus." *Works,* 3:507–8

155. Wesley exhibits some ambibuity on this point during this period. In his sermon *Salvation by Faith* (1738), III.1, Wesley had first said, "We speak of a faith which is necessarily inclusive of all good works and all holiness" ("inclusive" was changed to "productive" in later editions); *Works,* 1:125. In his Preface to *Hymns and Sacred Poems* (1739), he refers to "faith contradistinguished from all holiness, as well as from good works." Between these two works, in the sermon on Free Grace (April 1739, §18), Wesley argued against predestination because it is destructive of holiness and good works. *Works,* 18, 3:550–51.

156. In the preface to the second extract of his *Journal,* Wesley speaks of those who had found "the beginning of that salvation, being 'justified freely'"; but in the fall of 1739, while he and Charles were at Oxford, "certain men crept in among them unawares, greatly 'troubling and subverting their souls.'" *Journal* (Preface), §§8–9, *Works,* 18:219.

157. *Journal, Works,* 19:117. From the Moravian view, Wesley was appealing to "those who were unsound and wished to remain so." Hutton, "Beginning of the Lord's Work," p. 188.

158. 9 November 1739, *Journal, Works,* 19:121. Wesley continued to attack this problem head-on, as seen by his preaching to the society on 1 January 1740 on the text, "Be still and know that I am God." *Journal, Works,* 19:134.

159. The story is told by Wesley without names, but the person is most likely his mother. See 3 September and 10 November 1739, *Journal, Works,* 19:93, 120–21.

160. 11 November 1739, *Journal* (Curnock), 2:319n. From the Moravian perspective (James Hutton's view), "Wesley became hostile, partly through our imprudent behaviour towards him, partly from inablility to bear that he should be less thought of amongst us

than Brother Molther. In short he broke off from us, contradicted our teaching publicly, but we contradicted his only quietly. He took away from us almost all the women folk who then belonged to us but only some fourteen men. He became our declared enemy." "Beginning of the Lord's Work," p. 188. Wesley's final organizational break with the Moravians came on 23 July 1740; *Journal, Works,* 19:161–63. Hutton sarcasticly refers to the separated group as rapidly forming "a 'sect' in which the Saviour does not hinder them." "Hutton's Second Account," *Proceedings WHS* 15 (1926):211.

161. 31 December 1739, *Journal* (Curnock), 2:329. Towlson claims that doctrinal differences between Wesley and the Moravians would not have resulted in such controversy and disruption if not for the personal friction between Wesley and the Moravian leadership. *Moravian and Methodist,* pp. 116–17.

162. *Works,* 19:132

163. Wesley was beginning to sense the worst side of "enthusiasm," the subjective judgmentalism that cannot be challenged. In this context, he continually falls back upon his more traditional authorities as guides to measure the validity of personal experience: Scripture, the primitive church, and the teachings of the Church of England.

164. Ibid., 2:329–30. Wesley also points out in his memorandum against Molther that, as for propagating the faith, we should not use guile, deception, or "describing things a little beyond the truth in order to their coming up to it; much hurt has been done by this method, many "now wholly unsettled and lost in vain reasonings and doubtful disputations," many brought into "unscriptural stillness," "many being grounded on a faith which is without works, so that they who were right before are wrong now." *Works,* 19:132–33

165. See the second extract of his *Journal* published in the fall of 1740 to show that the Church of England and the "true" Moravians both disagreed with these false teachings perpetuated by some Moravians, under whose influence he had been in May 1738. *Journal* (Preface), *Works,* 18:218–20, 260–61; *Letters* (5 August 1740), *Works,* 26:24–30.

166. *Journal, Works,* 19:151.

167 Letter to John Clayton? (28 March 1738?), *Works,* 25:615.

168. 23 July 1739, *Journal, Works,* 19:82; 19:32.

169. Letter to John Clayton? (28 March 1738?), *Works,* 25:615. Later in this same letter he draws a larger picture on the same principles, using the familiar phrase, "I look upon all the world as my parish," explained thusly, "that in whatever part of it I am, I judge it meet, right, and my bounden duty to declare unto all that are willing to hear the glad tidings of salvation." Ibid., 25:616. Earlier, Wesley had used a similar rationale in a letter to his father explaining his reasons for staying at Oxford rather than taking the Epworth living, and to John Burton explaining his reasons for going to Georgia; ibid., 25:399, 439.

170. This idea of *simul iustus et peccator* is not yet clearly or consistently developed by Wesley at this time, but is reflected in his idea that justification and sanctification free the person from the guilt and power, though not the remains, of sin. *Works,* 1:123n, 124; 25:318, 575. Cf. Sermon 43 (1765), "The Scripture Way of Salvation," III.6, *Works,* 2:164–65 (this sermon is one of the best summaries of Wesley's mature theology).

171. During this period, Wesley exhibits a tendency to draw a rather sharp contrast between the formula of the *General Rules* with the formula of Romans 14:17. Letter to Henry Stebbing (25 July 1739), §6, *Works,* 25:671; see also 24 November 1739, *Journal* (Curnock), 2:321. See above, at nn. 74, 122.

172. *Homilies,* "Of Salvation," Pt III; and "Of the salvation of mankind," §15, in Wesley's *The Doctrine of Salvation, Faith and Good Works* (1738).

173. ". . . Joy, though not *unfelt,* yet *unspeakable* and full of glory." Letter to Henry Stebbing (25 July 1739), *Works,* 25:671. Wesley is beginning to deal more explicity with the manner of interpreting how one knows and understands the sensible operations of the Holy Spirit. In 1741, he further develops the relationship between inward and outward

religion, pointing out that the "power of godliness" cannot be without the "form": "Outward religion may be where inward is not. But if there is none *without* there can be none *within*." Sermon 150, "Hypocrisy in Oxford," II.2, *Works*, 4:400.

174. Ibid. Wesley here and elsewhere equates "feel" with "know" (and implies that to learn from Holy Writ is to know): "You will know you are under the guidance of God's Spirit the same way, namely, by *feeling it in your soul*; by the present peace and joy and love which you feel within, as well as by its outward and more distant effects." Ibid. See also Charles Wesley on sensible operations of the Holy Spirit (e.g., "feeling the Spirit of Christ") in Sermon 3, "Awake Thou that Sleepest," III.8–9, *Works*, 1:155–56.

175. 13 December 1739, *Journal*, *Works*, 19:128.

176. Or, as John put the question to Charles in 1747, "Is justifying faith a sense of pardon?" His own answer was no on several counts, followed by the summary comment, "It is flatly absurd. For how can a sense of our having received pardon be the condition of our receiving it?" By that time he had been pressed hard in this and other matters on more than one occasion over the past two years by John Smith. Letter (31 July 1747), *Works*, 26:255.

177. He had already used the eye metaphor: Christians are more enlightened, their eye is "more clear and single," they look "beyond the veil of the material world," the eyes of their understanding "being enlightened." Sermon 17 (1733), "Circumcision of the Heart," Sermon 147 (1734), "Wiser than Children of Light," *Works*, 1:405; 4:364. John's sermon on "A Single Eye," Charles transcribed as "A Single Intention," an easy change given the comment in the sermon, "The intention is to the soul what the eye is to the body." He would soon begin referring to having "new eyes to see and new ears to hear." Sermon 148 (1736), *Works*, 4:373; cf. 1:306, n. 34.

178. A concept that first appears in the sermon Charles Wesley preached in 1742, "Awake Thou that Sleepest" (I.11). In 1744, Wesley uses the same phrase in "Scriptural Christianity" (I.1–2); that same year he also refers to faith as "the eye of the newborn soul" as well as the ear, the palate, and the feeling of the soul, each image supported by a passage of Scripture. *Appeals*, §§6–7, *Works*, 11:46–47.

179. By 1741, the Wesleys could say, "Neither dare we affirm, as some have done, that all this salvation is given at once. There is indeed an instantaneous, as well as a gradual, work of God in his children; and there wants not, we know, a cloud of witnesses who have received in one moment either a clear sense of the forgiveness of their sins or the abiding witness of the Holy Spirit. But we do not know a single instance, in any place, of a person's receiving, in one and the same moment, remission of sins, the abiding witness of the Spirit, and a new, a clean heart." Preface to *Hymns and Sacred Poems* (1740), *Works* (Jackson), 14:326. Cf. above, at n. 83. By 1747, Wesley also felt that the biblical term "sanctified" did not mean "saved from all sin," and that such use was not proper without adding a modifier such as "wholly" or " entirely." He goes on to say, "Consequently, it behooves us to speak almost continually of the state of justification; but more rarely, at least in full and explicit terms, concerning entire sanctification." *Minutes* (17 June 1747), *Works* (Jackson), 8:294.

180. At the conference of 1746, Wesley answered the question, "Wherein does our doctrine now differ from that we preached when at Oxford?" with only two main points: "(1) We then knew nothing of that righteousness of faith in justification; nor (2) of the nature of faith itself as implying consciousness of pardon." Minutes (13 May 1746), *Works* (Jackson), 11:290. John Deschner points out that Aldersgate was not a "theological conversion": "Rather the old theology was reborn that night, reconciled to God, and a lifelong process of theological sanctification, so to speak, began. The theology of his student days . . . was cut off its old tree and grafted onto a new one." *Wesley's Christology* 2nd Edition, Revised (Dallas: Southern Methodist University Press, 1985), p. 197.

181. Sermon 2 (1741), "The Almost Christian," *Works*, 1:131–41.

182. Minutes (2 August 1745), Q. 20, *Works* (Jackson), 8:284.

183. Ibid., Q. 15, 8:283–84. Wesley was occasionally quite candid about the changes in his thinking over the years, even admitting in 1768 that he had not only "relinquished several of my former sentiments," but also "during these last thirty years I may have varied in some of my sentiments or expressions without observing it." *Letter to Dr. Rutherforth,* I.3, *Works,* 9:375. James W. Fowler, looking at Wesley's growth through stages of faith-development, sees these changes as part of his transition to a more "Conjunctive" faith in middle life after the rather prolonged transition to the "Individuative-Reflective" stage was completed with his experiential appropriation of the doctrine of justification by grace through faith. "John Wesley's Development in Faith," in M. Douglas Meeks, ed., *The Future of the Methodist Theological Traditions* (Nashville: Abingdon, 1985), pp. 183–92.

184. Although the sharp theological distinction is not yet attached to the distinction between justification and sanctification, this terminology appears as early as Sermon 1 (1738), "Salvation by Faith," and Sermon 5 (1746), "Justification by Faith," *Works,* 1:122–23, 191.

185. "Thou shalt be saved; first from the guilt of sin, having redemption through his blood; then from the power, which shall have no more dominion over thee; and then from the root of it, into the whole image of God." Sermon 116 (1788), "What is Man?" *Works,* 4:26.

186. 2 Tim 3:5.

187. Acts 10:35.

188. §2, in *Works,* 9:69.

189. *A Plain Account of the People Called Methodists,* IV.2, in *Works,* 9:265.

190. *A Letter to the Rev. Dr. Rutherforth,* I.4, in *Works,* 9:376.

191. Sermon 67, "On Divine Providence," §18, *Works,* 2:543. He also associates this phrase with the definition of true saving faith: "such a divine conviction of God and of the things of God as even in its infant state enables everyone that possesses it to 'fear God and work righteousness.'" Sermon 106, "On Faith," I.10, *Works,* 3:497.

192. Sermon 89, "The More Excellent Way," §5, *Works,* 3:255–56.

193. Minutes (13 May 1746), *Works,* 11:287–88. See also an early use of this distinction in Sermon 9 (1746), "The Spirit of Bondage and of Adoption," §2, *Works,* 1:250.

194. Sermon 117, "On the Discoveries of Faith," §13, *Works,* 4:35; cf. n. 26 above. This changing perspective led Wesley in 1774 to alter his earlier *Journal* accounts of 1738, adding qualifications to his earlier claims that before Aldersgate he had not been converted, did not have faith, was not in a state of salvation, was a child of wrath, and was building on the sand. *Works,* 18:215n, 235n, 242n, 245n, 248n.

195. Sermon 106, "On Faith," I.11, *Works,* 3:497. Bernard G. Holland refers to this "faith of a servant" as "suppliant faith" and points out that John Wesley distinguishes between that and the "faith of a son" as well as another level of "saving" faith. Holland, however, does not follow Wesley's own development, but rather confuses faith with assurance and fails to distinguish adequately between justification and sanctification in his description of the Wesleyan typology of faith. "The Conversions of John and Charles Wesley," *Proceedings WHS* 38 (1971):46–53.

196. See Wesley's comment to Thomas Rutherforth (28 March 1768): "Therefore I have not for many years thought a consciousness of acceptance to be essential to justifying faith." *A Letter to the Rev. Dr. Rutherforth,* I.4, *Works,* 9:376. Wesley even went so far at one point to say to Samuel Walker (19 September 1757), "Assurance is a word I do not use because it is not scriptural." *Letters* (Telford), 3:222; and to Dr. Rutherforth (1763), "Some are fond of the *expression;* I am not—I hardly ever use it" (although "a consciousness of being in the favour of God . . . is the common privilege of Christians fearing God and working righteousness"). *Works,* 9:375. See Yates, *Doctrine of Assurance,* pp. 133–34 for an attempted explanation for Wesley's tendencies toward overstatement in the matter of terminology.

197. Robert Southey, *The Life of Wesley* (New York: W. B. Gilley, 1820), 1:258. Cf. Sermon 3, "Awake, Thou that Sleepest," III.6, *Works*, 1:154.

198. First seen in Charles Wesley's sermon, Sermon 3, "Awake, Thou that Sleepest," I.11, *Works*, 1:146. Charles here used the Greek phrase for "evidence of the Spirit"; John frequently translates the text "evidence and conviction."

199. This was the text of his two sermons on "The Witness of the Spirit," written twenty years apart. Sermons 10 and 11 (1746, 1767), *Works*, 1:267–98. See also his other main treatment of the subject in Sermon 12 (1746), "The Witness of Our Own Spirit," *Works*, 1:299–313.

200. This point is developed most fully in Sermon 130, "On Living Without God," especially §§9–11, *Works*, 4:172–73. See also Rex D. Matthews, "Religious Epistemology," pp. 4–9.

201. See especially *An Earnest Appeal* (1743), §32, *Works*, 11:56–57; and Sermon 119, "Walking by Sight and Walking by Faith," *Works*, 4:48–59. Richard Brantley parallels what he calls "Wesley's spiritual sense" with Jonathan Edwards's "religious sense" and sees it as analogous with Locke's finite sensate means of knowing the religious unknown (as well as being "the major English antecedent of the Romantic imagination"); *Locke, Wesley, and the Method of English Romanticism*, p. 100. Frederick Dreyer has pointed out that Wesley's concept of the "spiritual senses" is "a peculiarly eighteenth-century solution to an epistemological problem," drawing a parallel with Francis Hutcheson's "moral sense." "Faith and Experience in the Thought of John Wesley," p. 26. Nagler sees "religious empiricism" as the most important contribution of both Wesley and Pietism; *Pietism and Methodism*, p. 176. Matthews points out, however, that there is no real precedent for Wesley's "transcendental empiricism," the wedding of the notion of "spiritual senses" to a rigorously empiricistic epistemology. "Religious Epistemology," p. 55–56.

202. See his comment in *A Plain Account of Christian Perfection* (1763), §8, which recognizes that Aldersgate itself was not an experience of full assurance for him. *Works* (Jackson), 11:370; see above, at n. 120.

Runyon—Importance of Experience

1. See especially, Jennings 1988a.

2. Cf. Rex D. Matthews, "'With the Eyes of Faith': Spiritual Experience and the Knowledge of God in the Theology of John Wesley," in *Wesleyan Theology Today*, ed. Theodore Runyon (Nashville: Kingswood Books, 1985), pp. 406–15; and *idem*, "Religion and Reason Joined: A Study in the Theology of John Wesley" (Harvard University Th.D. thesis, 1986).

3. *A Survey of the Wisdom of God in the Creation, or A Compendium of Natural Philosophy* (5 volumes), 5th edition (corrected 4th ed.) (London: Maxwell & Wilson, 1809), Volume V, pp. 149–96.

4. Volumes 5–7 (1782–4).

5. Sermon 69, "The Imperfection of Human Knowledge," §I.4, *Works* 2:570–1.

6. Sermon 117, "On the Discoveries of Faith," §2, *Works* 4:29.

7. "An Earnest Appeal to Men of Reason and Religion," §32, *Works* 11:57.

8. See fn #1.

9. *Works* 18:226.

10. *Journal* (13 May 1738), *Works* 18:238–9.

11. *Journal* (24 May 1738, §11), *Works* 18:247–8.

12. Ibid., §12, p. 248.

13. Ibid., pp. 248–9.

14. For the following three quotes see: *Luther's Works*, VI (Philadelphia: Muhlenberg Press, 1932), pp. 451–2.

15. *Journal* (24 May 1738, §14), *Works* 18:250.

16. See especially: Albert C. Outler, *John Wesley* (New York: Oxford University Press, 1964), pp. viii-ix; and *idem*, "John Wesley's Interests in the Early Fathers of the Church," *Bulletin of the United Church of Canada Committee on Archives and History* 29 (1980–2):5–17.

17. Outler, *John Wesley*, p. 9 fn 26.

18. Ted Allen Campbell, "John Wesley's Conceptions and Uses of Christian Antiquity" (Southern Methodist University Ph.D. thesis, 1984), p. 170.

19. See his Letter to Count Zinzendorf and the Church at Herrnhut (5–8 August 1740), *Works* 26:24–31.

20. *Journal* (3 Sept. 1741), *Journal* (Curnock) 2:489. For English translation see Outler, *John Wesley*, p. 369.

21. Sermon 64, *Works* 2:500–10.

22. *Journal* (3 Sept. 1741), *Journal* (Curnock) 2:490. For English translation see Outler, *John Wesley*, p. 371.

23. Sermon 24, "Sermon on the Mount, IV," §II.2, *Works* 1:539.

24. *Journal* (24 May 1738, §11), *Works* 18:248.

25. *Journal* (6 June 1738), *Works* 18:254.

26. Cf. *Journal* (4 January 1739), *Journal* (Curnock) 2:125.

27. Letter to Samuel Wesley, Jr. (23 Nov. 1736), *Works* 25:487.

28. *Journal* (25 Jan. 1738), *Works* 18:213 fn 95.

29. *Letters* (Telford) 7:120.

30. *Letters* (Telford) 7:61.

31. Sermon 10, "The Witness of the Spirit, I," §I.8, *Works* 1:274.

32. Letter to Melville Horne (1788), quoted in Robert Southey, *The Life of Wesley* (New York: W.B. Gilley, 1820), 1:295.

33. Theodore H. Runyon, "A New Look at 'Experience'," *Drew Gateway* 57.3 (1988):44–55. An earlier discussion of "orthopathy" is found in the author's "Conversion—Yesterday, Today and Tomorrow" (unpublished), Emory Minister's Week, January 17, 1984. Cf. Gregory S. Clapper's term, "orthokardia" in *John Wesley on Religious Affections* (Metuchen, NJ: Scarecrow Press, 1989).

34. Sermon 24, "Sermon on the Mount, IV," §§I.7 & II.2, *Works* I:537, 539.

Schmidt—"Strangely Warmed"

1. Jennings 1988a, p. 22.

2. Albert C. Outler, *John Wesley* (New York: Oxford University Press, 1964), p. 52.

3. See the excellent discussion of the successive generations of Wesley interpreters in Richard P. Heitzenrater, *The Elusive Mr. Wesley*, vol. 2 (Nashville: Abingdon Press, 1984), pp. 159–212.

4. John Whitehead, *The Life of the Rev. John Wesley, M.A.*, vol. 2 (London: Stephen Couchman, 1796), p. 44.

5. Heitzenrater, *Elusive Mr. Wesley*, 2:172.

6. Whitehead, *Life*, pp. 40, 53.

7. Heitzenrater, *Elusive Mr. Wesley*, 2:175.

8. Albert C. Outler, "A New Future for Wesley Studies: An Agenda for 'Phase III,'" in *The Future of the Methodist Theological Traditions*, ed. M. Douglas Meeks (Nashville: Abingdon Press), pp. 36–7.

9. Cf. Heitzenrater, *Elusive Mr. Wesley*, 2:178.

10. Henry Moore, *The Life of the Rev. John Wesley*, vol. 1 (New York: N. Bangs and J. Emory, for the Methodist Episcopal Church, 1826), p. 78.

11. Moore, *Life*, 2:223.

12. Ibid., title of chapter, p. 198.

13. Rev. L.[uke] Tyerman, *The Life and Times of the Rev. John Wesley, M.A.: Founder of the Methodists*, vol. 1, 5th ed. (London: Hodder and Stoughton, 1880), Preface, v.

14. Heitzenrater, *Elusive Mr. Wesley*, 2:185.

15. Tyerman, *Life and Times*, 1:175–76.

16. Ibid., p. 180.

17. Ibid., p. 182.

18. Ibid.

19. Ibid., p. 184.

20. Outler, "Wesley Studies," p. 39.

21. Maximin Piette, *John Wesley in the Evolution of Protestantism* (New York: Sheed and Ward, 1937; French original: 1925), cf. pp. 234, 305ff.

22. Heitzenrater, *Elusive Mr. Wesley*, 2:198.

23. George Croft Cell, *The Rediscovery of John Wesley* (New York: Henry Holt and Company, Inc., 1935), Preface, viii; pp. 28, 361.

24. Heitzenrater, *Elusive Mr. Wesley*, 2:200; Umphrey Lee, *John Wesley and Modern Religion* (Nashville: Cokesbury Press, 1936), pp. 101–4.

25. William Ragsdale Cannon, *The Theology of John Wesley* (New York: Abingdon-Cokesbury Press, 1946), pp. 68, 117.

26. Ibid., p. 249.

27. Thomas Jackson, *The Centenary of Wesleyan Methodism* (New York: Mason and Lane, 1839). The quotation is from a review of the volume in *Methodist Review*, 1839, 225. (Quoting from *Minutes* of General Conference, 1838.)

28. Ibid., p. 228.

29. See George Smith, *History of Wesleyan Methodism*, vol. 3: *Modern Methodism*, 2nd ed. rev. (London: Longman, Green, Longman, and Roberts, 1862), pp. 360–91; and E. Benson Perkins, "Centenary Fund," in Nolan B. Harmon, ed., *The Encyclopedia of World Methodism* (United Methodist Publishing House, 1974), 1:432.

30. Smith, *Modern Methodism*, pp. 360–61.

31. Ibid., p. 364.

32. Nathan Bangs, *A History of the Methodist Episcopal Church*, vol. 4 (New York: Carlton & Porter, 1841), p. 295.

33. Ibid., p. 296.

34. Frank Baker, "Wesley Day," *Encyclopedia of World Methodism*, 2:2510–11.

35. Ibid., p. 2511.

36. A. S. Graves, "Wesley's Variations in Belief, and the Influence of the Same on Methodism," *Methodist Review*, March 1887, pp. 192–211. (Quotation is on p. 196.)

37. Outler, "Wesley Studies," pp. 41–52; see also M. Douglas Meeks, "The Future of the Methodist Theological Traditions," intro. to volume by the same name, p. 19.

38. (Nashville: Methodist Publishing House, 1938). Page numbers in the next three paragraphs refer to this work.

39. See their essays above in this volume.

40. Outler, *John Wesley*, p. 17.

41. Martin E. Marty, Lecture at Iliff Week of Lectures, 1979.

42. Outler, "Wesley Studies," p. 44

Gunter—The Holiness Movement

1. Cf. Melvin E. Dieter, *The Holiness Revival of the Nineteenth Century* (Metuchen, NJ: The Scarecrow Press, 1980).

2. Timothy Merritt, *The Christian's Manual, A Treatise on Christian Perfection* (New York: N. Bangs and J. Emory for the Methodist Episcopal Church, 1827).

3. John A. Roche, *The Life of Sarah A. Lankford Palmer*, introduction by John P. Newman, Bishop of the Methodist Episcopal Church (New York: George Hughes, 1898), p. 10.

4. Dieter, *Holiness Revival*, p. 27.

5. For a comprehensive study (900+ pages) of the historical development of these denominations, see Charles Edwin Jones, *A Guide to the Study of the Holiness Movement* (Metuchen, NJ: The Scarecrow Press, 1974).

6. This thesis is not his dominant concern, but one may discern these strands of emphasis in Charles E. Jones, *Perfectionist Persuasion: The Holiness Movement and American Methodism, 1867–1936* (Metuchen, NJ: The Scarecrow Press, 1974), esp. chap. one, "Methodism's Peculiar Doctrine," pp. 1–6.

7. Cf., Donald Dayton, *Discovering an Evangelical Heritage* (New York: Harper & Row, 1976).

8. C. F. McKee, "Aldersgate Still Happens." *Preachers' Magazine* 55.1 (1979):9, 60. The person giving the testimony did not in all likelihood attach the Aldersgate terminology to the published title of the article on his testimony of entire sanctification, this being the prerogative of the editor. The editor of the magazine later became a professor at a holiness college and currently serves as academic dean in a holiness Bible College.

9. See the various articles in the May 1988 issue of the United Methodist periodical *Circuit Rider*, devoted to the 250th anniversary celebration of Aldersgate.

10. Cf. the essay by Schmidt in this volume.

11. Gentry 1979.

12. This presupposition also informs Peter Gentry's *Heritage of the Warmed Heart: Our Holiness Roots* (Kansas City: Beacon Hill, 1986.)

13. David Cubie, "Placing Aldersgate in Wesley's Order of Salvation." Unpublished version of Cubie 1989.

14. Ibid., pp. 2, 3.

15. Ibid., p. 5.

16. Ibid.

17. Ibid., p. 17.

18. Ibid., p. 20

19. Ibid., p. 34.

20. Ibid., p. 35.

21. Cubie makes the case that Wesley's "designated successor," John Fletcher, taught a twofold structure by describing the "baptism of the Holy Spirit" as the "second definite work of grace;" but even Fletcher did not identify Aldersgate as the moment of entire sanctification for Wesley. To unravel the difference of opinion among holiness scholars on this point would require a separate essay.

22. Rob L. Staples, "John Wesley's Doctrine of Christian Perfection: A Reinterpretation" (Unpublished Th.D. Dissertation. Pacific School of Religion, 1963).

23. Ibid., p. 197.

24. Ibid.

25. Ibid., pp. 198–99.

26. Ibid., p. 200.

27. Herbert McGonigle, "Significant Wesleyan Milestones," *Preachers' Magazine* 63.3 (1988):32–36.

28. Ibid., p. 33.

29. Ibid.

30. *The Journal of Charles Wesley, M.A.*, edited by Thomas Jackson (Reprint: Kansas City, MO: Beacon Hill, 1980), I:91

31. McGonigle, "Milestones," p. 34.

32. Ibid.

Maddox—Tradition-History

1. Maser 1978, pp. 35–6.

2. The most helpful surveys of these issues are: Baker 1963, Maser 1978, and Weyer 1988a. For treatments championing a conversionist reading, see: Cell 1937, and Collins 1989b.

3. Maser has argued that repetition of Aldersgate within the *Journal* would not have been appropriate from a literary point of view (1978, p. 40). While this is possible, it does not explain the absence of explicit mention in Wesley's sermons—particularly awakening sermons. For an argument similar to Maser, based on an historical analysis of the genre of spiritual autobiography, see W. Reginald Ward, "Introduction," *Works*, 18:24–43.

4. The classic expression of this hermeneutical tension is Hans-Georg Gadamer's image of interpretation as a "fusion of two horizons." For a brief summary of this notion and an analysis of some of the issues involved, see Randy L. Maddox, "Hermeneutic Circle—Vicious or Victorious?" *Philosophy Today* 27 (1983):66–76.

5. For this and our subsequent characterizations of twentieth-century Wesley studies, cf. Albert Outler, "A New Future for 'Wesley Studies': An Agenda for 'Phase III'," in *The Future of the Methodist Theological Traditions*, pp. 34–52, ed. M. Douglas Meeks (Nashville: Abingdon, 1985).

6. Cf. the evaluation of Ward, "Introduction," *Works* 18:94–8.

7. This concern is most evident in the biography by John Whitehead. However, similar tones are found in those by Thomas Coke, Henry Moore, John Telford and Richard Watson. The only biography that reads Aldersgate as evidence of Wesley's inclination to enthusiasm is that by the "outsider" Robert Southey. For brief insightful characterizations of all of these biographies, see Richard Heitzenrater, *The Elusive Mr. Wesley* (Nashville: Abingdon), II:172ff. See also the essay by Schmidt in this volume.

8. For further details on Wesley commemorations, see the Schmidt essay in this volume; Kenneth E. Rowe, "Celebrating Aldersgate: Historical Reflections," unpublished address given at Drew University, May 1988; and Randy L. Maddox, "Celebrating Wesley—When?" *Methodist History* 29 (1991).

9. Cf. John Wesley, *The Complete English Dictionary*, 3rd ed. (London: Hawes, 1777).

10. Robert Brown, *John Wesley's Theology: The Principle of It's Vitality and It's Progressive Stages of Development* (London: Jackson, Walford, and Hodder, 1865), p. 14.

11. One of the most glaring examples of such a "de-Anglicanization" of Wesley was Thomas Jackson's omission of Wesley's extract of the Anglican *Homilies* from the "standard" edition of Wesley's works, even though Wesley had included it in his own last collected edition.

12. The best example is James H. Rigg. Cf. his *The Living Wesley*, 3rd ed. (London: Charles H. Kelley, 1905; first edition, 1874), pp. 115–21. See also Luke Tyerman. *The Life and Times of the Reverend John Wesley, M.A.* (London: Hodder & Stoughton, 1871), Vol. I, pp. 179ff.

13. For "high-church" readings reacting to the de-Anglicanization of Wesley, see: Richard Denny Urlin, *John Wesley's Place in Church History* (London: Rivington's, 1870); and Frederick Hockin, *John Wesley and Modern Wesleyanism*, 3rd. ed. (London: J.T. Hayes, 1878).

14. The two classic Catholic studies that presented this argument are: Augustin Leger, *Le Jeunesse de Wesley. L'Angleterre Religieuse et Les Origines du Methodisme au XVIIIe Siècle* (Paris: Libraire Hachette et Cie, 1910), pp. 77–82, 350, 364; and Maximin Piette, *John Wesley in the Evolution of Protestantism* (New York: Sheed and Ward, 1937; French original: 1925), pp. 234, 305ff. For a similar reading see Laura Petri, *John Wesley* (Stockholm, 1928), p. 259. For a sympathetic Methodist review of Leger, see Beet 1912.

15. This term was actually suggested by a Methodist, Umphrey Lee (*John Wesley and Modern Religion* [Nashville: Abingdon-Cokesbury, 1936], p. 103, 58–9). The term was then adopted by several Catholic scholars. One example is Jean Orcibal, "The Theological Originality of John Wesley and Continental Spirituality," in *A History of the Methodist Church in Great Britain*, Vol I:90, eds. R.E. Davies and E.G. Rupp (London: Epworth, 1965).

16. There are some exceptions among Catholic scholars. Perhaps the most dramatic "conversionist" reading of Aldersgate by a Roman Catholic scholar is Brendan Byrne, S.J., "Ignatius Loyola and John Wesley: Experience and Strategies of Conversion," *Colloquium: the Australian and New Zealand Theological Review* 19.1 (1986):54–66.

17. The best examples of a championing of an "empirical" Wesley are: George Eayrs, *John Wesley, Christian Philosopher and Church Founder* (London: Epworth, 1926); and Frank Wilbur Collier, *John Wesley Among the Scientists* (New York: Abingdon, 1928). For their comments on Aldersgate, see Eayrs, p. 90; and Collier, p. 56. Examples of a Schleiermacherian reading of Wesley are: Herbert B. Workman, *The Place of Methodism in the Catholic Church* (New York: Methodist Book Concern, 1921), esp. pp. 23–6; and George Croft Cell, *The Rediscovery of John Wesley* (New York: Henry Holt, 1935), esp. pp. 46–51. For Cell's description of Aldersgate as the "masterkey to (Wesley's) mature doctrine of Christian experience," see p. 92. N.B., Cell actually presented an intriguing blend of a Schleiermacherian emphasis with the emerging Neo-Orthodox concerns.

18. See the entire issue of *Religion in Life* 29.4 (1960). For a critical perspective on this emphasis, see Claude Thompson, "Aldersgate and the New Reformers," *Christian Advocate* 6.10 (1962):7–8.

19. Lee 1937 & Rattenbury 1938 are both framed as extended rejections of the Catholic reading of Aldersgate. They also register various concerns with the Liberal reading. A clearer rejection of Liberal emphases is J. Ernest Rattenbury, *Wesley's Legacy to the World* (London: Epworth, 1928), pp. 80ff.

20. Besides Lee 1937 & Rattenbury 1938, other examples of this general reading of Aldersgate include: Bond 1938, Cameron 1955, and Schofield 1938. This reading is particularly amenable to those who tried to stress Wesley's similarities to the Reformers, whether Luther (Martin Schmidt & Philip Watson) or Calvin (William Cannon). Cf. Cannon, *The Theology of John Wesley, with Special Reference to the Doctrine of Justification* (New York: Abingdon-Cokesbury, 1946), p. 68; Schmidt 1938a, esp. pp. 54, 75; Schmidt 1938b, pp. 137–41; and Watson, *The Message of the Wesleys* (New York: Macmillan, 1964), p. 7.

21. One of the first to make this distinction is Matthieu Lelièvre, *La Théologie de Wesley* (Paris: Publications Méthodistes, 1924), pp. 8, 27. While Rattenbury emphasized the importance of Wesley's "Protestant conversion" during March of 1738 as setting the scene for Aldersgate, he reserved the phrase "evangelical conversion" to cover something more like the emphasis on assurance to be treated later.

22. Henry Elderkin, "The Bi-centenary of John Wesley," *Experience* 12 (1903):81–7; here, p. 87.

23. Cf. a pamphlet published by the Fellowship: John Arundel Chapman, *John Wesley's Quest* (London: Epworth, 1921). The description of the Fellowship is on the cover. The discussion of Aldersgate is on page 2.

24. Cf. the article on "Wesley Day" in *Encyclopedia of World Methodism*, ed. Nolan B. Harmon (Nashville: United Methodist Publishing House, 1974), II:2510–1. In 1951 this observance was moved to "Aldersgate Sunday."

25. The addresses presented are collected in Clark 1938. Clark's leading essay particularly stresses the idea of Aldersgate as a crisis conversion. For a survey of some of the other essays, see Schmidt above.

26. These are collected in the *London Quarterly and Holburn Review* 163 (1938):168–224 (includes Platt 1938). Cf. the emphasis on the role of experience in religious life on pp. 171, 175, 179, 197, 211, 219.

27. Williams 1938. Note his claim that at Aldersgate Wesley found "a new faith" (297), and that Aldersgate commemorates an "experience" (299).

28. Joy 1937 organizes his biography of Wesley around his search for spiritual experience, his finding the same (Aldersgate), and his "having and doing." Watkins 1937 is a missions study volume which deals with Wesley only at the beginning, but stresses his crisis conversion (19). Nuelsen 1938 reads Aldersgate as Wesley's foundational salvation experience (*Heilserlebnis*, p. 4) and as a great turn in his life (12). However, he stresses that Wesley was as pious before his conversion as after (23) and that Wesley does not reduce religion to feelings (15ff).

29. Cf. Leslie F. Church, "Two Birthdays—and Their Celebration," *London Quarterly and Holburn Review* 178 (1953):82–4. For more on these points, see Maddox, "Celebrating Wesley."

30. See especially, Arnett 1964, Edwards 1963a & 1963b, Rott 1963, Sommer 1963, and Wood 1963.

31. In an editorial by William P. King, "Aldersgate Recurrent," *Christian Advocate* (Nashville) 99 (8 April 1938):421.

32. This was particularly true in America. A good illustration is the American *Book of Discipline*. In the original 1785 edition this included Wesley's account of the rise of Methodism which traces it back to the Holy Club in 1729. In 1790 this section was moved to the opening address of the Discipline. But, in 1948 this "historical statement" was replaced by one emphasizing Wesley's Aldersgate experience! Cf. Frank Baker, *From Wesley to Asbury* (Durham: Duke University Press, 1976), pp. 164–5.

33. One of the earliest examples of this reading is Eltzholtz 1908. For further details on the holiness movement and this reading of Aldersgate, see the essay by Stephen Gunter in this volume.

34. For a detailed discussion of events (including Aldersgate) identified by Wesley's successors as his testimony to entire sanctification, see John L. Peters, *Christian Perfection and American Methodism* (Grand Rapids, MI: Zondervan, 1985), pp. 201–15.

35. For an insightful study of the development of Pentecostalism from Wesleyan holiness roots, see Donald W. Dayton, *Theological Roots of Pentecostalism* (Grand Rapids: Zondervan, 1987). Dayton summarizes the current scholarly debate over the appropriateness of the identification of the "baptism of the Holy Spirit" with Wesley's "entire sanctification" on pp. 184–5.

36. The best example of a Pentecostal reading is probably Fadiey Lovsky, *Wesley: Apôstre des Foules, Pasteur des Pauvres* (Lausanne: Foi et Victoire, 1977), esp. pp. 31, 158, 163. Cf. Lovsky 1947. For a reading arising out of the German Catholic Charismatic movement that identifies Wesley's Aldersgate experience in this way, see Lucida Schmieder, *Geisttaufe: Ein Beitrag zur neueren Glaubensgeschichte* (Paderborn: Ferdinand Schöningh, 1982), pp. 75, 93.

37. For a convincing proof that Wesley rejected the suggestion that the "baptism of the Holy Spirit" was an event in Christian life subsequent to justification, see M. Robert Fraser, "Strains in the Understanding of Christian Perfection in Early British Methodism" (Vanderbilt University Ph.D. thesis, 1988), pp. 382ff.

38. For an explicit (conversionist) reading of Wesley as a "twice-born" man, see Ross W. Roland. "The Continuity of Evangelical Life and Thought." *Religion in Life* 13 (1944):245–53.

39. For examples of this reading throughout the time period, see: Bashford 1903, p. 784; Green 1909, pp. 33, 43; Bradfield 1938; Lewis 1938; Vivian H. H. Green, *The Young Mr. Wesley* (New York: St. Martin's Press, 1961), pp. 271, 288; and Arthur Yates, *The Doctrine of Assurance with Special Reference to John Wesley* (London: Epworth, 1952), chapter 1.

40. At the time of Aldersgate Wesley assumed that assurance *must* accompany conversion; hence, he viewed Aldersgate as his conversion! Later he becomes convinced by his observations of the Methodist revival that one can be a Christian without having full assurance. On reflection, he corrected the *Journal* account to portray himself as in that situation prior to Aldersgate. Cf. Yates, *Doctrine of Assurance*; and the essay by Heitzenrater in this volume.

41. Cf. Richard P. Heitzenrater, "The Present State of Wesley Studies." *Methodist History* 22 (1984):221–33.

42. Of particular note are: James W. Fowler, "John Wesley's Development in Faith," in *The Future of the Methodist Theological Traditions*, pp. 172–92, edited by M. Douglas Meeks (Nashville: Abingdon, 1985); and Donald M. Joy, "Toward Christian Holiness: John Wesley's Faith Pilgrimage," in *Moral Development Foundations*, pp. 207–32, edited by D. M. Joy (Nashville, TN: Abingdon, 1983). Also interesting, but more idiosyncratic, are: Thorvald Källstad, *John Wesley and the Bible: A Psychological Study* (Bjärnum, Sweden: Bjärnums Tryckeri, 1974); and Robert Moore, *John Wesley and Authority: A Psychological Perspective* (Missoula, MT: Scholars Press, 1979).

43. For two helpful discussions of the process of such a fusion in theological reflection, see: Anthony C. Thiselton, *The Two Horizons* (Grand Rapids: Eerdmans, 1980); and Werner G. Jeanrond, *Text and Interpretation as Categories of Theological Thinking* (New York: Crossroad, 1988).

Select Bibliography

Compiled by Randy L. Maddox and Kenneth E. Rowe

NOTE: This bibliography is limited to works that deal specifically with Aldersgate. The Tradition-History also notes several other sources that make reference to Aldersgate, within a larger context.

Anonymous (Editor)
1854 "When did the Rev. John Wesley Become Savingly Converted?" *Wesleyan Methodist Association Magazine* 17:256–70.

Arnett, William Melvin
1964 "What Happened to Wesley at Aldersgate?" *Asbury Seminarian* 18.1:6–17.

Arnett, William Melvin *et al.*
1964 *Methodism's Aldersgate Heritage*. Nashville: Methodist Evangelistic Materials.

Baker, Frank
1963 "Aldersgate 1738–1963: The Challenge of Aldersgate." *Duke Divinity School Bulletin* 28 (May):67–80.

Bashford, Joseph Whitford
1903 "John Wesley's Conversion." *Methodist Review* 85:775–89.

Beet, Joseph Agar
1912 "John Wesley's Conversion." *Proceedings of the Wesley Historical Society* 8:3–6.

Bond, Robert
1938 "The Image of the 'Warmed Heart'." *London Quarterly & Holburn Review* 163 (sixth series, 7):168–71.

Bradfield, W.D.
1938 "What Christ is to Us: An Aldersgate Interpretation." *Christian Advocate* (Nashville) 99:522–3, 619–21.

Cameron, Richard M.
1955 "John Wesley's Aldersgate Street Experience." *Drew Gateway* 25.4:210–19.

Clark, Elmer T.
1938 *What Happened at Aldersgate?* Nashville: Methodist Publishing House.
1950 *The Warm Heart of Wesley*. New York: Association of Methodist Historical Societies.

Collins, Kenneth Joseph
1988 "The Continuing Significance of Aldersgate: A Response to 'John Wesley *Against* Aldersgate.'" *Quarterly Review* 8.4:90–9.
1989a "Albert Outler and Aldersgate." In *Wesley on Salvation*, pp. 55–64. Grand Rapids: Zondervan.
1989b "Twentieth-Century Interpretations of Aldersgate: Coherence or Confusion?" *Wesleyan Theological Journal* 24:forthcoming.

Cubie, David Livingstone
1989 "Placing Aldersgate in Wesley's Order of Salvation." *Wesleyan Theological Journal 24.*

Denman, Harry
1963 "What Aldersgate Means to Me." *Together* 7.5 (May):23–4.

Edwards, Maldwyn L.
1963a "The Significance of Aldersgate for the Present Day." *Methodist Recorder* (May 2):7.
1963b "'Aldersgate' and the Three Freedoms." *Methodist Recorder* (May 9): 4.

Eltzholtz, Carl F.
1908 *John Wesley's Conversion and Sanctification*. Cincinnati: Jennings & Graham; New York: Eaton & Mains.

Funk, Theophil
1963 "John Wesley nach 'Aldersgate'." *Der Evangelist: Sonntagsblatt der Methodistenkirche in Deutschland* 114:267.

Garrison, Webb B.
1960 "The Myth of Aldersgate." *Christian Advocate* (Chicago) (May 12):7–8.

Gentry, Peter
1979 "What Happened at Aldersgate?" *Preacher's Magazine* 55.1:8, 59–60.

Green, Richard
1909 *The Conversion of John Wesley*. London: Francis Griffiths.

Heitzenrater, Richard Paul
1973 *John Wesley and the Road to Aldersgate.* Lexington, KY: Kentucky Methodist Heritage Center.
1988 "Aldersgate: Evidences of Genuine Christianity." *Circuit Rider* 12.4 (May): 4–6.

Holland, Bernard George
1971 "The Conversions of John and Charles Wesley and Their Place in Methodist Tradition." *Proceedings of the Wesley Historical Society* 38:45–53, 65–71.

[Jackson, Thomas]
1838 "Mr. Wesley's Conversion." *The Wesleyan Methodist Magazine* 61:342–54.

Jeffery, Thomas Reed
1960 *John Wesley's Religious Quest.* New York: Vantage Press.

Jennings, Theodore Wesley
1988a "John Wesley *Against* Aldersgate." *Quarterly Review* 8.3:3–22.
1988b "Reply to Kenneth Collins." *Quarterly Review* 8.4:100–05.

Joy, James Richard
1937 *John Wesley's Awakening.* Chicago: Methodist Book Concern.

Kennedy, Gerald
1963 "Aldersgate and 1963." *Christian Century* 80:677–8.

Kissack, Reginald
1939 "Wesley's Conversion. Text, Psalm and Homily." *Proceedings of the Wesley Historical Society* 22:1–6.

Klaiber, Walter
1988 "Bekehrung und Heilserfahrung in der Bibel." In *Im Glauben Gewiss: Die bleibende Bedeutung der Aldersgate-Erfahrung John Wesleys,* pp. 40–8. BGEmK 32. Ed. Studiengemeinschaft für Geschichte der Evangelisch-methodistischen Kirche. Stuttgart: Christliches Verlagshaus.

Lacour, Lawrence
1963 "Aldersgate and Authority." *Christian Advocate* 7.11 (May 23):7–8.

Lawson, John.
1987 *The Conversion of the Wesleys.* Wesley Fellowship Occasional Paper #2. Derbys, England: Moorley's Bookshop; reprint, *Asbury Theological Journal* 43 (1988):7–44.

Lee, John D.
1937 "The Conversion-Experience of May 24, 1738, in the Life of John Wesley." Boston University Ph.D. thesis.

Lewis, Edwin.
1938 "Wesley Before Aldersgate Street." *Christian Advocate* (Nashville) 99:644.

Lovsky, Fadiey
1947 "La 'Conversion' de Wesley." *Foi et Vie* 45:574–84.

McIntosh, Lawrence D.
1969 "John Wesley: Conversion as a Continuum." *Mid-Stream* 8:50–65.

McKenna, David L.
1988 "That Amazing Grace." *Christianity Today* 32 (May 13):22–3.

McNeill, John T.
1939 "Luther at Aldersgate." *London Quarterly & Holburn Review* 164 (sixth series, 8):200–17.

Mansfield, Herbert W.
1953 "The Wesleys and Aldersgate." *Methodist Magazine* (London) (July):296–8.

Marquardt, Manfred
1988 "Heilsgewissheit. Eine systematische Besinnung." In *Im Glauben Gewiss: Die bleibende Bedeutung der Aldersgate-Erfahrung John Wesleys*, pp. 49–57. BGEmK 32. Ed. Studiengemeinschaft für Geschichte der Evangelisch-methodistischen Kirche. Stuttgart: Christliches Verlagshaus.

Maser, Frederick E.
1978 "Rethinking John Wesley's Conversion." *Drew Gateway* 49.2:29–53.

Mather, P. Boyd
1963 "John Wesley and Aldersgate 1963." *Christian Century* 80:1581–3.

Míguez Bonino, José.
1983 "Conversión, hombre nuevo y compromiso." In *La Tradición Protestante en la Teología Latinoamericana*, pp. 207–18. Ed. José Duque. San Jose, Costa Rica: DEI.
English: "Conversion, New Creature and Commitment." *International Review of Missions* 72 (1983):324–32.
Reprint: in *Faith Born in the Struggle for Life*, pp. 3–14. Ed. Dow Kirkpatrick. Grand Rapids: Eerdmans, 1988.

Miller, M.

1854 "The Life and Times of John Wesley." *Wesleyan Methodist Association Magazine* 17:276–86.

Nelson, James D.

1988 "The Strangeness of Wesley's Warming." *Journal of Theology* (United Seminary) 92:12–24.

Neulsen, John L.

1938 *Das Heilserlebnis im Methodismus.* Zürich: Christliches Vereinsbuchhandlung.

Outler, Albert Cook

1963 "Beyond Pietism: Aldersgate in Context." *Motive* 23:12–16.

Platt, Frederic

1938 "The Work of the Holy Spirit." *London Quarterly & Holburn Review* 163 (sixth series, 7):175–8.

Rattenbury, J. [John] Ernest

1938 *The Conversion of the Wesleys.* London: Epworth.

Raymond, B.P.

1904 "Wesley's Religious Experience." *Methodist Review* (NY) 86:28–35.

Rott, Ludwig

1963 "John Wesleys Heilserfahrung am 24 Mai 1738." *Der Evangelist. Sonntagsblatt der Methodistenkirche in Deutschland* 114:247–8.

Roux, Théophile

1938 *La Conversion évangélique de Wesley.* Paris: Dépôt des Publications Méthodistes.

Sackmann, Dieter

1988 "Heilsgewissheit Heute. Predigt zu Römer 8,16." In *Im Glauben Gewiss: Die bleibende Bedeutung der Aldersgate-Erfahrung John Wesleys,* pp. 58–63. BGEmK 32. Ed. Studiengemeinschaft für Geschichte der Evangelisch-methodistischen Kirche. Stuttgart: Christliches Verlagshaus.

Schmidt, Martin

1938a *John Wesleys Bekehrung.* Bremen: Verlagshaus der Methodistenkirche.

1938b "Die Bedeutung Luthers für John Wesleys Bekehrung." *Luther Jahrbuch* 20:125–59.

1938c "Zum Gedächtnis von Wesleys Bekehrung." *Sächsisches Kirchenblatt* 21 (n.s. 2):165–7.

Schofield, Charles Edwin
1938 *Aldersgate and After*. London: Epworth.

Selleck, J. [Jerald] Brian
1988 "Aldersgate: A Liturgical Perspective." *Doxology* 5:35–44.

Smith, H. H.
1930 "BC and AD in John Wesley." *Methodist Quarterly Review* (Nashville) 79:713–15.

Snow, M. Lawrence
1963 "Aldersgate Mythology." *Christian Advocate* 7.21 (October 20):7–8.

Sommer, Carl Ernst
1963 "John Wesleys Weg nach Aldersgate." *Der Evangelist: Sonntagsblatt der Methodistenkirche in Deutschland*. 114:234–5.

Sommer, Johann Wilhelm Ernst
1938 "John Wesleys Heilserlebnis in seiner Bedeutung für die Mission." *Evangelisches Missions Magazin* n.s. 82:342–51.
1953 "Die Bedeutung der Heilserfahrung John Wesleys." *Wort und Tat. Zeitschrift für den Dienst am Evangelium* 7:51–7.

Ten Methodist Bishops
1963 *Twentieth Century Aldersgate*. Nashville: Methodist Evangelistic Materials.

Thomas, G. Ernest
1962 *Abundant Life Through Aldersgate*. Nashville: Methodist Evangelistic Materials.

Urwin, E. C.
1938 "The 'Warmed Heart' and its Social Consequences." *London Quarterly & Holburn Review* 163 (sixth series, 7):211–14.

Vickers, John A.
1988 "The Significance of Aldersgate Street." *Epworth Review* 15.2:8–14.

Voigt, Karl Heinz
1988 *Hat John Wesley sich am 24. Mai 1738 bekehrt?* EmK Heute 57. Stuttgart: Christliches Verlagshaus.

Watkins, William Turner
1937 *Out of Aldersgate*. Nashville: Publishing House of the Methodist Episcopal Church, South.

Westbrook, Francis
1963 "The Music of Wesley's Conversion." *Choir* 54:39–40.

Weyer, Michel

1988a "Die Bedeutung von 'Aldersgate' in Wesley's Leben und Denken." In *Im Glauben Gewiss: Die bleibende Bedeutung der Aldersgate-Erfahrung John Wesleys*, pp. 7–39. BGEmK 32. Ed. Studiengemeinschaft für Geschichte der Evangelisch-methodistischen Kirche. Stuttgart: Christliches Verlagshaus.

1988b "Die Aldersgate Erfahrung John Wesleys." *Ökumeniche Rundschau* 37: 311–20.

Williams, M.O., Jr.

1938 "The Warmed Heart: Aldersgate Then and Now." *Chinese Recorder* 69:296–300.

Wood, A. [Arthur] Skevington

1963 "Lessons from Wesley's Experience." *Christianity Today* 7:720–2.

1988 *Wesley & Luther*. East Sussex, England: Focus Christian Ministries Trust.

Yost, Clark R.

1938 "What the Aldersgate Experience Was." *Christian Advocate* (Joint edition: May 19, 1938):41.

Young, Frances

1988 "The Significance of John Wesley's Conversion Experience." In *John Wesley: Contemporary Perspectives*, pp. 37–46. Ed. John Stacey. London: Epworth.

Yrigoyen, Charles

1988 "Strangely Warmed." *Interpreter* 22.3 (April):11–13.

Yrigoyen, Charles, editor

1988 *Celebrating The 250th Anniversary of Aldersgate: Suggestions for Local Congregations*. Madison, NJ: General Commission on Archives and History of The United Methodist Church.